W9-DDG-074

THE NEXT
GOVERNMENT
OF THE UNITED STATES

THE NEXT
GOVERNMENT
OF THE UNITED STATES

WHY OUR INSTITUTIONS
FAIL US AND
HOW TO FIX THEM

DONALD F. KETTL

W. W. NORTON & COMPANY   NEW YORK · LONDON

Copyright © 2009 by W. W. Norton & Company, Inc.

All rights reserved
Printed in the United States of America
First Edition

For information about permission to reproduce selections from this book,
write to Permissions, W. W. Norton & Company, Inc., 500 Fifth Avenue, New York, NY
10110

For information about special discounts for bulk purchases, please contact
W. W. Norton Special Sales at specialsales@wwnorton.com or 800-233-4830

Manufacturing by Courier Westford
Book design by Chris Welch
Production manager: Anna Oler

Library of Congress Cataloging-in-Publication Data

Kettl, Donald F.
The next government of the United States : why our institutions fail us
and how to fix them / Donald F. Kettl. — 1st ed.
p. cm.
Includes bibliographical references and index.
ISBN 978-0-393-05112-4 (hardcover)
1. Administrative agencies—United States—Management. 2. Executive
departments—United States—Management. 3. United States—Politics and
government—21st century. I. Title.
JK421.K4815 2009
351.73—dc22   2008038584

W. W. Norton & Company, Inc.
500 Fifth Avenue, New York, N.Y. 10110
www.wwnorton.com

W. W. Norton & Company Ltd.
Castle House, 75/76 Wells Street, London W1T 3QT

1 2 3 4 5 6 7 8 9 0

For Mildred
and all those who worked so hard to care for her

For those who suffered because of Hurricane Katrina
and those whose imagination and leadership brought them relief

CONTENTS

PREFACE

This book evolved through a long and meandering process. It began with conversations in the late 1990s suggesting that big changes in American government were emerging but that their shape was anything but clear. The genesis continued with an observation that monumental forces periodically bring fundamental change to the workings of American government without dramatically transforming the foundation of the American system. The search for an explanation of these observations, and an effort to discern the future of American politics through the fog of great uncertainty, led to the book.

In the late summer of 2001, I began writing in earnest. On a Labor Day weekend trip back from the West Coast, I was busily composing. The last sentence I pounded on the computer before the flight attendant asked me to turn off the laptop was this: "Big changes are coming. It's not clear whether they will be quiet and subtle or sudden and dramatic, but they're coming nonetheless." A week later, the horrible events of September 11 answered that question. They also framed the book's basic questions in sharper relief. Political commentators repeatedly argued that, with the terrorist attacks, everything had changed. But what had, in fact, fundamentally changed? How was the future likely to be different from the past? Were the changes likely to ripple past homeland security into other policy areas? And where were these forces likely to take American democracy?

Policy makers promised they would learn the lessons of September 11, but the painful aftermath of Hurricane Katrina's August 2005 strike on the Gulf Coast showed that the system was struggling with many of the same problems. In the midst of all these large-scale policy puzzles, my wife and I were quietly facing a series of tough decisions in caring for her mother, Mildred, whose health was deteriorating and who needed care through several government programs. All these cases shared surprising similarities that shaped a conclusion: American government was facing some tough, inescapable problems, and it was becoming painfully clear that the government we had was not a good match for the problems we were trying to solve.

I began exploring that notion with government officials, and I found surprising echoes of the same puzzles in unexpected places, from Philadelphia's streets to space missions. This book grew out of my observations and conversations. The book's methodology, in fact, is unusual. It is the product of an evolving dialogue with hundreds of government officials over more than a decade. I regularly lecture to government officials, and after many presentations individual government workers have come up to me with their own stories. One conversation was with a senior FBI official; another, with senior officials in the US Department of Transportation. Homeland security officials in Los Angeles and local government officials in Wisconsin shared their experiences. I am deeply indebted to my dialogues with these many government officials, at all levels, for their help in developing and refining the evidence that shapes this book.

At its core, this book is an argument, based in observations about American government—most important, about that government's future. Research into September 11 and Katrina injected pessimistic notes. However, the encouraging energy and innovation of so many officials, in government and among its many partners in the private and nonprofit sectors, make the book an optimistic one. Government can indeed rise to the challenges of the information age, but achieving that goal will require new ways of adapting America's enduring pragmatism to the tough problems of the twenty-first century. Failing to rise to that challenge will only undermine the prospects that American democracy will endure. The stakes are large in building the next government of the United States.

ACKNOWLEDGMENTS

As this book took shape along its winding course, I accumulated many debts. I am grateful to Roby Harrington at Norton for the long conversations that helped give this project shape and for his unwavering support, even when the contours of the project were anything but clear. Norton's Mollie Eisenberg provided superb editorial guidance, and Stephanie Hiebert proved an excellent copy editor. Exceptionally thoughtful reviews of the manuscript from Ron Daniels, John DiIulio, Charles Goodsell, Anne Khademian, and Donald Moynihan provided invaluable comments for sharpening the book and its argument. Both are vastly better for their keen insights and pointed suggestions.

My wife, Sue, was along for every step of this long journey. She listened to the stories, tested their lessons, and provided the touchstone for what rang true. No one could ask for a better partner or friend.

Finally, I am indebted to the legions of officials, in government and out, who have been working to find new strategies to solve the problems they face. They are often so busy trying to figure out how to do their jobs that they might not recognize the bigger picture but, step-by-step, they have been inventing the next government of the United States.

THE NEXT
GOVERNMENT
OF THE UNITED STATES

1

MILDRED AND KATRINA

Mildred

Let me tell you about Mildred.

Mildred was a spry ninety-one-year-old, born in east Texas to a mother and father who had worked hard on the land. As a young woman, she had often spent summers in the cotton fields and moved down the rows with her eyes to the skies, imagining what it would be like to fly. After reading about Amelia Earhart's adventures, Mildred decided to take flying lessons. In the barnstorming days of the 1930s, novice flying was much different from today. The aircraft were less stable and not as forgiving, and there were not many instruments beyond a couple of gauges in the cockpit and the pilot's eyes. Mildred was a young widow with two very young children at the time, and her own mother was afraid that flying was a bit too much adventure. She stopped her lessons just short of her first solo flight but she never lost her taste for wings.

During World War II, Mildred worked at the Bryan, Texas, Army Air Corps base as office manager. One of the fliers rotating through the base caught her eye. He was a young lieutenant named

1

Al, just back from forty-seven missions over Germany in a B-17 heavy bomber in the Mighty Eighth Air Force. The standard tour for B-17 crew members in the early years of the war was twenty-five missions. Especially in the first phase of the air war, German fighters often picked off bombers, and antiaircraft batteries around critical targets were fierce. The odds of winning membership in the Army Air Corps's "Lucky Bastards Club," an honor bestowed upon fliers who made it through those twenty-five missions, were low—just one chance in five, according to some estimates.[1] Al completed his twenty-five missions and then flew twenty-two more, before being shipped back to the States for a breather—and to be retrained for what many analysts feared would be a brutal Pacific campaign.

Al was dark and handsome, an Italian from one of the old neighborhoods of New Haven, Connecticut, which made him an exotic figure in Texas. He quickly proved popular with the women staffing the air base, including Mildred. But Mildred sensed that being too direct would not work with Al. Instead, she ignored him, which proved infuriatingly irresistible to him. As the war wound down, Mildred and Al were the last two employees on the air base. She stayed to organize the files; he, to shut down the military facilities. They closed the base and opened their relationship, which soon blossomed into marriage. The fledgling US Air Force, which had spun off from the Army after the war, sent Al to tour West Coast bases to assess their management and readiness, and Mildred tagged along. Al soon won a promotion and a transfer to the Pentagon, as the Army Air Corps split off into the new US Air Force. And soon thereafter, their daughter, who one day would be my wife, was born.

Al's Air Force career took the family around the world. They moved from Washington to El Paso, and then to San Francisco, before setting out to far-off Guam, where Al was a navigator on the new-generation B-52 intercontinental bomber, which carried nuclear weapons. The family moved from Guam to Maine—a culture shock as big as one could imagine—where Al helped open a new Air Force base. He retired from the service after his Maine assignment, but he and Mildred continued to move periodically, from Maine to Texas, then to New York and Connecticut, and on to Virginia, Tennessee, and Wisconsin. At age eighty-two, Al developed a quick-spreading cancer that soon took his life, and we buried him at Arlington National Cemetery.

Soon after the funeral, we noticed that Mildred was having a harder time remembering things, from what she had done the day before to how long her eggs had been in the refrigerator. The long-term memories of her early years remained strong and vibrant, but her short-term memory was failing. She needed more prompting to accomplish her daily activities. She was always glad for telephone reminders, but then she would sometimes forget to hang up the phone. It was sadly becoming clear that she was having a hard time taking care of the basic tasks of daily life on her own.

We struggled to manage the challenge that so many families share: a wonderful senior citizen who prized her independence but who could no long safely live alone. We tried assisted living—a facility where the older residents lived in their own apartments but received help from the staff with meals, housecleaning, and bathing. But Mildred, now in her late eighties, proved increasingly unsteady on her feet. After a few weeks in assisted living she fell, was hospitalized, and came home, only to fall again the same evening and have to ride the ambulance again back to the emergency room.

The hospitalization cycles told everyone, health care providers and family members alike, that Mildred needed twenty-four-hour skilled care to assist her with basic living and help her in and out of bed. Another fall could cause a serious head or hip injury, which at best would gravely affect her quality of life and at worst could end it. But residence in a facility that offers such care costs $75,000 or more per year. Mildred's Social Security check and her survivor's pension from Al's military service did not begin to cover the cost. The family had no choice but to apply for assistance from Medicaid, a program in which the federal and state governments share the cost of health care for poorer Americans. Under Medicaid's rules, Mildred would surrender her monthly income to the program. In return, the program would pay for her nursing-home and medication expenses. Medicaid and Medicare, the companion program for doctor and hospital care for senior citizens, would share her medical costs.

Mildred was certainly not alone. Millions of elderly Americans either have no savings or find their assets quickly depleted by the high cost of nursing-home care. Mildred was thus the face of the federal budget's shifting priorities. Medicare and Medicaid, along with Social Security, accounted for four out of every ten dollars of federal spending by 2006. Congress had enacted Medicare and Medicaid in 1965 to launch a new approach to medical care. For decades, the United States had flirted with proposals for a universal health care system, of the sort that many other major industrialized nations have. But fears of socialized medicine—of government control over the care that patients receive and how much doctors and hospitals are paid—had always blocked the effort.

President Lyndon B. Johnson, however, made the expansion of health insurance a central part of his War on Poverty: Medicare, to pay doctor and hospital bills for persons over the age of sixty-five; and Medicaid, to pay for health care for poorer Americans. It was not a universal system, since it did not cover younger Americans or those who did not meet the income guidelines. Nor was it truly a system. In fact, to satisfy critics who had long raised the specter of socialized medicine, the government itself did not provide the care. Instead, the federal and state governments funded for-profit and nonprofit hospitals, clinics, and health care providers, reimbursing them for the costs they incurred in caring for patients. The strategy vastly expanded the reach of government without directly increasing its size.

Moreover, although government revenues fund the program, the money flows through a highly complex pipeline. Federal tax revenues and individual payroll tax contributions pay for Medicare. For Medicaid, the federal and state governments split the costs. The federal government funds a basic basket of services. Each state can add other services, including more care for younger Americans, more alternatives for physical therapy, and many other options. Medicaid is thus not one program but many, with a different package of benefits (and a different level of cost) in each state. As more Americans live longer, more seniors have drifted into nursing homes because they need additional care. Over time, nursing-home benefits for seniors have become a larger share of Medicaid, and Medicaid pays nearly half of all nursing-home expenditures in the United States.[2]

At this point we lived in Pennsylvania, and the application process for Mildred was detailed but not overly difficult. There were three parts. The nursing home's medical staff had to certify that Mildred needed twenty-four-hour care, which her medical history made easy. The family had to document her monthly income, which the military retirement and Social Security bank deposits provided. And the family had to detail her assets during the previous few years. The program limited benefits to those with little income and few assets. To qualify, some families had spent years redistributing assets from older to younger family members. Federal regulations, designed to make sure clever families did not bilk the government, limited asset transfers. New businesses, in turn, sprang up to skate just within the boundaries of the federal rules, and the federal government countered with new regulations. It soon became a complex back-and-forth battle.

None of this affected Mildred. Her medical team (whose bills were paid by Medicare) knew that, without round-the-clock care, she would continue to fall. Her monthly income was easily below the Pennsylvania limits for nursing-home coverage through Medicaid. And years of subsisting on that meager income had left almost nothing in the bank. It was an easy application process for her because her family filled out all the forms, and for the government because she easily met all the standards.

Mildred's approval was quick, but the process was surprising. The federal government paid much of her Medicaid support, but the state administered the program. In Pennsylvania, Medicaid was one of the largest and fastest-growing items in the state budget, but as Mildred's application wove through the process, *she never met a single government employee.* Not one. The government was committed to funding a very expensive program of care, but Mildred did not encounter the government. Her family had but a single contact with a government employee—a form sent by a government worker that required a signature before being mailed back. Everything else relied on nongovernment employees. An employee of a nonprofit agency under contract to the state of Pennsylvania completed the required interview to assess Mildred's status. Private physicians, reimbursed by Medicare, certified her medical condition. The financial certifications all occurred long-distance. The government, federal and state, committed to paying for Mildred's care—for as long as she lived and remained eligible, for whatever she needed—without ever laying eyes on her.

Every element of Mildred's care was a step in an intricate ballet of intertwined organizations, all of them connected indirectly, at most, with the government. A registered nurse at her nursing home (paid by Medicaid) oversaw Mildred's care and arranged for regular visits by a private physician (paid by Medicare). The physician wrote prescriptions for her medications, which a private-contract pharmacy filled (with the costs shared by Medicare and Medicaid). A private dentist-on-wheels program regularly visited to take care of her teeth (through Medicaid payments). A nursing-home staff nutritionist monitored her weight and diet (because loss of appetite is a major cause of dehydration and hospitalization and weight loss can increase the risk of falls and make them more serious). A social worker managed supportive care. A physical therapist helped provide daily exercise, even though Mildred was wheelchair bound. Medicaid paid for all this, as well as for Mildred's meals and for the nursing aides who helped her with dressing and bathing. Medicaid paid for her wheelchair and her walker, as well as any other medical supplies she needed. Medicare paid for the cataract surgery she needed, and Medicaid paid for the private transport service that took her back and forth for the preoperative appointments and for her operation.

For the staff of the nursing home, the hardest work was assessing each patient's constantly changing condition. Many of the residents were in varying stages of Alzheimer's or other forms of dementia and, as one experienced social worker once told me, "If you've met one Alzheimer's patient, you've met—one Alzheimer's patient." The Alzheimer's diagnosis often conveyed a false sense of uniformity, when in reality the progressive loss of memory, and all of the human functions connected with it, is different in everyone who suffers from it. Some of those with progressive dementia, like Mildred, simply become more quiet, with less and less memory of things—even recollections of conversations just seconds before. Her world simply became smaller, bit by bit. Others become combative or noisy or aggressive. For some, Alzheimer's eventually leads to the failure of key organs. For others, dementia is a progressive disconnection from the world without obvious physical results, except for a gradual weakening of the joints and the risks that come from being sedentary. The staff therefore often had to rely on their experience and experiments to determine what was most likely to work for each resident.

Moreover, residents rarely remained stable. Lapses and recoveries were unpredictable, so the staff had to be vigilant (in noticing what was happening) and creative (in guessing what was most likely to work for each resident). One day, the staff noticed that Mildred seemed more anxious than usual. They discovered that she was developing a serious systemic infection that immediately required antibiotics. Another day, Mildred seemed listless and sleepier than usual. The staff checked her vital signs and discovered that she had a low fever. But as the day wore on, she became more listless. The staff checked again and her fever had spiked dangerously, rising a degree an hour. Her nurse called for an ambulance (a private transport vehicle, paid for by Medicaid), telephoned her doctor (paid by Medicare, who was able to get her into a crowded emergency room, funded by Medicare, that had been closed that day because of a heavy patient load), and administered acetaminophen (paid by Medicare) to start bringing down her fever. At the emergency room, doctors did blood tests and took urine cultures, and they discovered that Mildred had developed a major urinary tract infection morphing into sepsis, an extremely serious systemic infection, as well as the beginning of pneumonia. The hospital team of physicians and nurses deployed its full arsenal of intravenous fluids and antibiotics and, after a few days in the hospital (paid by Medicare), an ambulance (paid by Medicaid) took Mildred back to her bed in the nursing home (paid by Medicaid). Had it not been for the alert team of nurses on her floor, who read in her languid behavior the signs of a brewing crisis, there would not have been a return trip. She probably would not have lived through the night.

Mildred's tale is complicated enough. For the staff on the floor, however, there were fifty Mildreds, each with a distinct set of problems, each in a different condition from the week before, and each facing yet a different condition the week after. The staff's job was to monitor each resident, to gauge what each one needed, and to make sure she got it. (Most of the time it was *she*—the overwhelming number of residents were female.) Sometimes that meant trying to encourage someone to eat who had no appetite, to encourage someone sitting alone to take part in activities, or to cajole a resident having a bad day into being more pleasant.

The quality of care that the millions of nursing-home residents receive is only as good as the staff, the many other partners (from doctors and hospitals to nutritionists and volunteers), and the ability of case managers to weave all these pieces together and to repeat this feat millions of times each day. Mildred was lucky. Her care was very, very good. When she died, after two years in the nursing home, her good friends on the staff shed as many tears as her family members and streamed to her funeral. Their hard work had unquestionably lengthened her life and vastly improved its quality.

THE MILDRED PARADOX

At the core of Mildred's care was a central paradox: she went through the entire application process and then received all of her care for two years through two of the fastest-growing programs in the federal budget, yet she never encountered a single government employee. The high quality of her care, funded but not provided by the government, in the face of this *Mildred paradox* highlights important problems. Many nursing-home residents are not as lucky. They might not be blessed with as high a quality of care, or a problem might slip through one of the many cracks in the system, to fatal effect. Federal investigators in 2008 found that many nursing homes had serious deficiencies. State inspectors, charged with overseeing the quality of the system, often missed warning signs. In nine states, inspectors did not discover problems ranging from malnutrition and bedsores to overmedication and patient abuse more than one fourth of the time. If Mildred got good care, hundreds of thousands of other nursing home residents did not receive the care that they needed, that their families expected, and that the government often was paying for.[3]

The nation's exposure to such problems is growing. More Americans are living longer. Census Bureau analysts expect that the over-sixty-five population will double by 2030, when almost one fifth of the population—72 million people—will be older than sixty-five. The "old old"—those aged eighty-five and over—are the fastest-growing part of the American population.[4] Good nutrition and health care earlier in life are helping many more Americans reach retirement age. For a generation, Medicare has funded high-quality care that helps older Americans live longer. Add the rapidly aging baby boomers to the mix, and it is clear that there will be many, many more Mildreds in the nation's future. Most of the boomers are not saving nearly enough to fund their retirement expenses, let alone the soaring cost of nursing-home care. The government will face huge costs and fewer workers to pay the taxes to cover the bill.

Just what is the government's role in all this? Part of the answer is financial. Medicare and Medicaid account for a huge and growing piece of all federal spending. However, the Centers for Medicare and Medicaid Services has just 4,400 employees to run the two programs: 0.2 percent of federal employment to manage 20 percent of the federal budget. This is the product of the Mildred paradox. Government does not so much run the Medicare and Medicaid programs as leverage them. Trying to leverage such complex programs without directly controlling the service delivery system is the hidden puzzle inside governance in the twenty-first century. The tremendous difficulty of doing this well, and doing it repeatedly, is one of the major challenges facing government.

The federal and state governments leverage these programs through a vast and hugely complex network of intermediaries. Neither the federal nor the state government provided any of Mildred's care or directly paid any of the bills. Her caregivers submitted their bills to financial management companies—Medicare-related expenses for physicians went to one company in Madison, Wisconsin; hospital-based expenses paid by Medicare went to Omaha, Nebraska. Medicaid-related expenses were processed through a Camp Hill, Pennsylvania, company. A Columbia, South Carolina, company processed her prescription drug costs, from a Pennsylvania pharmacy based in Moon, near Pittsburgh, with which the state had contracted to secure the best possible prices. Each of Mildred's service providers—the nursing home, hospitals, doctors, pharmacies, ambulance providers, physical therapists, dentists, and others—had their own back-office staff whose job was to sort out her bills and send them to the proper financial management company. Each of these private companies reviewed the bills for compliance with the Medicare and Medicaid program guidelines. (Was the charge for a particular test an allowable cost? Was the daily room charge within the standards? Were prescription drugs ordered from the lowest-cost supplier?) Each financial management company billed the federal and state governments for the allowable costs, sent payments to the providers, and mailed a regular printed (but largely indecipherable) report to the family.

THE MILDRED COROLLARY

Beyond the Mildred paradox is the *Mildred corollary*: throughout her care—whose taxpayer-borne costs totaled hundreds of thousands of dollars—no one was in charge. No one was coordinating the full range of services she received. The government's costs were the mostly accidental total of the services her care providers ordered: which specialists she saw, which tests she got, which treatments she received. No one was budgeting the cost of her care, and no one was keeping track of the total amount spent to improve her quality of life. Mildred had a primary physician who did a remarkable job of coordinating her care, but when she went to the hospital for emergencies, the hospital team took over. When she moved back to the nursing home, her primary physician resumed oversight of her care. Every trip to the hospital produced changes in her medications. Because her nursing-home physician also covered other facilities, he was not at the nursing home all the time, so the nursing staff sometimes had to make the call on what supplemental assistance she needed. The Mildred corollary put a heavy burden on her family: to the degree there was any overall case manager, it was her family, who had to make important health care decisions without the benefit of health care training.

Those who had the most training had no ultimate power of coordinating her care; those who coordinated her care were not medical experts. There was no budget for her care. The cost, borne mostly by taxpayers, was the total of whatever the health care professionals decided. These accumulating decisions shape the one fifth of the federal budget that goes to Medicare and Medicaid, with millions of such networks, different for each service recipient. They all share the Mildred paradox of government service payment without government service provision, and the Mildred corollary of government spending without government control of the decisions that shape the costs and quality of care. The government, federal and state, sets the reimbursement rate for care, but it has little control over who orders which services. Budget experts sometimes speak euphemistically about "uncontrollable spending" and "entitlements." The underlying meaning of these arcane terms is that a large share of the public budget goes to goods and services that the government, at best, manages and controls indirectly. The solvency of Social Security looms as a major issue for the nation's fiscal future. But even more important is the spiraling cost of government-paid health care, where the biggest problems blossom out of the Mildred paradox and its corollary.

For those who loved Mildred, the central question was this: Who is responsible for ensuring that she receives the best care possible? For the taxpayers paying the bill, the question was this: Who is in charge of Mildred to make sure that we are getting our money's worth for the public dollars spent? The answer, in both cases, was no one. Mildred lived within a loosely coupled network that worked remarkably well, but no one was in charge of it. In other nursing homes, the paradoxes sometimes strained the system to the breaking point. Physicians might be slow to respond to a nurse's request for evaluation. Shift coordinators might fail to pass along their trouble list of patients to watch out for. Nutritionists might not work with the physicians. Overworked nursing assistants might not attend to a resident's toileting. Life is very fragile in its last stages, and it takes little to shatter that fragility. We have constructed a system that bets the quality of life on a system in which no one is in charge.

For Mildred, the story ended in January 2007. The disease process gradually weakened her to the point where she refused food and, eventually, liquids as well. A cycle of hospitalizations left her weaker and weaker, until her body finally gave in. But her spirit remained strong until the end, with a small smile crossing her lips as family members visited. At age ninety-one and a half, she died at midday on a sunny winter day, with some of her best friends—the team that cared for her at the nursing home—around her.

Mildred's story is about one person, but it is a case that continues to play itself out millions of times a day. Next let's consider the case of Hurricane Katrina, which played itself out only once but affected millions of people. It turns out to be a story with the same lessons.

Katrina

"Ohmygawd it's arriving," an obviously worried Jon Donley posted on his blog as the hurricane bore down on New Orleans.[5] Donley is the founding editor of NOLA.com, the web affiliate of the city's *Times-Picayune*. He had holed up with his colleagues in the paper's hurricane bunker waiting for the storm to hit, and he told his readers that, without power or air conditioning, the situation was quickly getting worse. "The scene out the windows is frightening, and it's just beginning," he wrote. "Gusts slamming the big windows, and people reflexively ducking, knowing they've got to break. Trees whipping as if they're about to be uprooted. There is a tooth-grinding whistle from the wind . . . if it keeps up, I'm going to climb up there with my trusty roll of duct tape." Reports began arriving of shattered windows in high-rise hotels and water rising in the French Quarter.

Then the Seventeenth Street levee failed and publisher Ashton Phelps ordered the staff to evacuate. "Frantic now . . . scooping cameras and gear into camera bag, jerking out network cables and power supplies and cramming my remaining clean shirt and shorts into the bag (stinking to high heaven like everyone else, but want to save the clothes against the time we find showers). Adrenaline pumping . . . now it's against time." They hopped onto delivery trucks, which rode high through the water. They spotted a "huge fire in the lower Garden District area of Uptown . . . big building, thick smoke . . . pillars of smoke rising here and there. Fumes are rising off the water, and the air in this 'bowl' is hazy with smoke—sometimes choking."

Donley transformed his blog into both a home for news bulletins and a clearinghouse for information about the storm's victims. Hundreds of tales of New Orleanians poured in, along with messages from desperate family members trying to track down loved ones. The fears and worries of the city's residents, and of countless friends and relatives across the country, played themselves out in Donley's blog. It was heroic work, which contributed to the Pulitzer Prize the paper won for its coverage of what ultimately became the single biggest administrative failure in American history.

No one had intended for government to fail so badly. When the storm ferociously struck the Gulf Coast in late August 2005, government at all levels and a host of voluntary organizations rolled into action. To a truly remarkable degree, thousands of workers put their skills to work to aid millions of victims, especially the many thousands left terrified and isolated in flooded New Orleans. There had been storms before, so government agencies knew what they had to do. And in the aftermath of the September 11 terrorist attacks, government planners had resolved that their response to the next large event, whatever its cause, would prove even better.

Despite these pledges, however, government did fail. Thousands of New Orleans residents were stuck for days at the Superdome, without food, water, shelter, evacuation, or hope. A few blocks away, at the city's convention center, the story repeated. Desperate residents echoed the same unanswered question: Where was their government? Why could a government that had rushed aid to Asian tsunami victims a year before not do as much for its own citizens? Even the Bush administration's public affairs apparatus, as good a machine as ever worked from the White House, fumbled the presidential response.

Two weeks later, still struggling to regain his footing, Bush flew into New Orleans for a photo op. He stood in Jackson Square, in front of a beautifully lit Saint Louis Cathedral, to tell the city's residents, "We will do what it takes, we will stay as long as it takes, to help citizens rebuild their communities and their lives."[6] But years later, many of the city's most seriously damaged neighborhoods remained devastated. The French Quarter had sprung back to life, but many city neighborhoods beyond the tourist core remained virtually untouched. City residents were furious that Bush's 2007 State of the Union address did not contain a single mention of Katrina. "I almost broke my TV, knocked it off the stand," said one disappointed refugee. Louisiana Governor Kathleen Blanco noted that the speech was supposed to be about Bush's domestic priorities. "It's not even on his radar," she complained.[7]

The failure spawned three separate government investigations: a quiet one by the Bush White House and very public ones in each house of Congress. It would have been perversely reassuring if the reports had found dishonesty, malfeasance, or sheer stupidity at the core of the problem. At least that problem could have been fixed by firing the miscreants, changing the law, and hiring smarter people. But the saddest fact about the Katrina debacle is that it occurred despite the best efforts of government employees, at all levels. All involved had tried their best. They had run their plays by the book. They had followed their procedures and rolled out the prescribed resources. They might have been following the book, but with Katrina it turned out to be the wrong book.

The Federal Emergency Management Agency (FEMA) and its administrator, Michael Brown, were easy scapegoats. Director Brown had had no previous experience in running large-scale disaster management programs. He had previously worked for the International Arabian Horse Association and had joined the Bush administration to work for Joe Allbaugh, a longtime friend who had managed Bush's 2000 presidential campaign and had followed Bush to Washington as FEMA director. When Allbaugh left FEMA, Brown took over as director but, as Katrina revealed, without the "operational awareness"—a sense of how to size up the situation on the ground and deploy the right response—that emergency management requires.

FEMA's problems, however, ran far deeper. Hurricane Katrina was not only intense but inflicted damage over hundreds of miles. In Mississippi, the storm surge lifted large casinos and deposited them across a highway. In Louisiana's bayou country, some towns simply disappeared. Katrina rearranged fragile barrier islands and shifted the navigation channel down the Mississippi River. Even without the failure of the levees in New Orleans, it would have ranked as one of the most destructive hurricanes in American history. But the levee failure transformed Katrina from a major disaster into a gut-wrenching catastrophe.

Why would people build a large city in such a vulnerable place? When French settlers established a settlement there in the early 1700s, the Mississippi had already become a major trade route, so whoever controlled the mouth of the mighty river could shape commerce. Picking a site for controlling commerce, however, was a tough job. The delta was very flat, much of it was below sea level, and the river often changed course. Those characteristics set up an inevitable collision between two irresistible forces: man's desire to tame the mouth of the river to fuel the economy and Mother Nature's underestimated power. Geographer Peirce Lewis called it an "inevitable city on an impossible site."[8]

In 1965, Hurricane Betsy made Lewis's point. The category 3 hurricane drove a monstrous storm surge across Lake Pontchartrain. Water spilled over the top of the existing flood control system and into many of New Orleans' neighborhoods, in some cases up to the rooftops. President Lyndon B. Johnson quickly jumped on Air Force One and flew to the city, where he promised immediate help. Congress passed the Flood Control Act six weeks later and launched the construction of a massive protection system. Betsy was the benchmark. Engineers knew that stronger hurricanes were possible, including the dreaded category 5 strike. But they were starting virtually from scratch and understood that category 5 protection was impossible in the short run. Better to start with a system that would defeat a Betsy-like category 3 storm as a first step, members of Congress reasoned. Other communities were battling for their own flood control projects, and getting enough money for a stronger system was politically impossible.

The Army Corps of Engineers, the nation's flood control experts, built 125 miles of interlocking channels, drainage canals, dikes, levees, walls, dams, and pumps. The corps designed the system to channel the river and keep it within its banks and, if water intruded into the city, to pump it out. The "system" in fact was not a single structure but an interlocking network of facilities that stretched for miles along the river. Because of the interconnected elements, the system was only as good as its weakest part—and only as good as its bet that human engineering could outsmart Mother Nature.[9] Complicating the job was the inescapable fact of New Orleans. With most of the city below sea level, any break in the system would cause the city to fill up like a bathtub. The levees were a calculated bet: that Mother Nature would not throw anything stronger than a category 3 storm at the levees and that the levees would hold.

As Katrina wound itself up, it emerged as the planner's worst fears: a category 5 storm aimed directly at the city. At almost the last minute, however, two very good things (at least for New Orleans) happened: The storm weakened to a category 3, the level for which the levees promised protection. Then the storm jogged slightly to the east and took aim at the Louisiana–Mississippi border. Hurricanes tend to pack their biggest punch in their northeast quadrant, where the winds and storm surge are usually strongest. The change of course left New Orleans with the weaker winds in the northwest quadrant. The storm was very bad, but it was of the order for which the system was supposed to provide defense. In the first hours, the system held. Several of the city's most famous restaurants, including Antoine's, suffered serious damage. The storm spun off a tornado, which shattered windows in the Hyatt hotel. Most of the city was without power. The streets were wet—but not flooded.

In the city's Lower Ninth Ward, however, the Louisiana National Guard soon picked up ominous clues that serious trouble was on the way. An airman stationed at the guard's barracks there reported by phone that there were just puddles in the parking lot. But then the airman interrupted the call. "Would you hold the line a minute?" he asked Major General Bennett Landreneau, the guard's commander. "I need to look at something." After a few seconds, he got back on the line. "I don't know why," he said, "but there's probably a foot of water on Claiborne Street" in front of the barracks. Then he interrupted himself. "Sir, there's two feet of water on Claiborne Street."

It got worse. "Cars are beginning to float out of the parking lot. There's a river of water moving into this area," he told the stunned general. General Landreneau knew there was only one explanation: the levees had failed and water was pouring into New Orleans. Electric power at the National Guard barracks soon failed, first as the city system went down and then as the backup generators went underwater. Their communication systems began to fail and the high-water trucks, each packed with communication gear, were lost to the rising water. About 300 soldiers, stationed on the front lines to rescue anyone stranded by the storm, now needed to rescue themselves.[10] A quick survey of the levees soon revealed the worst. The system had failed in several spots and water from Lake Pontchartrain, pushed by the receding storm's winds, was pouring through. Soon 80 percent of the city was flooded, in some places to a depth of twenty feet.

How had this happened? Katrina, after all, had hit as the category 3 hurricane the levees were designed to protect against. But
Katrina had proven devilish. Her winds—and the storm surge they
drove—had come at the city from the rear, with waves pushed
across Lake Pontchartrain, up against the levees and down the
drainage canals. At multiple points the protection systems had
failed, in part because the levees and floodwalls in some places
were not built to the proper heights and in some places engineers
had failed to account for settling that occurs over time, a phenomenon called *subsidence*. Pilings to support the walls did not go deep
enough into the ground to support the walls. Together, "overtop-
ping" and "underseepage" had eroded the structures and scoured
away the foundations at several places—and the water had come
pouring in at a frightening pace. To make things worse, new homes
had been built right next to the levees' base, and the roots of the
lovely shade trees had weakened the levees' foundations.[11]

New Orleans quickly found itself under multiple assaults—
water that came over the top of some levees, storm surges that
flattened the walls in other places, small leaks that allowed water
to enter elsewhere, and a pumping system knocked out by all the
water. The system had failed, in multiple places, and it had failed
catastrophically—in letting the water in, making it hard to get the
water out and providing residents a false sense of security that multiplied the damage by encouraging building into the floodplain.

According to a post-Katrina analysis by the National Academy
of Sciences, the vast flood control project was "not a single system
constructed as part of a unified plan." As the Army Corps of Engineers admitted, "the hurricane protection in New Orleans and
Southeast Louisiana was a system in name only."[12] It had sprung
up over time as federal, state, and local governments, "operating
with different mandates, levels of resources, and staff backgrounds
and capacities" had cobbled it together. "No single entity had been

fully 'in charge' of constructing and maintaining all hurricane protection structures," which complicated efforts to build, maintain, and repair it.[13] The system was a loosely coupled network where a breach anywhere threatened problems everywhere.

The lack of centralized control of the system frustrated angry residents searching for someone to blame. There was no single cause of the levee failure, no smoking gun pointing to a target at which to aim the anger of New Orleanians. Instead, the failure had a host of parents. The Army Corps of Engineers had not designed the levees strong enough or supervised their construction well enough. Private contractors had not built them strong enough. The state of Louisiana had not regulated them thoroughly enough. The local levee boards had not maintained them well enough. City zoning officials had allowed the construction of structures in floodplains and, in some cases, right up against the levees. Beautiful trees in the backyards of some of these homes had sprouted roots that had dug into the foundation of the levees and weakened them.

Once the levees failed, the water rose at a frightening pace. Residents who had failed to heed Mayor Ray Nagin's call to evacuate—those who had no transportation out of town, those who were too frail or ill to move, or those who had simply decided to ride out the storm—quickly found themselves trapped. Some terrified residents clambered up from the ground floor and, as the water continued to rise, retreated to their attics. As the water kept rising, they punched holes in their roofs and found themselves stranded. Some residents did not move fast enough. Others could not reach the roof. The rising waters washed others away. Soon, the television film crews began documenting bodies floating down the city's streets.

If there was any universal experience of those overwhelmed by the flooding, it was the sense of isolation. When the water rose, there were only a handful of passable streets. Some victims just hunkered down, unaware that their small neighborhood was part of an epic tragedy stretching hundreds of miles and being viewed on television around the globe. Many residents said later that, once they had finally managed to find a room in a hotel or with friends and family, they were stunned to see the vast expanse of the damage. All they had known was that they were stuck on their block and could not move.

Many people headed for narrow stretches of dry ground at the Superdome and the convention center. As thousands of people huddled there, food and water supplies gave out and sanitation disappeared. Some were older New Orleanians, without their medication and oxygen. Some were poor. All were stuck and their faces were overwhelmingly black. For days, they were mostly on their own, without emergency food and water or a strategy for evacuation. "It's like being in a Third World country," complained Mitch Handrich, a registered nurse manager in an overwhelmed public hospital. "We're trying to work without power. Everyone knows we're all in this together. We're just trying to stay alive."[14]

Compounding the tragedy—and the sense of outrage—was the enormous presence of news crews. If reporters and their camera operators had figured out how to get into the city and send back video, why couldn't the government get in with help? And why had the federal government—with warehouses full of military Meals, Ready-to-Eat (MREs) designed to be parachuted to troops anywhere in the world, and with thousands of helicopters—failed to get the basic supplies of life to so many people who were so obviously starving?

The breakdown of civil order compounded the human suffering. In many neighborhoods, gangs roamed the streets and looted stores. Meanwhile, the city's command and control system was shattered. At least one fourth of the city's police officers had simply walked off the job. Many of the officers were victims themselves, homeless and worried about their families. For the officers still on the streets, half of the patrol cars were out of service and for the remaining cars gas was scarce. The police were running out of ammunition and radios did not work, because the storm had blown down the antennas. Police headquarters was under water. The mayor, Ray Nagin, was marooned with key staffers at the Hyatt hotel with no telephone for two days and only sporadic radio contact. New Orleans was as close to the collapse of civil order as any American city has ever come.

In Baton Rouge, Governor Kathleen Blanco was trying from ninety miles away to get a clear fix on just what was happening. She urgently called on federal officials for help. "Look, we need everything you've got" was her plea. "Send us everything. Let's not debate over what we need. We need everything you have. Please send it to us as fast as you can."[15] Mayor Nagin gave interviews to CNN on the street in front of his hotel begging for help. The federal government had massive amounts of emergency food, water, and medical supplies, along with a large fleet of helicopters and supply vehicles with which to deliver them. Officials from agencies such as the departments of Transportation, Housing and Urban Development, and Health and Human Services offered help. But the help just did not arrive. State and local officials had trouble defining just what they needed beyond "everything." Federal officials waited for the right requests, submitted in just the right way. In the meantime, thousands of people were suffering, and some were dying.

Federal officials had long anticipated that a serious problem, from a nuclear attack to a huge earthquake, might require them to come to the aid of a major American city, but the question of who can deploy troops in the states is surprisingly complex. The founders knew that they needed to reassure nervous states that federal troops would not impose a new kind of tyranny. In fact, in his essay "Federalist No. 29," Alexander Hamilton had reassured his readers that the new Constitution had no provision "for calling out the posse comitatus" (a local sheriff's power to arm citizens for law enforcement). That, he said, would prevent the federal government from imposing military rule over the states. The Stafford Act (1988) reasserts the primacy of the states in disaster relief and requires the governor to ask for help before the federal government sends in troops. However, a long tradition rooted in the Insurrection Act of 1807 gives the president power to deploy federal troops if necessary to execute the law. Disaster planners had also long worried about how to respond if a disaster made it impossible for the states to ask for help quickly enough.

At best, the federal government's emergency role and legal powers have been murky, especially in deploying troops in the states. That ambiguity, in turn, slowed the federal response to Katrina. Federal attorneys tussled over who needed to file which forms before federal agencies could respond, whether the federal government could dispatch troops before the governor asked, and what to do if state and local officials became so overwhelmed by disaster that they lost the ability to ask, or failed to request help in a timely way.

FEMA took the brunt of the blame. It was the federal government's lead disaster agency, and Michael Brown was its most visible public face. Critics charged that he was more worried about appearance than results. His press secretary e-mailed him with fashion advice. "Please roll up the sleeves of your shirt, all shirts," she said. "Even the president rolled his sleeves to just below the elbow. In this [crisis] and on TV you just need to look more hard-working."[16] President Bush flew into Alabama and applauded FEMA Director Michael Brown, saying "Brownie, you're doing a heck of a job." That clearly was not true; by any imaginable standard, Brown and FEMA had failed.[17] In his own defense, Brown later claimed that he had tried to get the Department of Homeland Security (DHS) and the White House to respond, but that he had trouble getting DHS officials to move—or even to answer the phone. The explanations did little, however, to deflect blame away from Brown, and the president's "heck of a job" comment stuck to him like radioactive flypaper.

In reality, FEMA does not have the capacity to solve mega-problems on its own. It is a relatively small agency, with just 8,000 employees to cover the entire nation. Many of them are world-class experts, but big problems quickly swamp their powers. Part of FEMA's mission is to secure surge capacity—that is, to round up the additional help it needs when large problems like Katrina swamp its resources. Short of a megabureaucracy, staffed by tens of thousands of additional employees and backed by billions of dollars of supplies (the bulk of which would go to waste or would remain unused most of the time), it is impossible to imagine how Katrina would not have overwhelmed the capacity of any single organization to respond.

Katrina's victims, of course, had no patience for a debate on the intricacies of federalism or of organizational complexity. Marooned by the thousands, with their plight televised around the world, they simply wanted help. Their plaintive cry was, Why does the government seem so powerless to provide the aid we need?

Mismatch

It would be hard to imagine two more different cases than Mildred and Katrina. At their core, however, they share a singular reality: many of the most important problems we face simply do not match the institutions we have created to govern them. In fact, Mildred and Katrina are two different versions of the same story. Both cases show that we have interlocking public–private–nonprofit systems that lack adequate governance or a clear government role (the Mildred paradox); and multiple systems, responsible for important issues, in which no one is in control (the Mildred corollary). Each is a story of how big problems outstripped government's ability to respond—and how, too often, people suffer because the government does not respond quickly enough.

The loosely coupled parts of the system treated Mildred well. A remarkably broad range of health care workers came together to provide the care she needed, when she needed it, from emergency medication to a regular dose of love. Mildred, of course, was lucky; many nursing-home residents do not enjoy the same level of care. Their quality of life, and how long they live it, depends critically on how well the disjointed system that cares for them comes into sync. In the Gulf Coast, however, many of the elements of the system remained unconnected, and millions of storm-stricken residents paid the price.

As we shall see throughout this book, American government has a rich tradition of vibrant democracy. But it is struggling, with greater frequency and with ever greater failure, to cope with twenty-first-century problems. The growing complexity of the service delivery systems make it increasingly difficult to ensure that public programs work effectively and efficiently. This is the central issue raised by the Mildred paradox: government programs with less government service delivery. As more public programs are delivered by private and nonprofit actors, and as many more public programs rely on intricate public–private–nonprofit partnerships, it is ever harder to make sure the right dots are connected well.

As the coming chapters will bear out, we long ago created a theory of how to manage government programs well, but that theory rested on the assumption that government itself would run the programs. Reality has gradually but steadily drifted away from this foundation, and the further it has drifted the harder it has been to ensure that programs work well. The truly remarkable thing about Mildred's case was the high quality of care she received, for her caregivers found a way to weave a safety net to ensure that she did not fall through. The unremarkable thing about Katrina is that it revealed, on a grand and globally broadcast scale, what happens when the service system fails to match the problems it's trying to solve or the models long developed to solve them. Unfortunately, such problems are growing—and so, too, are the problems of government performance. Government is hard to run because government's tools are out of sync with the jobs it is trying to accomplish.

These performance problems increasingly are spilling over into fundamental problems of governance. The Mildred corollary—public programs in which no one is in charge—poses enormous issues for our elected officials and the governments they are trying to lead. In Mildred's case, no one was truly in charge of her care. With Katrina, the government's response proved sluggish because no one was in charge of making government move. The lack of leadership frustrated citizens seeking accountability and members of Congress looking for the responsible party. Identifying the cause of the slow response proved impossible because responsibility was broadly shared but only loosely connected. Michael Brown made an obvious and very attractive target for everyone's frustration, but he was right about one thing: it was unfair to hold him solely to blame, for many others shared responsibility. Government is hard for elected officials to govern and for citizens to hold accountable because responsibility has become so diffuse.

From time to time throughout American history, as we shall see, we have encountered such mismatches. In the past, we were lucky enough to restructure government and its tools to create a government that worked. We now face as big a governance challenge as American government has had in its long history, because it is subtly losing its grip on its most fundamental purpose: effective government that is accountable to citizens. Can America rise once again to the challenge of adjusting to a new age?

A government that fails to adapt will create a chilling future. Pessimists and cynics have regularly warned about the rise and inevitable fall of American democracy. Mildred and Katrina offer stark warnings that, without a fresh approach to governance, the cynics might be right. As baby boomers multiply Mildred tens of millions of times, and as a growing population crams ever more Americans into small spaces, failures will cascade into millions of homes with devastating results. It is impossible to escape the conclusion that government is not up to the problems we expect it to solve. Continued failure to solve these problems not only threatens serious consequences for citizens—it threatens to erode the very foundation of American government.

Still, this book is an optimistic one. We have encountered big challenges to governance before in our history. When America has faced these problems in the past, when government has fallen out of sync with the problems it has been charged with solving, we have reinvented it. Mildred and Katrina help frame the problems we increasingly face and the ones we must solve. As we shall see in Chapter 2, the cases of Mildred and Katrina are but a microcosm of a far larger set of forces we face. We have reached the point, quite simply, where we need to invent the *next* government of the United States.

2

NETWORK CHALLENGES

To make policy in America, policy makers traditionally created programs and assigned an agency to run them. The model is a vending machine: decide what to buy; insert money in the slot; wait for a hidden mechanism to process the cash and work the internal levers; enjoy the service that is dispensed. In a medical emergency, family members call 911 and wait for the paramedics to arrive. Citizens put their garbage at the curb and expect sanitation workers to take it away. At age sixty-five, retiring workers file a form and wait for monthly Social Security checks to start. If intelligence officials identify a terrorist target, the president expects to be able to give an order to military forces and have the target disappear. Pay taxes, elect public officials, create programs—and wait for services.

The model disguises the system's complexity, but there is no reason why citizens (or even presidents) need to grapple with all the details. When buying cars or getting money from an ATM, citizens do not need to know the thousands of steps along the car assembly line or the interconnected computer and telephone networks that feed the armored cash dispenser. For government programs, they do not need to know all the elements of Medicare or how 911 dispatchers decide which ambulance to send to which scene. All that matters is that the engine starts when they turn the key, that the money comes out when they insert their card, that they are cared for when they are sick, and that they receive emergency services when they are in need.

With the rise of Mildred- and Katrina-style policies, however, it has become increasingly difficult for citizens to know how and where to connect with their government, especially the part of government that spends their money and provides them with services. It has become equally hard to design a machine that reliably dispenses high-quality services and for policy makers to hold the whole system accountable. If a pharmacist does not realize that he is part of government when he is filling prescriptions, if a senior citizen can complain about government's hands on her Medicare, if health reform collapses in complexity because of its own weight—it is surely easy to understand why citizens feel disconnected from government, alienated from its key decisions, and confused about why it is so hard to make it work well. It becomes increasingly easy for everyone to deal with government from a distance, paying the money out as demanded (while complaining about taxes) and accepting the services provided (often without realizing they come from the government), feeling alienated from government (despite so often being part of the government service system). The vending-machine model both hides the complexity of the mechanisms inside government and distances citizens in their interactions with it. Despite the growing complexity of public programs, citizens and policy makers alike continue to look on government as a straightforward vending machine, in which government produces the services that government delivers. Inside the machine, however, the mechanisms are vastly more intricate in ways that challenge the assumptions underlying the vending-machine model.

Mildred and Katrina are prime examples of a large and growing array of public programs that rely on distributed networks instead of traditional hierarchies to deliver services. Policy makers still create a program and assign it to an agency to manage. To run these programs, however, government is relying increasingly on intricate relationships among federal, state, and local governments; among public, private, and nonprofit players; and between American and international organizations. Scholars have called this "government by proxy" and "government by network."[1] This line of research has produced some powerful new insights into the emerging issues of collaborative governance.[2] These networks created the Mildred paradox and its corollary—the growing role of nongovernment players providing public services and the inability of any single player to control the system and hold it accountable.

The rise of this new networked strategy creates new problems for getting results, not only for Mildred and Katrina but for a large and growing array of other issues. These networks raise three large challenges: for the boundaries of public programs, for the complexity in how these programs work, and for the puzzles of making the programs accountable to citizens and elected officials alike. The issues we saw in Chapter 1 are but microcosms of far broader challenges that the rise of network governance creates for American government.

Boundaries

Many of the central puzzles of government are problems of boundaries. What functions should government perform, and which of these should be left to the private sector? For the functions that government takes on, should the federal, state, or local government do the work? Which government bureaucracy should be responsible for performing the job? Americans have always worked on—and fought over—government boundaries. Those boundaries have become ever more critical as the connections between programs and problems have increased in range and scope.

Boundaries play multiple roles in American government. Boundaries define what a particular problem means, and what it does not. They shape what responsibilities government officials have and what jobs are left to others. They separate what lies inside government from what is outside. They are about the identity of government itself and how government relates to its citizens.

For the nation's founders, the most important battles revolved around questions of boundaries. How much power should government have over civil society? Within government, how much power should flow from the states to the national government? Within the national government, after the struggles under the Articles of Confederation to make government strong enough even to maintain public safety, they battled over how to create and apportion power. Congress might have been "the first branch" of government, and Hamilton might have argued in "Federalist No. 29" that the judiciary was "the least dangerous branch." But how much power should they put in the executive branch—and how could they ensure effective government without increasing the threat of tyranny? The founders never fixed the boundaries firmly—they have been less like fences than points in a tug-of-war, in which the balance of power constantly changes with the rise and fall of competing forces. American government has always been more about the contest than about resolving the issues that shape it.

Today's administrative system began to take its recognizable shape in the late nineteenth century, when the Progressives sought the best way for doing hard things well, and for doing good things predictably. The core of the strategy rested on creating routines for tackling problems. Consider the way fire departments respond to emergency calls. When a fire truck rolls to the scene of a fire, firefighters do not spill out of the truck like clowns from a circus clown car. Their training instills discipline, with each firefighter charged to perform separate tasks defined by clear boundaries and specific processes. Some firefighters immediately check on the source of the alarm. Some search for trapped victims, while others ready the hydrant and hoses and ladders. A careful look at the scene of a fire reveals an intricately choreographed response built on boundaries that come from decades of experience and training. Efficiency and effectiveness depend on creating routines that break down very hard jobs into manageable tasks that can be reliably accomplished.

Such routines drive most of government's work, and most of the time they serve government—and taxpayers—well. For example, more than fifty million Americans receive monthly Social Security payments, with a virtually perfect accuracy rate. More than four fifths of citizens doing business with the Social Security Administration rate their experience "excellent," "very good," or "good."[3] The Coast Guard breaks ice through the Great Lakes during the winter to ensure that heating oil reaches the chilly climes. Newspapers never headline "Mail Delivered Yet Again Today" or "Social Security Checks Arrive by the Millions." But that, in fact, is the core story of most of government's work: *what government does regularly, it tends to do well*. The same is true of all complex organizations, public or private. High performance typically hinges on building strong, effective routines.

Mildred and Katrina, however, confound this strategy, because their distinctly nonroutine problems challenged routine procedures. Some of FEMA's biggest problems in New Orleans came about precisely because the agency followed its routines. In nursing homes, nurses explain, nothing is ever routine. Just as no two Alzheimer's patients are alike, no two patients in a nursing home need the same pattern of care. Moreover, whatever worked the last time—for a hurricane or a nursing-home patient—might not work the next, because problems morph so quickly. Even though FEMA's managers had retooled the agency following September 11, it failed after Katrina because its next September 11 was not a terrorist attack but a catastrophic hurricane. Disaster planners can forecast with certainty that they will face another large-scale event. They cannot forecast what it will be, however, so focusing too narrowly on the past in planning for the future carries enormous risks.

It is becoming increasingly hard for government to solve problems because the problems themselves confound the boundaries created to solve them. In fact, *it is no longer possible to assign responsibility for any fundamental problem to a single government agency—and no single agency can control or manage any problem that matters.* The problems have become too large and the administrative strategies too complex for any single agency possibly to encompass or control them. In fact, it was the triumph of routines over self-evident problems that crippled FEMA's response to Katrina. Government agencies continue to hone their routines, but the routines increasingly fall short of the core missions that those agencies seek to accomplish. Quite simply, no single agency on its own can manage any important problem. Solving any important problem requires a multiorganizational strategy.

It is not surprising, therefore, that we struggle to make government work. We are increasingly attacking problems that fail to match our map of governance. In the 1970 movie classic *Patton*, two soldiers in George Patton's army, rushing forward to capture Berlin, have stopped their tank to puzzle over where they are and where to head next. "This place isn't on the map," one solder says. "You know why?" the other replies. "We've run clear off the map." That is precisely the situation in which the officials charged with Mildred and Katrina found themselves. They had big problems to solve and no map to follow. One longtime disaster expert explained that the problem of dealing with Katrina was like "landing an army at Normandy with a little less shooting."[4] For the nurses coming to work at Mildred's nursing home, the situation was more prosaic but no less important. They could only guess what challenges their day would bring.

We seek to manage complex government programs by establishing standard routines. Our management textbooks tell us how to create routines, but we have no book, no map to tell government officials how to adapt to so many problems that fail to fit our models. Indeed, the biggest tragedy of Katrina, arguably the biggest administrative failure in American history, is that no public official set out to make a mess of the response. The players tried hard and followed the book. In fact, the response to Katrina was a mess *precisely because* everyone was following the book, for the book did not fit the problem. Existing routines crippled the response instead of supporting it, and the system proved sluggish in navigating problems that were not on the map.

Natural disasters like Katrina have an uncommon ability to confound the boundaries we draw to contain them. FEMA, for example, had built its organization on regional offices, but Katrina split FEMA's organizational seam by making landfall almost precisely at the boundary between Regions 4 and 6 (see Figure 2.1). The storm inflicted enormous damage on both sides of the boundary, but FEMA's response depended on where the victims lived—that is, on which side of the boundary they were located. Department of Homeland Security investigators found that the Atlanta regional office had coordinated services more effectively

FIGURE 2.1   Katrina—and FEMA's Regional Structure

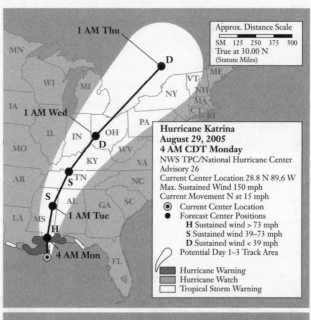

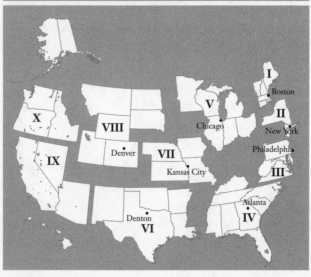

than had the Denton regional office, based just outside Dallas. Denton's struggles to deal with the disaster compounded New Orleans' problems.[5] In fact, the regional director had not even visited the state before the storm struck.[6]

These huge problems might tempt FEMA to restructure its regional boundaries to prevent such coordination problems in the future. The next storm, however, might prove just as uncanny in splitting a new seam—or FEMA's next major challenge might not be a storm but a major earthquake, or perhaps a terrorist attack or biological disaster. Relying on boundaries to control and solve problems and then reorganizing when an agency's response falls short are often-repeated pathologies of American government. The pathologies constantly handicap government's ability to learn and adapt because no set of boundaries can contain many problems and because the best solutions often require bridging boundaries instead of drawing them.

We have passed the point where we can manage problems by trying to bound them. The problems will not adapt to our institutions; we must adapt our institutions to the problems. Indeed, Michael Brown's fundamental problem in New Orleans was that he had come to town to manage FEMA, instead of focusing on solving problems. The problems did not cooperate with the boundaries FEMA had drawn, and only effective action across the boundaries began cracking Katrina's back. We repeat that problem constantly, and our recurring failure to devise strategies for problems that cross organizational boundaries compounds the crises we face.

Government deals with many routine issues. It also faces distinctly nonroutine challenges. The nonroutine challenges are becoming far more frequent, far more dominant, and far more threatening. The current government of the United States follows the Progressives' model for managing the routine, and it manages routine issues relatively well. However, the nation is facing a rising tide of nonroutine challenges that do not fit routine governance strategies. The combination of problems that refuse to stay within the boundaries of existing programs, policy makers' instincts to attack new problems by redrawing old boundaries, and the problems' stubborn insistence on challenging these new boundaries have combined to create a never-ending cycle of failed policies. As we shall see in later chapters, the mismatch of the Progressives' approach and new problems is the fault line separating twentieth-century approaches from the imperatives of twenty-first-century governance. The issues have become larger because the boundaries set to contain them do not fit the problems we must solve.

Complexity

Driving this problem forward is the growing complexity of public programs and a broader agenda of issues that the public views as government's responsibility. We seek better pollution control and fewer greenhouse gas emissions. We want safer cars and stronger infant safety seats. When tainted hamburger meat or bacteria-contaminated green onions sicken diners, citizens ask how this could have happened—and why government did not stop it. Citizens demand government action to make their spinach salads and toy trains safe from contaminants, their airports secure from terrorists, their bridges protected from collapse, their water safe to drink. They want the weather service to provide pinpoint accuracy in forecasting tornado strikes. Tough new problems, like preventing terrorism, have grown atop difficult old ones, like reducing poverty.

Consider Mildred. At the beginning of the twentieth century, few people had to worry about care in their old age. In 1900, the average American lived just forty-seven years.[7] When the federal government created the Social Security program in 1935, the choice of sixty-five as the retirement age was not arbitrary—it was about how long most Americans lived. There has long been a national debate about caring for older citizens. In 1795, for example, Thomas Paine argued that the nation needed to create an old-age pension,[8] but it took until the mid twentieth century for Social Security to emerge. The program's benefits gradually expanded to include individuals who had not worked and to provide a cost-of-living adjustment for beneficiaries. From that base came Medicare and Medicaid, and expansion of these programs from hospital care to nursing-home coverage. The emergence of new programs only fed the public's appetite for more government action.

As the programs grew, the federal government's share of health spending exploded, from 25 percent of the total in 1960 to 45 percent in 2005. By 2030, 22 percent of the American population will be eligible for Medicare, up from 9.5 percent in 1970. Mildreds will multiply by the millions. The strategy of relying on private service providers for the large public program sidestepped the issue of socialized medicine, but it came at the cost of enormous organizational complexity.

The programs shaped a new puzzle: how could government control a program it funded but did not operate? This arrangement flipped the standard organization chart on its head. Most organizations picture themselves as a pyramid, with a large number of employees at the bottom tapering to a small number of policy officials at the top. For the Centers for Medicare and Medicaid Services (CMS), the federal agency charged with managing both programs, the picture was the reverse. Just 4,500 federal employees manage—more properly, leverage—the work of more than 1.1 million health care providers, who in turn serve seventy-four million Americans (see Figure 2.2). Within this upside-down structure, federal "management" is at best loose and indirect. The

FIGURE 2.2   Organization Strategy of the Centers for Medicare and Medicaid Services

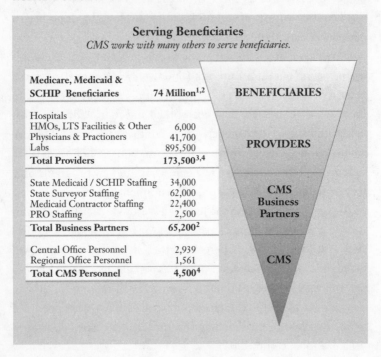

Serving Beneficiaries
CMS works with many others to serve beneficiaries.

Medicare, Medicaid & SCHIP Beneficiaries	74 Million[1,2]	BENEFICIARIES
Hospitals HMOs, LTS Facilities & Other	6,000	
Physicians & Practioners	41,700	PROVIDERS
Labs	895,500	
Total Providers	**173,500[3,4]**	
State Medicaid / SCHIP Staffing	34,000	
State Surveyor Staffing	62,000	CMS
Medicaid Contractor Staffing	22,400	Business Partners
PRO Staffing	2,500	
Total Business Partners	**65,200[2]**	
Central Office Personnel	2,939	
Regional Office Personnel	1,561	CMS
Total CMS Personnel	**4,500[4]**	

federal government can write rules and count the dollars going out the door. It can try to leverage the health care network, but it can scarcely *direct* the programs in any significant way.

Now consider Katrina. Until 1950, there was no overall federal emergency policy. Instead, the government responded, case by case, to individual storms and typically had to wait for Congress to pass separate legislation for each disaster. With the passage of the Disaster Relief Act of 1950, a sharper strategy emerged. If the president decided that state and local governments were overwhelmed, he could declare a disaster and federal agencies would provide help without having to wait for congressional authorization. The act thus elevated the importance of disaster relief and shifted power to the executive branch for putting government's vast capacity to work.[9]

After World War II, the fear of a nuclear attack further strengthened the federal government's hand in disaster relief. During the war, state governments had been responsible for civil defense, from plans to ensure the continuity of government to response in case of attack. The cold war, however, brought what President Harry S. Truman called "the potential damage of devastating nuclear weapons."[10] That made emergency response an issue of pressing national concern. Truman established the Federal Civil Defense Administration to ensure that the nation was prepared to respond to a nuclear attack—a step that pulled many responsibilities that had once rested with state and local governments to the federal level. Centralization continued with the creation of FEMA in 1978 and passage of the Stafford Act in 1988, which laid out the standards for national control in case of major disasters.

The central issue was finding the balance between national power (especially for ensuring effective response in case of nuclear attack) and state and local autonomy (especially for ensuring control over their communities). But the questions continued to echo: When should the national government assert control? How long should it wait to assess whether an attack—or a major storm—immobilized state and local officials, and how strong was the national interest in ensuring at least a basic capacity for state and local governments to respond? On the other hand, how could state and local governments protect their autonomy? The intricacies of American federalism, always difficult to resolve, became even more complex after September 11, as federal planners worried that a major attack could wipe out the local command structure and leave citizens exposed to escalating dangers.

To make things worse, few Gulf residents had purchased flood insurance. Some residents had simply neglected to buy the insurance their lenders required. Government investigators charged that private insurance companies, responsible for selling government flood insurance, had soft-pedaled flood coverage to make it cheaper for individuals to qualify to buy homes. Buyers were not required to buy flood insurance if their homes were not in the hundred-year floodplain (the area that would be under water in a storm that hit, on the average, once a century). As bad luck would have it, the devastated Lower Ninth Ward was not in the floodplain, so when the levees broke and the pumps failed, the surge obliterated most of the neighborhood and few residents had insurance to rebuild their homes.

President Bush had promised to bring New Orleans back, but it was hard to deliver on the pledge because so few New Orleans residents had flood insurance and rebuilding all the homes would have drained the federal treasury of hundreds of billions of dollars. In fact, more than $110 billion in federal aid flowed to the Gulf.[11] The money arrived only after the disaster had occurred, only after the chance for private homeowners to buy insurance had passed, only after the chance to shore up the levees had disappeared, only after the storm had inflicted tens of billions of dollars in damage, and only after all the other options had disappeared. The federal government slid backward into its aid role.

The scale of Katrina's damage, coupled with the media's wall-to-wall coverage of government's failures, made a big government response inevitable. Katrina created a quasi entitlement with a deep political pull. The lesson: when bad things happen, Uncle Sam will ultimately play the good uncle. Uncle Sam's help, in turn, means that private interests, homeowner and business alike, often rebuild in the same disaster-prone spots, and often in ways that only increase the risks from future storms. Katrina's two-story-high storm surge, for example, had savaged Mississippi's Beau Rivage casino barge and left some of the structure as little more than splinters. On the first anniversary of the storm, however, the casino's owners proudly announced they were reopening a new, land-based casino at the same site, with 800 new employees and a larger promenade. A gambling-industry Web site called it one of the "biggest comebacks in gambling industry history" and proudly hailed upcoming headliners.[12] Analysts call this "moral hazard," the tendency of individuals to behave differently if they know someone else will bear the cost of their decisions.

The predictable flow of federal aid led to substantial private investment, even when private insurance companies pulled out. Some private insurers, burned by 1992's Hurricane Andrew in Florida and 2005's Hurricane Katrina, simply decided to stop selling hurricane insurance in Florida. Other companies hiked their rates substantially, but coastal residents rebuilt anyway. For example, Dauphin Island, Alabama, is one of the nation's most picturesque beaches. It has a little red schoolhouse, ferry service, a bird sanctuary, and fishing charters, along with miles of condos and beach houses and motels. According to one rental agent, it is "Alabama's undiscovered treasure."[13] But it is also hurricane bait. From 1979 to 2005, six hurricanes hit the island and the federal government paid out $21 million in insurance. When storms level vacation homes, owners deposit the checks and rebuild. Katrina leveled homes that were just being replaced after the previous storm—a storm that had obliterated 300 homes.[14]

On Topsail Island, along North Carolina's Atlantic coast, a series of storms deposited 125 acres of fresh sand. With new beachfront property rising up out of the water, developers and residents could not resist building new vacation homes on the emerging land. "We know that it's a fragile area, and the Lord gives and the Lord takes away," one sixty-two-year-old librarian told a *Wall Street Journal*

reporter. "But if someone gave you something, you would probably want to use it to do what's best for your children and grand-
children."[15] Building on what the Lord gave was one thing; when
storms took it away, however, residents expected to be compen-
sated, either through the federal flood insurance program or by aid
to replace what they had lost. Government, not the Lord, wrote
the checks.

These programs increased government's reach into private
decisions. New, larger government programs gradually expanded
government's role and fueled government spending. Policy
commitments—large, new, but no less real—emerged almost acci-
dentally, sometimes implicitly. In the process, government increasingly drifted into commitments it could not afford that proved
ever harder to manage.

How did this happen? Throughout the twentieth century, several currents collided to frame this new strategy. One current was
pragmatism. During World War II, the government faced the
massive challenge of a speedy shift from a peacetime economy,
still struggling to recover from the Depression, to a two-front war
against the world's greatest armies. The government could not simply buy off-the-shelf war matériel from private companies, because
most weapons simply did not exist. There were not enough planes,
ships, tanks, and ammunition to fuel the armed service's needs, and
government could not wait for the private sector to catch up on its
own. On the other hand, the government had no interest in building its own permanent defense establishment. That would have
limited its flexibility and committed it to a level of spending that it
knew it would not want to maintain when the war ended.

In the process, the government quickly developed an enormous
contracting operation. Mildred's husband Al developed a lifetime
fondness for Boeing, which had built his B-17 bomber. The plane
often suffered amazing damage but kept him alive on his missions

over Germany. Decades later, he talked about the remarkable accuracy of his bombsight, built by a company founded by a Swiss emigrant. Factories in Delaware produced thousands of landing craft for the D-Day invasion, and new factories sprang up to produce tanks and the ammunition they fired. Meanwhile, secret production began on a new atomic weapon, with government-owned but contractor-operated plants scattered around the country.

After the war, heavy reliance on contractors continued to provide weapons and support for the brewing cold war, as well as for the new space program. In fact, most of the early vehicles designed for the space program, including the Atlas rockets used in the first manned flights of the Mercury capsule, were originally built to deliver nuclear weapons. The contractor strategy, which had proven so successful during World War II, became the foundation for America's emerging global military role, as well as Eisenhower's famous warning about the "military-industrial complex." That experience, in turn, set the stage for contractors that built the interstate highway system and, in turn, cleaned up toxic waste sites and provided new information management. Pragmatism—the practicality of relying on skilled private companies to do work the government wanted done—drove much of the development of this complexity.

Practical politics was another driving force. Especially after World War II, Americans' appetite for government programs expanded rapidly. How could government do all the things people wanted without transforming America into a welfare state that its citizens were not prepared to accept? The answer lay in contractors. They processed Medicare and Medicaid claims without hiring legions of new federal bureaucrats. Ronald Reagan made an attack on government the signature element of his 1980 presidential campaign. "In this present crisis, government is not the solution to our problem; government is the problem," he said in his first inaugural address. He appointed two special commissions to recommend how to shrink government and increase privatization. The result? Not fewer government programs or less spending but, ironically, an acceleration of the trend toward relying on contractors to do even more government work. It was good politics: preaching the gospel of small government, restraining the growth of government employees, while expanding government's power and reach through more partnerships with private contractors.

Government did not get smaller. Its management strategies simply became more complex. Moreover, the rising role of private contractors had an important political value. Conservative ideologues have long argued that private business can do anything that government can do—only better and cheaper, without the burden of government's heavy hand. Contracting thus had a powerful force behind it. The federal government's spending on contracts grew from $203 billion in 2000 to $412 billion in 2006. At the Department of Homeland Security, procurement spending soared by more than 50 percent in just one year, as the department struggled to recover from Katrina and to meet its terrorism prevention mission.[16] The US military relied extensively on contractors for fighting the war in Iraq. In 2008, there were more defense contractor employees than American military forces in the country, and it is very hard to imagine how the Pentagon could have fought the war if it had faced the challenge of doubling the recruitment of soldiers to fight the war in a more traditional way.[17]

New contracting strategies further complicate these issues. Since the 1990s, government has been relying more on new megacontractors, called *lead systems integrators* (or LSIs), which are large private organizations that manage programs on government's behalf. LSIs, in turn, contract with other contractors and subcontractors who actually perform the work. The LSI approach streamlines the government's chores by giving government managers a single contact for intricate issues, and it provides the contractor network a single point of contact with the government. The government agency must rely on the LSI not only for contract supervision but also for policy planning and program design. The government, in short, shares its governance responsibilities with its LSI partner.

A large management consortium, United Space Alliance, is responsible for the space shuttle program. USA—NASA has always had a knack for acronyms—became a hybrid systems integration contractor formed from Boeing and Lockheed Martin, the companies on which NASA had long relied for its manned space missions. USA, in turn, managed the vast army of subcontractors who did virtually all the work and spent 90 percent of the shuttle's budget. In general, NASA knew only what USA collected, processed, and shared. As the investigation into the shuttle *Columbia*'s tragic disintegration in 2003 revealed, NASA had little capacity for independent judgment, and it could not know what it did not think to ask. When a contractor's engineers concluded that the shuttle was in no danger from the collision with the piece of foam, NASA had little choice but to accept the judgment. It did not have sufficient expertise of its own to do anything else. Not only did NASA depend on the contractors to operate the shuttle, but it had to rely on the contractors for critical judgments about the safety of the system.[18]

The same was true of FEMA's reliance on contractors. FEMA purchased most of the temporary homes for Katrina victims through a handful of large contractors. And during America's long war in Iraq, several large contractors, like Halliburton, managed much of the Pentagon's war support operations. The government has come to rely more on general management contractors to consolidate oversight over the far larger contractor community. It has created new kinds of contracts that move beyond the traditional approach of drawing up specifications and accepting bids, including indefinite-quantity/indefinite-price arrangements that create ongoing relationships between government and private companies without competition for price and quality. In some cases, the government has even contracted out the task of defining what it ought to buy from other private companies.

The Pentagon has relied heavily on this strategy, and it has created vast new business opportunities for large LSIs such as Halliburton and Boeing. The strategy helps the military branches, which have long complained that they do not have an adequate workforce for overseeing large contracts. It helps the military circumvent the stovepipes that often characterize its own procurement system and spreads performance incentives throughout the contractor supply chain.

As the GAO found in its investigation of one LSI, however, the approach also created "the most complex acquisition [that the] Army has ever undertaken."[19] The Army contracted with Boeing to oversee transformation of the military's ground-fighting capability, by replacing its existing vehicles with new equipment, both manned and unmanned, that would be linked by new information systems. Boeing designed the system and managed the contractors that would produce it, which gave it substantial strategic authority. The contract also reimbursed Boeing for its costs, making it difficult to manage and control its expenditures. The relationship, the GAO concluded in a masterpiece of understatement, "may pose significant risks to the Army's ability to provide oversight over the long term."[20] It put Boeing in the layer between the Army's policy makers and the contractors actually doing the work. It made Boeing the expert on the project, thereby shifting key management and accountability responsibilities from public to private hands. The Army countered that it did not have enough capacity to run the project on its own, but that argument only underscored GAO's worries. In addition, the government's reliance on private companies offering military services for hire—what P. W. Singer calls "corporate warriors"—was on the rise.[21]

Contracting, of course, is not just a federal phenomenon. State and local contracting has increased steadily as well, driven by ideological and efficiency imperatives. State and local governments traditionally relied on contractors for road construction and snow removal. Under pressure of reformers, who have contended that the market incentives of the private sector make it inherently superior to government for service provision, contracting has expanded into garbage collection and libraries, road maintenance and public safety. Moreover, in many local governments, contractors have taken over the service integrator role, especially in social-service programs. In Philadelphia, for example, one large contractor became the pass-through integrator for nearly $100 million, to finance scores of programs ranging from after-school care to reduction of youth violence. In Arizona, Lester Salamon explains, the state "contracts out the contracting out of mental health services," through "master contracts."[22] No one really knows how much of this contracting out of contracting occurs, but the anecdotal evidence is that the practice is significant and growing.

Some ideologues have gone a step further by contending that *anything that can* be privatized should be. Beyond that is the flexibility that private contractors can provide and the use of competition to promote efficiency. The result, E. S. Savas concludes, is that "the trend is unmistakably away from government and toward the other institutions—in a word, privatization."[23] Beyond the ideology is a powerful and irresistible pragmatic movement. As Jody Freeman argued, much of the story of government's expansion in the twentieth century is the tale of expanded public–private relationships to support the public's growing appetite for services.[24]

This trend has also led governments at all levels to rely increas ingly on nonprofit organizations. No one knows exactly how much public money flows through nonprofits. GAO estimated that federal spending through nonprofits amounted to $317 billion in fiscal year 2004, and hundreds of billions more come from state and local governments.[25] The nonprofit sector is growing—and so, too, is government's reliance on nonprofit organizations for service delivery. In part, this is because nonprofits bring close connection to the people being served and their managers typically have special knowledge of the area. Nonprofits also offer the government greater flexibility. Moreover, the rise of faith-based organizations has further spurred—and introduced new political battles into—government's service delivery partnerships.[26] These nonprofits deliver social services and economic development programs. They provide job training and health care. Nonprofits work in education, run botanical gardens, contribute to environmental preservation, help troubled individuals escape addiction, advance human rights, advocate on behalf of veterans, and run cultural exchange programs with citizens of other nations. The scope of their role is sweeping and increasing.

The political and administrative imperatives are inescapable, but the governance challenges are huge. Nonprofits tend to grow out of an intense commitment to their mission and connection with their community. Their goal is to do good, but their focus is not necessarily to serve as government's agents. From their point of view, the search is for resources to accomplish the mission. From government's point of view, the question is how to harness their capacity to serve public purposes.

As the GAO has pointed out, federal money for public goals can end up in nonprofit organizations through many paths (see Figure 2.3), vastly complicating the government's problem of ensuring that nonprofits stay true to the public purpose. Not only do they start with different—sometimes radically different—purposes, but

FIGURE 2.3 Examples of Paths That Federal Funds Take to Nonprofit Organizations

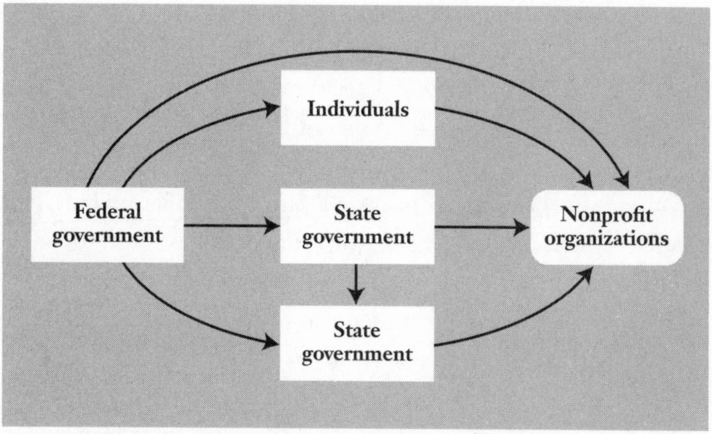

Source: Statement of Stanley J. Czerwinski, Director, Strategic Issues, U.S. Government Accountability Office, *Nonprofit Sector: Increasing Numbers and Key Role in Delivering Federal Services*, GAO-07-1084T (July 24, 2007), 8.

the money that provides the backbone of accountability can often come into the same organization through so many different paths that the cross-pressures are enormous and difficult to differentiate. Some nonprofits are fully dependent on a single government agency for all of their funds, but many receive funds from different sources, and the multiple funding sources multiply the number of funders who expect results—and the kinds of results they expect. That makes it hard for any single funder to call the shots. It makes it hard for nonprofits to sort out the expectations. And it creates opportunities for skillful nonprofit managers to play one funder against another, even if the funder is the government, which expects high performance and accountability for the taxpayer dollars invested in the nonprofit's programs.

The multiplication of sectors and service agencies further complicates the coordination of service delivery, because it becomes far harder to focus many agencies with different goals and funding streams on shared objectives. Moreover, many nonprofits receiving government funds are small, with limited capacity to manage their money, run the programs, and hire highly skilled employees to accomplish their work. They often have little patience with government's reporting requirements, because every dollar spent on complying with government rules is a dollar that cannot be spent on the organization's mission. Many nonprofits are in fragile financial condition, and leadership of the organizations remains a constant problem.[27] At all levels, government has become increasingly dependent on nonprofits for service delivery, and citizens interact increasingly with nonprofits in their daily lives. The flow of funds, competing goals and expectations, and the sometimes low management capacity of nonprofits all raise complex puzzles for the service system—problems that grow as the interconnections expand.

All of these contracting strategies have made government increasingly vulnerable to serious problems. Since 1990, the GAO has identified government programs that are especially vulnerable to fraud, waste, abuse, and mismanagement. The 2008 list, for example, contains twenty-seven programs, ranging from managing the Department of Homeland Security and modernizing the Department of Defense to transforming food safety programs and managing Medicare (see Table 2.1). The GAO's list highlights government's vulnerability to these increasingly complex arrangements, for every item on the list but one represents an intricate public–private partnership. The other item is strategic human capital: government's capacity to hire, retain, and direct the public officials who are responsible for managing everything else. The GAO's studies detail case after case of rising complexity cascading into growing problems of performance and rising levels of waste and mismanagement. The issues have become larger because the systems we created to pursue our ambitious policy goals have become far more complex. The increase in complexity has led to a shift of power, from public to private hands. The shift in power, moreover, has raised troubling questions about who is exercising sovereign governmental power.[28]

Since the end of World War II, the federal government has tried to solve this problem by drawing boundaries. It has encouraged contracting for functions in which the private sector can do the work more cheaply than the government can. It has tried to retain responsibility for "inherently governmental functions."[29] Contractors have taken on a growing array of services, and that concerns some observers. As David M. Walker, former head of the GAO, argued, "The closer contractor services come to supporting inherently governmental functions, the greater the risk of their influencing the government's control over and accountability for decisions that may be based, in part, on contractor work." That, he said, "may result in decisions that are not in the best interest of the government, and may increase vulnerability to waste, fraud, and abuse."[30] The difficulty of defining just what is an "inherently governmental function" has led several presidents and many contractors to stretch the boundaries, and that in turn has led to more contracting out for a dizzying array of functions—including some key decisions at the core of government's work.

The problem is that private business has become so sophisticated that almost anything can be contracted out, so drawing the line that demarcates government's core functions has become ever harder. Meanwhile, experienced government officials like Stephen Goldsmith, who led a major privatization effort while mayor of Indianapolis, have raised a troubling question: "what happens when government turns out not to be very good at inherently governmental work?"[31] Some of government's toughest critics argue that if almost *anything can* be contracted out, then almost *every-*

TABLE 2.1   GAO's High-Risk List

Addressing Challenges in Broad-Based Transformations

- Strategic human capital management
- Managing federal real property
- Protecting the federal government's information systems and the nation's critical infrastructures
- Implementing and transforming the Department of Homeland Security
- Establishing appropriate and effective information-sharing mechanisms to improve homeland security
- DOD approach to business transformation
- DOD business systems modernization
- DOD personnel security clearance program
- DOD support infrastructure management
- DOD financial management
- DOD supply chain management
- DOD weapon systems acquisition
- FAA air traffic control modernization
- Financing the nation's transportation system
- Ensuring the effective protection of technologies critical to US national security interests
- Transforming federal oversight of food safety

Managing Federal Contracting More Effectively

- DOD contract management
- DOE contract management
- NASA contract management
- Management of interagency contracting
- 2010 census

Assessing the Efficiency and Effectiveness of Tax Law Administration

- Enforcement of tax laws
- IRS business systems modernization

Modernizing and Safeguarding Insurance and Benefit Programs

- Modernizing federal disability programs
- Pension Benefit Guaranty Corporation single-employer pension insurance program
- Medicare program
- Medicaid program
- National Flood Insurance Program

Source: www.gao.gov.

thing should be contracted out. But to follow that advice would pull government even deeper into the accountability morass.

The GAO found that, at a major Army contracting center, contractors worked side by side with Army employees, doing the same job and differentiated only by the color of their badges. Contractors used government equipment and passed themselves off as government employees in communicating outside the contracting center. They often made major contracting decisions.[32] It was impossible to separate the role of contractors from the role of government employees—and it was impossible to tell who to hold accountable for what. The problem was not limited to defense facilities. At the Department of Homeland Security, contractors regularly communicated on behalf of the department and contractor employees used DHS e-mail addresses. Anyone connecting with the department from the outside could not tell whether the person at the other end was a government employee or a contractor.

Thus, the traditional approach—defining government's role by drawing lines around its core functions—no longer works, for two reasons: the private sector can often do whatever the government needs to have done, and the government often is not very good at either managing its own functions or overseeing its contractors. Why does it matter? Because the more the line between public and private roles becomes blurred, the harder it is to tell who is exercising government authority and to hold individuals accountable for the decisions they make. Contractors, for example, follow different lines of accountability than do government employees, and putting them in the same office doing the same job makes it impossible to use the accountability strategy that works best for the management tactic. The difficulty of producing reliable accountability raises a troubling question about what government is in the twenty-first century.

Accountability

Another consequence of the blurring boundaries and increasing complexity is a muddied accountability for public programs. Connected to the Mildred paradox (the rise of government programs provided through nongovernment agencies) and the Mildred corollary (a governance system in which no one is ultimately accountable for anything) is a fundamental problem: policy makers are increasingly insulated from the consequences of their decisions, and citizens' trust in government has faltered.

Consider the declining citizen trust in public institutions. A 2007 Pew Research Center survey found that nearly two thirds of those polled believed that "when something is run by the government, it is usually inefficient and wasteful." Public attitudes improved slightly and briefly following the September 11 terrorist

FIGURE 2.4   Public Attitudes about Government's Performance

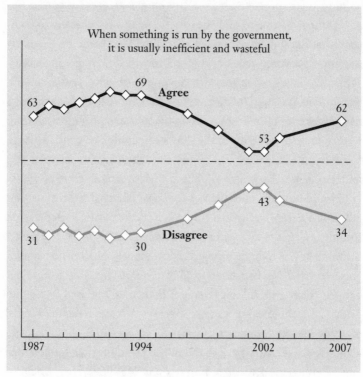

When something is run by the government,
it is usually inefficient and wasteful

Agree

63   69   62   53

Disagree

31   30   43   34

1987   1994   2002   2007

Source: The Pew Research Center for the People & the Press, *Trends in Political Values and Core Attitudes: 1987–2007* (Washington: Pew Research Center, March 22, 2007), 45, at http://people-press.org/reports/pdf/312.pdf.

attacks, when a rise in patriotism also prompted an increase in support for government and its programs. But within a few years, skepticism was rising back to the level that had endured for the previous twenty years (see Figure 2.4). In general, most members of the public just do not believe that government works well.[33]

These public opinion surveys represent the inevitable product of the Mildred paradox and its corollary. The growing difficulty of holding anyone accountable for anything also makes it harder for government to ensure high-quality work and for citizens to connect their tax dollars with what government gives them. We have slid into a growing array of programs in which no one is in charge. When problems occur, it is virtually impossible to identify who is responsible. It is hard for citizens to know where to go for help, and it is harder for public employees on their own to provide what citizens request. The result of the Mildred paradox and the Mildred corollary is a slippage in the vending machine's gears. Despite the remarkable breakdown surrounding the government's response to Hurricane Katrina, only FEMA Director Michael Brown lost his job. But a defensive Brown told a US House of Representatives committee that the manifest failure was not his fault.[34] Despite continued pleas to higher government officials, he said, he had not gotten the help he had asked for. His requests, he said, "just didn't happen. They just did not happen." Brown said he had argued to Andy Card, the president's chief of staff, that the federal government needed to move fast, but Card's response, Brown claimed, was, "We are going to have to follow the chain of command on this one." Card, he said, directed him to go to DHS Secretary Michael Chertoff and work through the department's lines of authority. In fact, Brown confessed to the committee, "I think that we as Republicans have made a fundamental error in creating this new bureaucracy [the Department of Homeland Security] that slows down the process." Pressed to explain why he had failed to produce results, Brown said,

> There is blame for everybody to go around. I want you
> to understand from my perspective, sitting in my shoes at
> that time, I am sitting there looking at now—and I know
> I've said Louisiana and New Orleans was dysfunctional,

but you know what? We were dysfunctional, too, because
the things that I was asking for wasn't occurring. And so
the whole thing became this dysfunctional mess.

Brown was frustrated, he said. "I couldn't make things happen."

Problems had rippled throughout the system. New Orleans
Mayor Nagin had pointed to state and federal officials. Louisiana
Governor Blanco had pleaded with federal officials to "send everything." Brown said he had asked the White House to help and
the president's aides had told him to work with the Department
of Homeland Security, which, Brown said, had told him to set up
operations in Baton Rouge and work through channels. It was a
catastrophe aggravated by slippage in leverage over action, the lack
of accountability for decisions, and the absence of consequences
for mistakes.

Of course, the New Orleans situation would have been far less
dangerous had the levees held. But Senate investigators found that
the breaks in the levees had followed breakdowns among the many
players in the levee system, which had set the stage for collapse
long before the storm struck. The Army Corps of Engineers, a
federal agency, had built much of the system. The Orleans Levee
District, a local agency, had local responsibility for maintaining
the system, and the Louisiana Department of Transportation and
Development was charged with state-level oversight, but they simply had not coordinated the maintenance and repair operations.
Over time, the levees had settled deeper and provided less protection, but there had been little repair work. The annual inspections
had been more like parties than engineering trips, as one former
levee district official explained:

> They normally meet and get some beignets [pastries] and
> coffee in the morning and get to the buses. And the colo-

nel and the brass are all dressed up. You have commission-
ers, they have some news cameras following you around
and you have your little beignets and then you have a nice
lunch somewhere or whatever. And that's what the inspections are about.[35]

When the levees broke, the three groups squabbled among themselves over who was responsible for the repairs and what emergency fixes were most likely to work. Those battles delayed the
efforts to stem the flooding for three days and further worsened
the damage.

No one intended to make these mistakes or to punish the city's
residents. But no one was in charge of solving the problems. The
bureaucratic tugs-of-war over what to do and who should do it
led to long, needless, and painful delays. Weeks after the city had
flooded, as displaced residents struggled to regain the rudiments
of their lives, one mother plaintively asked, "Where is the government right now? I don't know what to do."[36] The president had
flown to Jackson Square with a promise of help. Congress had
appropriated billions of dollars to fund it. Nonprofit and religious
organizations had contributed substantial assistance. Thousands
upon thousands of people had received assistance. Throughout
the area, however, the recurring theme among residents was that
they felt abandoned. "Don't forget us," was the recurring plea. The
inescapable fact was that government's programs were not working as government, at all levels, had promised. No one wanted to
fail, but no one was in charge of ensuring success.

Government programs do not align themselves easily or automatically, and when they fall out of sync, bad things can happen.
Such programs increasingly echo the old joke about helicopters:
"Helicopters are a collection of parts flying in relatively close formation while all rotating around a different axis. Things work well
until one of the parts breaks formation."[37]

The intricacies of American federalism further complicate the problem of accountability. Federalism is wonderfully designed to provide citizens multiple opportunities for representation, and it has played a critical role in balancing national control with local discretion. But it is not designed to get hard things done, quickly and cheaply. In fact, as Katrina showed, it sometimes makes it hard to get anything done at all.[38] Federalism is an American wonder—in part because it is wonderful at balancing competing interests across the country and in part because it is wonderful at blurring the lines of political responsibility. The intersection of the American constitutional separation-of-powers system with federalism ensures that no one is ever fully responsible for anything. Americans clearly relish the protections that their systems provide, but they increasingly chafe at the inefficiencies that the system produces. The growing complexities of twenty-first-century government increasingly impose punishing costs in exchange for the advantages of the system, and no cost is larger than the difficulty of holding anyone accountable for results.

Indeed, the boundaries between government and civil society in America are more blurred than anywhere else in the world, and those blurred boundaries are creating growing challenges for democratic government. Government administrators have responsibilities over programs for which they cannot control results. Elected officials promise things they cannot deliver. Citizens ask for government help that often seems a struggle, sometimes does not arrive at all, and makes them feel disconnected from their government. They complain about government, its costs and inefficiencies, yet they constantly ask for more. The growing dilemma of rising demands and hobbled capacity threatens to cripple government's ability to govern. The increase of these cross-pressures has undermined the ability of citizens and policy makers alike to hold government programs and their managers accountable.

The Challenges of Networked Government

American government has never suffered from low ambition. From providing long-term health care for older Americans to helping storm victims recover from their losses, government has proven itself generous and gifted with a broad, bold, impressive reach. But these generous instincts have generated programs that the nation cannot afford and that challenge our ability to manage and govern well. Since a small band of early Americans snuck aboard a ship to toss British tea into Boston Harbor, Americans have campaigned against Big Government. But deep down, they love it. They just prefer not to admit it, to themselves or to their neighbors.

To tackle these problems, we have created extraordinarily complex networks that are hard to manage, especially because they increasingly bring private and nonprofit organizations into the mission of doing public work. The problem of relying on agents is that their goals might not line up with the goals of those who hire them. The more boundaries the networks have to cross, the greater these goal conflicts will stretch, fray, and even break the pursuit of public ends. The nature of these networks, moreover, magnifies the government's problem of ensuring responsible government, since no one is in charge and, therefore, no one is accountable. It is little wonder that American government often seems to perform badly. The real miracle is that it works so well so often.

The implications for citizenship are just as profound. In his travels around America in the late nineteenth century, Alexis de Tocqueville noted the American disposition to form associations. The core of American government, he believed, was built on this special form of participative democracy. For a long time, this participation provided a subtle but important antidote to the fractioning of American politics. The founders sought to prevent the accumulation of too much power in any part of government. The energy of citizens, and the spirit of citizenship, provided the glue to hold the system together—to create a sense of nation and community that surmounted the institutional boundaries and conflicts. It was a model of *implicit activism*, of citizens voluntarily joining to connect with each other and, in the process, to provide the essential missing link for American government: a bridge across its boundaries.

With the rise of Mildred- and Katrina-style problems, however, that bridge developed serious problems. Robert D. Putnam pointed to the "disappearance" of civic America.[39] He has legions of critics, but there is no denying the strains in the body politic and its disconnection from civic life. Theda Skocpol quarrels about some of the data, but she points to the "generational disjuncture in the associational loyalties of many American adults, starting around the mid-1960s."[40] As Putnam, Skocpol, and many others have noted, large social forces were tearing at the fabric of American social life. Hugh T. Miller put it this way: "Deliberative governance has given way to spectator democracy."[41]

At the very time that citizens seemed increasingly disconnected from and cynical about government, more and more private citizens and private organizations were being drawn into the delivery of public services. Mildred- and Katrina-style problems were spreading, and with them the connection between government institutions and citizens was becoming frayed. We moved increasingly from implicit activism by citizens to *explicit passivism*: a growing expectation that government should solve citizens' problems, without an integrated public role, and through complex partnerships with private providers of public services.

The shift from implicit activism to explicit passivism has led to a paradox of "publicization," as private actors increasingly take on public roles.[42] The more government relies on private partners to assist in the delivery of public programs, the more these private actors become part of the public service system. Their role, how-ever, is rarely transparent, even to them.

A conversation I had not long ago with a pharmacist makes the point. As I waited to pick up two prescriptions, he was com-plaining about government and its problem of getting anything done, in the kind of conversation repeated thousands of times a day across America. One of the prescriptions was for me, paid by my university health insurance. At the time, I was an employee of the University of Wisconsin, so the benefits were paid by the state government through a private health insurance company. The other was for Mildred, who at the time was receiving prescription drug benefits as the widow of a retired Air Force officer, so the benefits were paid by the federal government through a private health insurance company. Mixed into the line were customers on medical assistance, Medicare, private insurance, and no insurance. The pharmacist, of course, had no idea who paid the bills for most of his customers. If the customer had an insurance card, credit card, or cash, he filled the prescriptions—at some moments an agent of the military, at other moments an agent of the state, at others simply a participant in the private market. All the while, he complained about the government, even though, in bits and pieces of his time, he was in fact part of the very system he was carping about.

That nugget is central to what makes networked government so hard to govern. American government has evolved to the point where most Americans do not recognize government when they see it. There are police officers, firefighters, emergency medi-cal technicians, garbage collectors, and snowplow operators, but these are local officials. There are members of the armed forces and diplomats, but these are relatively small in number. For the most part, government lives in the "nameless, faceless bureau-crats," the universal term of derision for those who do the public's work. Ronald Reagan loved to say, "I've always felt the nine most terrifying words in the English language are: 'I'm from the government, and I'm here to help.'"[43] The line always got big laughs and has been repeated endlessly by wags. But underlying the joke is a thinly veiled contempt for government and those who seek to do its work. The profound irony is that it is a snake that has bitten its own tail: as citizens laugh at Reagan's joke and complain about how poorly government works, they often fail to realize that, because of the increasingly blurry lines between government and the rest of society and the complex partnerships that produce government's work, they are complaining about themselves. That is the paradox of the pharmacist's carping, and the central paradox of citizenship in modern America.

In short, our problems and the consequences for failing to manage them well have combined to create a quiet crisis in American government. We have evolved a networked governance system challenged by a fundamental problem: what we seek to accomplish is out of sync with our capacity for delivering it. That conclusion lies at the core of the tales of Mildred and Katrina and, as we shall see, of many other arenas as well. We have more government, reaching further and deeper, without effective governance, and we have too many programs whose results too often fall short of our reach. For more than two centuries, our traditions and strategies served us relatively well. But as our ambitions have grown and our society has become more complicated, the gaps have grown larger and more dangerous. We want a responsible government, but too often it acts irresponsibly. That is the puzzle we take up in the next chapter.

3

IRRESPONSIBLE GOVERNMENT

For Lindsay Huckabee, the challenges of coping with networked government were almost too much to bear. Huckabee lived with her husband and four children in Pass Christian, Mississippi, near where Katrina made landfall and where the storm's surge—more than thirty feet—flattened virtually the entire town. The storm wiped out the town's McDonald's and left only a sign to mark where the police department had once stood. The Harbor View Restaurant disappeared. So did most of the harbor. A year and a half later, the town still lacked a supermarket. Providing housing so that workers could return to their jobs—and trying to restore the jobs to begin with—slowed the town's recovery.

The family's apartment had been completely under water, and they called FEMA for help. They got a travel trailer as a temporary home. FEMA then promised that, if they could clear a lot and provide septic, water, and power service to the site, FEMA would bring a mobile home. They managed just that in Kiln, Mississippi, twenty-two miles down the road, and they moved into their new home two and a half months after the storm hit. "We were very excited and felt very blessed," she remembered later. But then everyone in the family began getting sick. Three of the children developed frequent nosebleeds. Lindsay was pregnant and developed migraines and premature labor. After being born a month early, her son, Michael, suffered from clogged sinuses and coughed through much of the night.

Michael's older sister, Lelah, struggled even more. After moving into the FEMA trailer, she came down with recurring ear infections and repeated nosebleeds, and she was twice hospitalized for pneumonia. Nothing in the medical arsenal—allergy tests, MRIs, surgery to insert tubes in her ears, steroids, allergy medications, nasal sprays—helped doctors diagnose or solve her problem, and she missed forty-two days of kindergarten. One day, Lindsay came home to discover Lelah's arms and shirt covered in blood. Her ear, nose, and throat doctor asked a pointed question: was the family in a FEMA trailer? When the doctor heard the answer, the prescription was pointed: get out as soon as possible. But the family had no other place to go, so they decided to tough it out.

Almost a year and a half after the Huckabees moved into the trailer, the Sierra Club paid to test the air quality. The test showed a formaldehyde level of 0.18 parts per million, a level that researchers believe significantly increases the risk of cancer and respiratory problems. In Germany, Denmark, and the Netherlands, this level of exposure would require immediate remediation. In the United States, there is no formaldehyde standard for homes, but the Occupational Safety and Health Administration (OSHA) warns of the risks of long-term exposure at this level. Lindsay called FEMA and had to work through five different officials until the agency agreed to replace the trailer with one that was "formaldehyde free." To be safe, the family did a test on the new home and discovered a level of 0.108 parts per million, much lower than the first test. When Lindsay called to inform the agency, a FEMA representative pointed to the lower levels and confidently asked, "So we are good, right?" Lindsay wasn't so sure, because the level was still above the recommended exposure limit of 0.10 parts per million. She became all the more concerned when, a few months later, her husband visited the dentist. The exam uncovered a mass, which a CT scan revealed to be a tumor—a relatively common growth but in a very rare location.

"What makes me so angry," she told a congressional committee, "is that FEMA is providing trailers to disaster victims that they have 'inspected' and deemed safe without truly ensuring they are." She continued, "I do not want to believe that FEMA knew about the formaldehyde when they issued these homes, but I do know that when it was brought to their attention, they spent little effort to fix the problem. Instead, people were made to feel that they were being too picky." In fact, a congressional hearing later revealed, one manufacturer that supplied 50,000 FEMA trailers knew that some of its homes were emitting 45 times the formaldehyde set in the federal standard, but it told neither the government nor the trailers' residents.[1] The FEMA trailer, Lindsay hoped, would give the struggling family a chance to get back on its feet. Instead, with the bills for doctors and prescriptions, "we are actually moving backwards."[2]

Formaldehyde exposure is a common problem in many homes, and it is part of the chemical cocktail that creates the "new car smell" that car buyers often crave. In the FEMA trailers, the formaldehyde came from the adhesives used to assemble the trailers' cabinetry, especially in the glue used to manufacture the fiberboard. FEMA knew that formaldehyde complaints were growing. When a couple suspected that formaldehyde might have caused the death of their baby girl, a FEMA official visited the trailer. The smell, the official said, made her "nose burn." After a resident in another trailer died, a teleconference among twenty-eight officials, from FEMA and five other agencies, recommended testing and investigation. A FEMA official concluded that formaldehyde was probably at the root of the death and planned to install monitors to gauge the formaldehyde level. Another said simply, "This needs to be fixed today." But the agency's attorneys stopped the plan because, as one FEMA attorney said in an e-mail, an investigation "could seriously undermine the Agency's position in the litigation and that is not acceptable." One FEMA attorney explained the position on conducting tests: "Once you get results and should they indicate some problem, the clock is running on our duty to respond to them." If testing the trailers might reveal formaldehyde risks, FEMA's general counsel suggested a simple alternative: "that we do not do testing." Tests on the suspected problem "would imply FEMA's ownership of this issue."[3]

FEMA had bought the trailers from a private contractor. It had supplied them to Katrina's victims. But its officials refused to accept any responsibility for the agency's actions. House Oversight and Government Reform Committee Chairman Henry A. Waxman was scathing in his criticism. The committee had found "an official policy of premeditated ignorance," he said. "Senior FEMA officials in Washington didn't want to know what they already knew because they didn't want the moral and legal responsibility to do what they knew had to be done. So they did their best not to know." Waxman concluded that the findings were "sickening." FEMA's behavior, he said, "was the exact opposite of what government should be."[4]

Soon after Katrina hit, federal officials knew they were facing a housing problem of monumental proportion. The storm had displaced 700,000 people and destroyed or damaged 300,000 homes. The disaster ranged over 90,000 square miles across the Gulf. Visitors to the area in the weeks afterward knew from the television stories how devastating the storm was. But observers returning from the region came away saying they were not remotely pre- pared for the sheer scale and scope of the damage, with heavily damaged homes and stores stretching for miles. FEMA had been badly stung by the criticism of the agency's initial response, and top officials were determined not to stumble again in providing emergency housing.

The FEMA strategy has long been to buy travel trailers and manufactured housing for persons displaced through disasters. And rather than taxing its staff with company-by-company nego- tiations in the middle of a crisis, FEMA typically negotiated con- tracts in advance with a handful of big prime contractors, who could subcontract the work to housing manufacturers. The names of the big contractors might not be known to most Americans, but insiders know them as big players: Bechtel, CH2M Hill, Fluor, plus the Shaw Group from Baton Rouge. The prime contractors cre- ated Web sites for manufacturers to register and do business with FEMA. They did not build or install the trailers themselves. They operated as FEMA's intermediaries with the builders and install- ers. FEMA did not do the work. It did not even contract for the work. It contracted with contractors who managed the work, in an echo of the lead systems integrator approach that we explored in Chapter 2. So, much as the case for Mildred and her nursing home, government itself did not perform most of the work it paid for.

The contractors were enthusiastic about the business, and such enormous sales came along rarely.[5] At the peak, they were cranking out 120 travel trailers a day. FEMA buyers snapped up as many homes as they could find—3,500 manufactured homes and another 5,200 travel trailers. Tens of thousands of new homes descended on the region. In fact, one FEMA housing administrator sent an e-mail telling everyone, "Purchase until I say stop." But that is where the problems started. The administrator told everyone to buy but did not tell them what to buy. The homes flooded the area but FEMA had not arranged for where to put them. In some communities, FEMA spent money to prepare sites but failed to coordinate with local officials for the necessary zoning and utilities. In other communities, the sites were found to be contaminated and could not be used. Some proposed sites required more renovation than program requirements allowed FEMA to do. FEMA spent $8.5 million preparing sites that could not be used. In other communities, FEMA was slow to process the applications for homes, so units that were available went empty.

Moreover, FEMA's own rules prohibit putting manufactured homes in floodplains. This was scarcely a case of red tape. No one wanted to put flood victims at risk of having their temporary housing float away with the next storm. That put FEMA at the hub of a monumental miscalculation. Thousands of homes were heading to the region, but Katrina's victims could not use most of them because their destroyed homes were in floodplains. FEMA, for example, ordered 60,000 travel trailers and shipped in 5,000 manufactured homes from its inventory. Local FEMA officials could find only 100 places to put the modular homes, all to house emergency personnel. They found 2,600 sites in Louisiana and 2,000 in Mississippi. But the rest of the housing units sat in white-elephant lots around the region, including 10,000 at the Hope, Arkansas, municipal airport. The Hope homes had cost $300 million, plus another $3 million per year to be stored. Another 12,000 homes sat at ten other storage sites throughout the southeast. In all, FEMA bought 120,000 trailers.

Some of the homes became damaged because they were not stored properly. Others warped. FEMA did not know what to do with the homes, and the agency faced quiet but fierce opposition from manufacturers who feared that FEMA's dumping so many homes on the market would destroy their businesses (even though their businesses had been artificially inflated by the post-Katrina FEMA buying boom).

As FEMA's lawyers tried to deflect the agency's "ownership" of the formaldehyde problem, the inspector general charged with investigating their management concluded that he could not determine who was responsible for having made the buying decisions. Richard L. Skinner told a congressional committee that he had found initial e-mails that gave a green light for buying "until I say stop." After that, his office "could not locate subsequent e-mails that provided the specific number of temporary housing units to be purchased or who made the final decision to purchase."[6] FEMA ended up hundreds of millions of dollars in the hole, holding an inventory of tens of thousands of housing units that it could not use and did not know how to dispose of. Its inspector general could not determine who had made the decision or who should be held accountable for the problem.

FEMA's lawyers tried to build a shield against complaints from people who had moved into the trailers and had become sick, but the shield did not work for long. Under enormous pressure from scientists in February 2008, FEMA accelerated the effort to move all the hurricane victims out of the trailers. The US Centers for Disease Control (CDC) had tested 519 of the trailers and found that, on average, formaldehyde exposure in the trailers was five times the level in most homes. In some trailers, the CDC found levels fifty times as high. "We do not want people exposed to this for very much longer," said CDC official Mike McGeehin, director of a CDC division that focuses on environmental hazards.[7] CDC Director Julie Gerberding bluntly told reporters, "We're making the recommendation that all of the people in these situations be relocated to safer, permanent housing as quickly as possible."[8] As a *New York Times* editorial concluded, "Just when you thought the federal government could not possibly outdo its incredible record of ineptitude in the handling of the victims of Hurricane Katrina, it contrives, against all odds, to make yet another colossal mistake."[9]

With toxic trailers piling up and 63,000 unused trailers sitting in lots, FEMA struggled to dispose of the trailers. Storage alone was costing at least $36 million per year. Under pressure from the trailer manufacturers, Congress passed a law forbidding FEMA from donating the trailers to the public, even though it was hard to give them away. Manufacturers also pressured FEMA to limit auctions of the trailers. Dennis Harney, executive director of the Indiana Manufactured Housing Association-Recreation Vehicle Indiana Council, warned that the auctions "could have a devastating effect on Indiana," which produces two thirds of the nation's recreational vehicles. One plan to sell 46,000 trailers would have flooded the market with about 30 percent of the industry's annual production, according to some estimates.[10] FEMA slowed the auctions; the trailers they were able to sell fetched just forty cents on the dollar.

In the end, FEMA found government agencies willing to take some trailers. In Gettysburg, Pennsylvania, one trailer became a mobile spay and neuter clinic for pets. Philadelphia planned to use another trailer to store emergency flashlights, and another trailer became a mobile emergency response unit for the Harrisburg region. But the state's emergency management office still had ninety-one trailers it was struggling to dispose of. As Steven Kelman, a Harvard professor who had formerly headed the federal government's procurement operations, concluded, "The most parsimonious account of what went wrong was that they had a contracting organization in place that was stuck in the 1980s and they never took advantage of the reforms from the '90s."[11] The system was no match for the problems of the twenty-first century.

GAO investigations later found an estimated $1 billion in fraud in the housing relief effort. FEMA had mailed a $6,000 check to one person who listed a vacant lot as the address damaged by the storm. Some prisoners had wrangled checks, and one clever person had received three rental assistance checks for two different hurricanes on top of an $8,000 check for staying in a California hotel. FEMA had distributed 750 debit cards, worth $1.5 million, but the agency could not establish whether the cards had even gone to Katrina victims. Some legitimate recipients had used their Katrina debit cards to buy professional football tickets, a Caribbean vacation, and unspecified "adult entertainment." With tongue placed firmly in government-ese cheek, the GAO concluded that these expenses "do not appear to be necessary to satisfy disaster-related needs as defined by FEMA regulations."[12]

FEMA had drifted into a never-never land of big decisions with clumsy management and little accountability. Why? The DHS inspector general concluded that "FEMA attempted to use traditional solutions for non-traditional problems."[13] Faced with a nonroutine problem that required an adaptive solution, FEMA's officials saw it as a routine problem and applied traditional, hierarchical solutions. As always happens when government gets out of sync with the problems it is trying to solve, the result was disaster—not just the natural disaster of Katrina, but a perpetuation of FEMA's administrative disaster that had dogged it since Katrina had struck. Michael Brown was the public face of FEMA's problems, but the agency's problems were epidemic, rooted far more deeply in its operations.

American government has a complex system of checks and balances designed to ensure accountability. If one branch of government does not catch a problem, another should. The system can make government inefficient, but it is also supposed to make government responsive. However, the rise of the network challenges we saw in Chapter 2 not only court the administrative inefficiency of checks and balances—they also confound the quest for accountability and responsiveness. In some cases, our public institutions have contributed to the problem. In other cases, they have failed to rise to the challenge. In yet other cases, the problems slip through cracks in the system. Put together, these forces have undermined the responsibility of our governing institutions to govern.

Congressional Theater

Congress is responsible for part of the problem. By any measure, it is one of the world's great deliberative bodies. But at its core, Congress is a body of 535 individuals, each of whom seeks ownership of enough turf to make a case for reelection. The result is a lawmaking process dominated by tunnel vision that focuses on spending money, structuring government agencies for symbolic purposes, and advancing narrow political interests. This focus helps shape the congressional political game, but it handicaps Congress in dealing with the tough dilemmas of networked governance.

The Katrina problem was rooted in Congress's ongoing obsession with reorganizing FEMA and the rest of the homeland security apparatus. The September 11 terrorist attacks revealed substantial holes in the homeland security system, but congressional interest soon strayed from solving the problem to piling up symbolic points—to be seen as acting to "connect the dots," but without enough attention to ensure that the right dots were connected in the best way. This focus on restructuring over effectiveness, in turn, undermined Congress's ability to make good policy and oversee its execution. Those forces, according to Thomas E. Mann and Norman J. Ornstein, made Congress "a broken branch," a dysfunctional body where "bad process leads to bad policy." In fact, they sadly conclude, "The failure of both houses of Congress to do meaningful oversight contributed to the massive and unconscionable failures of the Department of Homeland Security and, after Hurricane Katrina, of its FEMA arm."[14]

The problems began soon after September 11. The attacks created a temporary truce on partisan attack, but as information emerged about the attacks, and especially about intelligence failures, members of Congress began talking about "connecting the dots" as a mantra. As Senator Joe Lieberman said in 2003, "We now know that the failure of our intelligence agencies to connect the dots on September 11th was the single greatest error among many glaring failures."[15] A Heritage Foundation analyst concluded that the "compartmentalization of data is the real reason the U.S. government failed to 'connect the dots' and predict the September 11 attacks."[16] The diagnosis was on target. The question was what medicine to prescribe.

The 9/11 Commission concluded that the problem lay in "structural barriers to performing joint intelligence work." The disciplines of the host of agencies collecting intelligence defined how they read the information. Structure, "not the joint mission," defined the approach and got in the way of "integrated, all-source analysis." Without that, the commission concluded, "it is not possible to 'connect the dots,'" because "no one component holds all the relevant information."[17] But members of Congress decrying the intelligence failure had only to look to Shakespeare for the explanation. "The fault," Cassius told Brutus in *Julius Caesar*, "is not in our stars but in ourselves."[18] The president is responsible for the faithful execution of the law, but Congress writes it. The president might appoint the heads of cabinet departments, but Congress must confirm them and Congress creates the overall structure within which they work. The pre-9/11 dots lay unconnected in part because the members of the intelligence community failed to share the information they had with each other. The fragmented structure of the intelligence community, which followed decades of decision making by Congress, created multiple roadblocks for that information sharing.

The multiplicity of players made it hard to ensure adequate coordination and control. Of course, the situation was so complex that no one could ever be fully in charge, but as one old Washington hand put it, "every discipline [and organization] thinks it's in charge of everything." Program officials cannot referee fights, and the dysfunctional environment in Washington gets everyone trapped in gotcha games, which get in the way of the mission. "Think about what you get in trouble for in this town—failure to follow a procedure, so you focus on fixing procedures," he explained. That leads to an accumulation of new rules and procedures like barnacles on a ship. "It's the small stuff you can't fix that gets everything bogged down," to the point that the big stuff never gets fixed at all. The resulting dilemma, he said, has helped fuel a "collapse of governance."[19]

Congress took on the "connect the dots" issue in 2002, and members pressed for a major reorganization. Senator Lieberman contended that "bold organizational change is demanded of us."[20] He picked up support from Republican Senator Arlen Specter: "The threat to our homeland and border security is so serious that the United States needs more than a presidential advisor." Specter said, "We require a cabinet-level secretary with the appropriate resources to further institutionalize the position and guarantee that the person holding the position has the legal authority to act."[21] President Bush, however, resisted the congressional plan for creating a new cabinet department for homeland security and argued instead for a beefed-up White House homeland security office. By late spring of 2002, congressional support, especially among the Democrats, was reaching critical mass. Bush had two choices: either members of Congress would force a restructuring plan on him, which would give them the policy initiative and the political credit for reform, or he could seize the initiative to craft a plan more to his liking. Just as Congress was about to pass the Homeland Security Act, Bush announced his support for the bill in a nationally televised address. It soon became *his* reform and, behind the scenes, Bush worked to flip the homeland security restructuring plan into an initiative that would also suit his other political objectives. He wanted to give the new department's managers more flexibility in hiring and firing employees and in structuring their work—a move that enraged the public employee unions, which was a key Democratic constituency. In a flash, Bush took over the Democrats' issue and reshaped it into a weapon aimed at their base, in a form they could not resist.

This high political drama, in the end, had little to do with connecting the dots. At the bill's signing ceremony in November 2002, Bush proudly said that, with the reorganization, "America will be better able to respond to any future attacks."[22] The new department brought together twenty-two different agencies. That restructuring, the reformers hoped, would improve coordination among them. But the bill did not merge the agencies responsible for intelligence, which is where the connect-the-dots problems lay. The DHS acquired responsibility for analyzing the data, but it was not in charge of collecting it or reviewing the raw data. The dots that most needed to be linked remained unconnected.

Congress got its new department. Bush got it in a way that undermined the Democrats. Homeland security managers got the challenge of making sense of the department's sprawling structure and multiple lines of accountability, especially on Capitol Hill. The White House counted eighty-eight separate committees and subcommittees with jurisdiction over the new department.[23] In the House alone, analysts found fourteen full committees and twenty-five different subcommittees that claimed jurisdiction over homeland security policy. Of the thirteen subcommittees of the Committee on Appropriations, ten exercised control over at least part of the budget.[24] The jurisdictions of the committees overlapped. Not only did the DHS find itself reporting to scores of committees, but multiple subcommittees often claimed ownership of the same issue. Committee and subcommittee hearings demanded representation by high-level DHS employees, and for a department located more than seven miles away from Capitol Hill, negotiating Washington's traffic just to reach committee hearing rooms was a constant logistical nightmare.

DHS Secretary Michael Chertoff complained that the burden of dealing with Congress's overlapping jurisdictions was severely taxing his staff. He estimated that the department would spend 15,000 work hours a year in preparing formal testimony, submit 535 reports, and give more than 2,000 briefings on Capitol Hill, with the burden "proliferating at an alarming rate." He added, "Arguably, the most important step Congress can take to improve operational effectiveness at DHS at this juncture is to streamline congressional oversight of DHS." For DHS officials, the burden was especially great because the department's headquarters was across town, near the vice president's mansion, more than seven miles away and at least a thirty-minute ride in the capital's heavy traffic, so every hearing and briefing meant an extra hour in the car. Congressional staffers had no patience for the argument, however. "We're doing our due diligence," one said. "Welcome to the world of oversight."[25]

That, however, is precisely the point. The overwhelming number of congressional committees and subcommittees that owned at least a part of the homeland security puzzle ensured that the DHS would never hear a consistent voice coming from Capitol Hill. The House created a Select Committee on Homeland Security, but the committee had no control over either policy or purse strings. As a result, Mann and Ornstein concluded,

> There has been no serious oversight of the DHS in either house. Perversely, the problem has been compounded by the incessant demands of the 88 congressional committees and subcommittees that, eager for political cachet and cover, have sought to grab a piece of homeland security jurisdiction by demanding that top DHS officials testify before them. The agency's top managers have spent a lot of time at Congress but almost none seriously examining the DHS' functions and performance.[26]

The restructuring layered new congressional jurisdictions atop old ones, created conflicting cross-pressures on agency officials, and demanded instant improvements on difficult problems. It made members of Congress feel that they were accomplishing something. It created a powerful new symbol—a department devoted to homeland security, with its own secretary—but it did nothing to alter the folkways of power within Congress. The executive branch—in structure, function, and budget—is the extended shadow of Congress itself, since Congress creates the structure, defines the function, and appropriates the budget. Solving homeland security problems would not be easy, members of Congress said as they were debating the issue. The biggest potential obstacle is "a four-letter word: T-U-R-F," explained California Democratic Representative Jane Harman.[27] What she did not say is that the toughest turf issues were on Capitol Hill.

Instead of rethinking the federal government's homeland security strategy, Congress shuffled executive branch boxes to create the new department, charged it with preventing another September 11, but then changed none of its own behavior that had made it so difficult for the dots to be connected. Congress then failed to effectively oversee the massive animal it had created. It is little surprise that DHS and its new stepchild, FEMA, failed to rise to Katrina's challenge. Then, within months after Katrina struck, at least thirteen different bills surfaced to reorganize FEMA yet again.[28] Congressional instinct for organizational restructuring was undying.

However, there is scant evidence that such tinkering improves the effectiveness of public organizations. In part, that is because few studies have looked at the impact of restructuring. Because the driving force for such changes is often political, the most important goals are met with the president's signature on the bill. Restructuring strategies to centralize control and power have rarely produced better management.[29] When the purpose is creating a symbol, passing the bill accomplishes the goal. Congress rarely follows through with the hard work needed to ensure that the new structure solves the problem that prompted it. The reason is circular. Congress tends to rely on symbolic restructuring because restructuring, not detailed policy oversight, better fits its political objectives. If Congress more effectively oversaw administrative actions to begin with, restructuring often would not be necessary. And once Congress moves the boxes, it rarely follows through to ensure that the new structure works. Congress most often pursues reorganization as a symbol, and symbols alone cannot get results.

In government, structure is about far more than efficiency. It is about the political importance that policy makers attach to certain missions. When Congress followed President Jimmy Carter's lead in transforming the Veterans Administration into the Department of Veterans Affairs in 1989, the signs and letterhead were updated, but little else about the agency changed. Does that mean that the reorganization did not matter? Of course not. Elevating the VA to cabinet status conveyed a higher sense of national purpose to care for veterans. Senator Spark Matsunaga applauded the change. "For the first time," he said, "the Veterans' Administration will have access to the president without an intervening party."[30] Having a high-level voice and a direct pipeline to top policy makers has long been part of the reorganization strategy. This is about symbols, but it is also about political clout. More political leverage—in this case, returning Vietnam veterans who argued that the nation was overlooking their needs—led to elevating the VA to a department, for the purpose of giving it more status.

All this scarcely means that organizational structure does not matter. Bringing related functions together can often improve their efficiency, because top managers can secure stronger coordination and provide better administrative support. There are often economies of scale for computer and information management systems, and agencies that assemble a critical mass of experts can often get stronger leverage over their missions. The DHS/FEMA restructuring ended up primarily a symbol of government's commitment to the homeland security issue. The most important dots—the intelligence apparatus—remained unconnected, and Congress's follow-up oversight imposed huge burdens on the DHS but produced little clear direction. It was little wonder that FEMA, brought into the new department to enhance its capacity, had found itself literally swamped by Katrina. Indeed, the Department of Homeland Security's own analysts found that the constant reorganizations had undermined FEMA's capacity to respond to tough problems.[31] Congress tried to strengthen FEMA for the future by looking to the past for clues about the future. It was like driving down a highway at seventy miles per hour, trying to steer by looking in the rearview mirror. That provided an ever-fading view of the past and inevitably caused FEMA to miss a curve and plow into a tree.

None of this proved much comfort to Lindsay Huckabee or her family. As David R. Mayhew argues in his classic, *Congress: The Electoral Connection*, members of Congress engage in casework, they take public positions, and they seek opportunities to claim credit for solving problems.[32] After September 11 and then again after Katrina, the push to reorganize the homeland security apparatus focused on structural questions that were opportunities for creating symbols, and on broad issues of policy widely separated from results. Once they had created the symbols, members of Congress were on to the next issue. They had little taste for details about how their decisions actually worked, except for a handful of members who worked to ensure that the sea of trailers oozing formaldehyde would not undermine the travel trailer business. Huckabee was left to fight on her own.

Members of Congress persist in their symbolic strategies and tactics for two reasons. One is because they can. In the face of an executive branch whose sheer size, mass, activity, and complexity are overwhelming, redesigning an organization's structure creates a sense of action. But as strong as members and their personal and committee staffs might be, they are no match for the professional firepower of executive branch agencies. Symbolic action creates a congressional imprint on policy without putting Congress into a game where it has a strategic disadvantage. The second reason that congressional members persist is that other tools are much harder to use. Members of Congress have budgetary control, of course, and they use it regularly to promote narrow pork barrel programs through earmarks. But it is far easier to add relatively small amounts of money to the nooks and crannies of federal agencies than it is to use the budget to shift basic policy. The core missions, along with the budgets that support them, are usually the product of long years of complicated deals. It is not easy to unwind those deals, as the Democratic Congress proved repeatedly in its unsuccessful battle to use the budget to force the Bush administration to shift its Iraqi war strategy. The budget can often be a blunt and clumsy instrument. It is hard for members of Congress to know enough about the details of administrative actions to steer them effectively, and it is deceptively hard for them to find the right instruments to reshape policy.

Members of Congress like to hold administrators accountable, but they are not held accountable for the quality of their oversight. Their decisions—the programs they create, the rules they write, the budgets they appropriate, the people they confirm, the oversight they perform (or fail to)—shape the crucial elements of government policy. In fact, members of Congress often play a stronger role in the lives of top executive branch officials than the White House does. The hideaway office of one Clinton administration cabinet secretary captured this reality perfectly. In a corner, with a head-on view of the Capitol's dome, was a treadmill, where the secretary could go to keep in shape, work out tensions, and be reminded constantly of where to focus attention. But although Congress plays a very powerful role in shaping the administrative life of American government, it has not played its role very effectively. In fact, its understandable political instincts have often pushed administrators in unhealthy directions. It aggravates what Theodore J. Lowi calls "legiscide," an instinct to bleed away congressional authority through delegation of excessive power to the executive. That, in turn, weakens Congress's capacity to learn and rule.[33]

Lindsay Huckabee struggled with the consequences. She had to work within the structure that Congress created, which did not connect well with her problems. FEMA officials had strong incentives to keep their heads down, because they knew that Congress would pay them little attention. They guessed right, until in 2007 Huckabee's plight caught the attention of Democratic staffers on the House Committee on Oversight and Government Reform, who saw an opportunity to spotlight the issue and further embarrass the Bush administration. The story continued the Democrats' narrative: that the Bush administration had been caught flat-footed by Katrina, had fumbled the response, and when help finally arrived, had come with trailers that made people sick. It was high political theater, but it did little to prevent Lindsay Huckabees of the future from suffering the same fate.

Presidential Leverage

The president, of course, is chief executive, and the executive branch apparatus was responsible for solving Lindsay Huckabee's problems. However, Katrina left the normally nimble Bush administration remarkably flat-footed. The initial response was clumsy, both politically and administratively. Neither the White House nor FEMA ever recovered. Michael Brown had gone to the Gulf to manage FEMA, and President Bush had counted on him to do so. What the Gulf needed was someone to solve the problem, not manage the program. Only when the political cost of the administrative failure became inescapable did the White House stir to action. Like Congress, the White House paid attention to management only to the degree that it presented political opportunity or threatened political cost. The president might be chief executive, but the scope of issues on which the president can exercise executive leadership is small, the choice is driven more by political than managerial demands, and the difficulty of finding the right levers for complex administrative problems is huge. The Katrina failures came because of the Mildred paradox and its corollary—the huge role for multiple organizations with no one in charge. There were complex problems that required interorganizational collaboration, and there was no collaborator in chief.

In reality, of course, even though the president is called "chief executive," the administrative role typically is relatively weak. The president can propose a budget, but Congress has to approve it. The president can recommend major restructuring of government, but Congress must enact it. The president can announce new policies, but moving them forward requires congressional assent. The nation's founders wanted to make sure that the president could never be king, but in the process they made it impossible for the president to serve as a real chief executive.

Even though the presidency provides strong executive powers, presidents often do not want to use them. With the exercise of power comes political responsibility for its impact. If the president asserted stronger ownership of problems, people would (rightly) hold the presidential team responsible for problems. From a political point of view, the balance of power with Congress provides great value, for it provides a ready (and true) explanation for policy failures. Republicans, for example, campaigned for years for a presidential line-item veto—the ability to excise individual items from large appropriation bills. That power, they said, would allow the president to make the tough decisions that Congress had proven it could not.

In 1985, Reagan challenged Congress on this issue. He called on members of Congress to slash $50 billion from government spending. "If there isn't enough courage to approve these cuts," he said, "then at least give me the authority to veto line items in the Federal budget. I'll take the political responsibility, I'll make the cuts and I'll take the heat."[34] Of course, since Congress never gave the president this power, the president has never had to stand up to such a challenge, and Reagan got what he wanted: talking tough but avoiding the need to back up the talk with the pain of peeling back the hard-won political compromises that lay beyond congressional spending decisions. The tilting-at-windmills campaign for a presidential line-item veto has been a staple of Republican presidential candidates ever since—a Reaganesque applause line with little chance they would ever have to act out the role. By both instinct and necessity, the president must focus on a relatively small handful of issues and try to shape them in the presidential image. The complexity of big problems and of the many potential instruments to solve them plays into the president's political imperatives.

George W. Bush employed many of those tools after September 11 to promote a historic concentration of power in the executive branch. Beyond strengthening intelligence, the administration increased the federal government's investigative powers and blocked new air quality standards to reduce climate change. The administration's management reform efforts, aimed squarely at linking performance measures with the budgetary process, also helped pull more power to the Office of Management and Budget (OMB, where the B side has always out-muscled the M side). The administration left office with a balance of power decidedly shifted toward the White House.

The contest between Congress and the Bush administration over FEMA and homeland security was epic. In the end, however, it did little to help Huckabee. Her problems lay far from the issues that most preoccupied the White House, and solving them required leverage that the president did not have—or that would have required substantial capital to marshal. The same was true for the wide collection of Mildred-style problems. For example, the Bush administration featured the Medicare and Medicaid programs in its last budget, but the focus was on restraining the growth of spending. The administration submitted plans for shrinking Medicare outlays by $178 billion over five years, with another $17 billion of cuts in Medicaid. There was little to improve the situation for the millions of seniors who relied on these programs. The fuzzier the boundaries were, the more complex the public programs became, and the harder it was to hold them accountable—that is, the more the challenges explored in Chapter 2 grew—the more disconnected the legislative and executive branches became from the programs they had created.

Presidents are uncommonly busy people, with daily intelligence briefings to digest between photo sessions with the winners of basketball tournaments and rallies to shore up their political base. Their principal job is to get elected, do what they must do to get reelected, and be true to the people who elected them. Thus, presidents inevitably focus on a handful of the big policy issues and on the issues of symbolic leadership that will stir people to act (or at least to vote). Given the time pressures and political realities of the job, that is a logical and inescapable imperative. Moreover, it is also reasonable for the White House staff to assume that it is the job of the 2 million federal employees to keep administrative problems off the president's desk. They quite naturally assume it is their job to make decisions and, once the decisions are made, to count on others throughout the executive branch to carry them out. When that assumption fails, when administrative problems scream to them from the front pages of newspapers and the lead stories of broadcast news, top officials insist on quick answers. They not only want the problems to go away; they want to root out forces that sidetrack them from their agenda. When it comes to managing policy problems, the White House typically is in a reactive mode. But that only further handicaps the executive branch from solving the problems to begin with. It is not surprising that the White House, regardless of the party controlling it, so often seems to be caught flat-footed on big problems.

Alarm Bells

My conclusion about the executive branch might seem cynical, but given the political incentives it is quite reasonable. The problem is that, when the alarm bells do go off, top White House officials have no choice but to jump on the problem. Nothing can more quickly damage a president's credibility and political standing than a cascading sense that no one is in charge. Like Katrina, alarm bells become instant crises and demand immediate responses. To make things worse, there is little time for anything but instinct and symbols. The problems cascade, government's response falls short, government looks weak, the media complain, and citizens are disappointed. But the balance of power that restrains the abuse of power by any branch of government also shields all the players from accountability. More problems demand concerted action, but when everyone is in charge, no one is in charge. Coordinated action falters, but no one is held accountable.

Such issues are critical to democracy in America, and they are growing. Many big issues tend not to have trip wires or early-warning alarms. And because solving the problem depends on leveraging the complex systems we saw in Chapter 2, it is hard for top officials to get satisfying results quickly. Often there is no single person the president can call to solve the problem because the problem spills out over multiple levels of government, multiple sectors of society, and, increasingly, across disparate nations.

Presidents thus tend to focus on issues that fly at a far higher altitude than Mildred- and Katrina-style problems. They do not have radar screens tuned to detect such problems at a long distance, where they can be defused before they land with an inescapable thud in the Oval Office. Big administrative problems often get a presidential response only after they have already exploded into political problems, and they then must first be tackled through political problems. The instinct to view administrative issues as political ones, in turn, only tends to weaken government's capacity to produce effective administrative results. The fact that government's main alarm system is inherently political widens the chasm between the politics and management of big, inescapable problems. It muddies the politics and worsens the management.

These forces also undermine the executive branch's ability to create a system that can get in front of problems to prevent them or manage them better. As such problems multiply, this presidential dilemma will only spread. Indeed, the lack of an alarm system coupled with little attention to management issues guarantees that the problems will proliferate and will present future presidents with even more difficult and dangerous problems. The Bush administration eventually made the political problem of Katrina go away, but its actions did little to lower the risk of future Katrinas.

The fundamental dilemma is that good management is not necessarily good politics. With Katrina, however, it is also clear that bad management has become bad politics. There might be little appreciation for government managers who struggle hard to perform well. It would be asking a lot for taxpayers to applaud public employees for doing their jobs. But in many ways, Katrina cast a longer shadow than September 11. Following the terrorist attacks, the president and Congress restructured government to avoid another September 11. The next September 11, however, was Katrina—a disaster that came as a surprise, oblique to the postattack reforms—and it proved how deep the consequences of bad management could run. Katrina might not have increased political support of good governance, but it demonstrated the impact of bad governance.

For Congress, the problem was both simpler and more damaging. Congress tended to jump in only after the problems multiplied and became inescapable, but then only because it presented an opportunity to engage in headline-grabbing oversight. Many of the problems stemmed from the very systems that Congress had created, but Congress had few incentives to root out these problems, let alone change its behavior that had contributed to the problems to begin with.

Wicked Problems

Government increasingly relies on policy strategies that, by their very nature, are hard for elected officials to govern. Moreover, the basic and understandable instincts of policy makers undermine the system's ability to perform. The combination of these forces creates a self-perpetuating cycle, of government programs that so often fall short of expectations, and disappointments that undermine confidence in government.

The nation's founders built a system that has proven remarkably resilient for more than two centuries—adept in its ability to adapt, lithe in its capacity to meet new challenges without breaking loose from the basic principles that have driven the nation. The founders drew lines—dividing government and society; dividing levels of government; dividing executive, legislative, and judicial institutions—to limit and, sometimes, to focus conflict. For generations, those boundaries worked remarkably well. They did not so much prevent catastrophic conflicts as constrain them, to define the turf on which Americans would fight to define the answers. Over time the boundaries would shift. The system's great strength was its ability to bend without ever fully breaking, even under the unfathomable pressures of civil war.

However, many of the most important policy issues facing the country, including Mildred and Katrina, create more than just fundamental governance challenges. Failure to address them poses serious consequences because so many of the problems are *wicked*.[35]

First, they allow *little time to react.* The Air Force scrambled jet fighters on the morning of September 11, but the jets did not reach Washington in time to stop the plane that crashed into the Pentagon. A small private plane seemed headed for the capital in May 2005. It turned out to be harmless, but even at its slow speed it was just minutes from the White House. After Katrina, thousands of refugees huddled around the New Orleans Superdome in search of the basics of life, and some individuals died when help did not arrive fast enough. For Mildred, quick decisions by her care team saved her life more than once. Police officers and firefighters, of course, have for centuries realized that quick response is the key to their jobs. But many of the problems facing modern government prove especially punishing if government does not respond quickly enough. The interconnectedness of the system requires a quick response to what often are small problems, before those problems become large disasters.

Second, *failures anywhere can quickly become problems everywhere.* With services so tightly interconnected, failures can soon ripple throughout the system. Relatively small levee failures in New Orleans put most of the city under water. The ability of terrorists in 2001 to sneak just a handful of weapons past a small number of airport security checkpoints allowed them to kill nearly 3,000 people and to cripple the nation. The interconnectedness of the government system multiplies the system's vulnerability.

Third, when failures occur, *the costs can be very high and can quickly spread very far.* In early 2008, rogue trading by a single person in a French investment management firm created a $7 billion crisis that rippled through the world's financial community. In fact, the consequences began appearing in international securities markets even before French bank officials knew they had a problem. American utility companies have discovered that tiny failures in the electric grid can bring widespread blackouts, like the one in 2003. A handful of pet prairie dogs in 2003 created a large monkeypox epidemic. With the interconnectedness of the government system—indeed, of all society—small problems can quickly become big problems and spread with devastating speed.

Government in the past often proved robust—sometimes slow to react but usually flexible in adapting to new problems. The wicked problems of this new generation, however, often span the seams of the nation's governing institutions, and government has often proved sluggish in adapting to them. The institutions and the problems they are charged with solving have often proved a dangerous mismatch. These wicked problems are occurring with greater frequency than ever before. They challenge the ability of political institutions to act, and when their response lags, the consequences can be immediate, large, and sometimes devastating.

American government is very good at political theater. It excels in drilling deep down into the details of the policy system. But it is far less effective at moving beyond the theater to uncovering the critical issues at the core. It is even less adept at finding the critical connections needed to ensure effective action across the seams of the policy system. In the months after September 11, "connecting the dots" became an overused cliché. However, the cliché was a perceptive diagnosis for the government's fundamental problems: dealing with the basic problems behind the symbols and building the horizontal strategies needed to connect vertical silos.

Just as seriously, the institutions have struggled to govern the tools they have created. As government has relied more on contracts, grants, and other indirect tools, it has not created oversight mechanisms capable of governing them. The OMB and White House staffs drill deep into the details of individual programs but struggle to ensure connections among them. It is little wonder that dots go unconnected, because there are precious few mechanisms at the top to link them. Congress, together with its vast network of committees, is even more fragmented. It has no mechanism to pursue oversight of crosscutting issues like homeland security or health care. Indeed, as problems become ever more wicked and interconnected, it is little wonder that Congress's appetite for earmarks has increased. The more those problems have grown, the more members of Congress have retreated into the things they can actually control.

Neither Congress nor the White House, under either party, has proven especially adept at looking around the corner to understand the next issue. The calculus of American government rewards quick political payoffs, from targeted earmarks to broad symbols. Many important and inescapable problems, from entitlement reform (for Mildred) to the development of sophisticated capacity in homeland security (for Katrina), require a longer-term vision with crosscutting solutions. Solutions to these puzzles, however, often require up-front financial investments—and political costs— in exchange for longer-term payoffs, which often seem uncertain and distant. The political system, of course, is designed this way. But the very separation-of-powers system that fuels these instincts and that aims at keeping any institution from becoming too powerful also is increasingly handcuffing government as a whole in its attempts to tackle big, inescapable, wicked problems.

This is an exceptionally dangerous combination: more problems require longer-term, crosscutting action; government has limited capacity for solving them; and failure to solve these problems exacts higher costs. With the rise of networked governance, this dilemma is sure to grow. America needs an increasingly nimble government that can adapt to pressing challenges. Instead, its governing institutions are proving sluggish—adapting and reaching for symbols instead of solutions. Of course, forecasters have for generations predicted the fall of American democracy. The growing gap between policy problems and the system's ability to solve them, however, is unquestionably drawing the nation's political institutions into ever-deeper patterns of dysfunction.

That is the real lesson of Lindsay Huckabee and her family. The instincts of the nation's most important political institutions made it far harder for government to respond to her problems to begin with. When the response—the new FEMA trailer—created its own problems, government proved just as sluggish to fix it and then immobilized in preventing the problem's spread. Both Congress and the White House stumbled in dealing with the key issues at the core of Mildred- and Katrina-style governance issues—the complex and interconnected set of organizations responsible for solving public problems and the fact that no one is in charge. It is little wonder that government so often seems to work so badly. Its politics have become twisted out of sync with what is required to make public policies work. We will explore the roots of this mismatch in Chapter 4.

4

ROUTINES AND REMEDIES

The performance of government, all too often, lags behind the promises it makes. Time after time, we try to solve problems before we understand them and, too often, we try to fit new problems to old routines. In the first days after Katrina struck, most of the frontline managers applied the approaches they had learned and practiced, but they struggled with routines that simply did not fit the problem. They went by the book—but the book did not fit the circumstances, and the mismatch proved disastrous.

By comparison, the system's relative success in dealing with Mildred began with a recognition that her case was a distinctly nonroutine situation ("if you've met one Alzheimer's patient, you've met—one Alzheimer's patient"). Her caregivers were constantly on the alert for signs and symptoms of subtle changes and proved imaginative in cobbling together new treatments. During one period, for example, Mildred would quickly tire after dinner and try to scoot in her wheelchair off to her bedroom, where her effort to slide into bed often ended with her falling to the floor.

The staff dealt with the situation by quietly parking the medicine cart in front of her door—to subtly block the entrance and keep her in clear sight. Instead of trying to force the problem to fit their routines, they adapted their routines to fit the problem.

The Routines of Governance

No problem is ever fully routine, but some problems are far more routine than others. Government attacks some problems through hierarchies and deals with others through complex networks. These differences produce a variety of strategies, depending on how routine the problem and how hierarchical the approach. Matching the wrong solution to the wrong problem invariably makes things worse. Consider the following four categories in light of the models outlined in Figure 4.1.

SLOPPY MANAGEMENT OF ROUTINE SERVICES

From their movie debut in 1912, the popular Keystone Cops proved incredibly imaginative, through scores of sketches, in turning even the most routine problem into total chaos. Their gag was that *anyone* watching could see that there was an easy and straightforward way of solving a problem to which the Cops could only bring mayhem. The Keystone Cops' creators, of course, did not design their slapstick as deep political theory, but they made an important point: doing things the hard and complex way when there is an easy, straightforward organizational solution is inefficient (and funny). Mismatching problems with solutions can cause big problems, the Keystone Cops proved over and over. They showed what happened when managers failed to adapt their systems to routine problems.

FIGURE 4.1   Models of Governance

		PROBLEM	
		Routine	Nonroutine
STRATEGY	Traditional/ technical/ hierarchical	Social Security Garbage collection	Katrina Pennsylvania I-78
	Nontraditional/ adaptive/ networked	Keystone Cops	Mildred Environmental programs

EFFICIENT MANAGEMENT OF ROUTINE SERVICES

In contrast to the incompetence of the Keystone Cops, government has transformed the management of many important but routine problems into well-oiled machines. Consider the distribution of Social Security checks. The agency makes payments to 50 million Americans per month. With remarkably few exceptions, the system is a work of art. Checks appear like clockwork in the bank accounts of recipients every month. For 80 percent of Social Security recipients, in fact, there is no check. Their payment goes through the banking network's direct deposit system right into their accounts, at a cost of just four cents (compared with forty-five cents to print and mail a check).[1] Developing a routine and applying it uniformly is the key to the payment system. No one wants to have two people under the same circumstances but living in different states receiving different payment amounts. No one wants recipients in Montana and Florida to receive different levels of service (let alone different answers to their questions). No one wants the payments to limp to recipients in New York but speed to those in Arizona. Social Security is a program in which the traditional hierarchical approaches to bureaucracy rule.

The same is true of the intricate routine of local garbage collection. Everyone knows what day of the week the garbage truck arrives. In some communities, there are rules for how the garbage has to be packaged, how much trash can be put out, and how recyclable materials have to be separated. The rules exist to streamline the routine, to ensure that garbage collection works smoothly and the costs stay low. In San Diego, for example, the city deployed global positioning system (GPS) devices to track its garbage trucks through geographic information systems and computer models. The sophisticated mapping system allowed the department's managers to determine first that it was best to concentrate all of the city's trash trucks on one of the city's five zones on each workday. The system determined where best to deploy the trucks and how to deal with problems (like homes where the trash cans are not visible from the street—the solution: provide drivers with computer-generated maps with the problems flagged). The city knew where all of its trucks were at any moment, and if a truck broke down, managers could reassign other trucks on the fly. If citizens complained about the service—for example, if they charged a garbage truck driver with speeding—managers knew from the GPS data whether that was true. The innovation dramatically improved efficiency, especially by reducing overtime. Within three years, San Diego officials estimated, the new system would save $1 million per year.[2]

This approach represents the very best of government's routine service function. Take a task, like distributing monthly Social Security benefits or picking up the trash. Then constantly refine the routine that produces the service. Innovate as opportunities present themselves, such as by using direct deposit to replace mailed checks or introducing GPS on garbage trucks. Tinker, refine, innovate, and tinker some more. For routine tasks, the vending-machine model characterizes both how things work now and how they can work better.

HIERARCHICAL APPROACHES TO NONROUTINE PROBLEMS

When agencies try to use routine approaches to nonroutine problems, the machine often breaks down or at least shudders as it tries to produce the service. The introduction of the Supplemental Security Income (SSI) program in 1974 provides a powerful case study. As Martha Derthick demonstrates in her classic, *Agency under Stress*, Congress and the president took an agency doing a very good job of administering the relatively routine Social Security and layered on top of it a new program, SSI, which has complex eligibility rules and requires a great deal of discretion. Years later, Derthick sadly reports, "SSI is still remembered inside the agency as a disaster."[3] The agency, well schooled in the mechanics of routinely calculating and distributing monthly checks, found itself profoundly challenged by the distinctly nonroutine nature of the SSI program. The problem, as Derthick crisply defines it, is that "the institutions of American government function in ways that are not conducive to good administration." The reason?

> Policymaking neglects administration. Policymakers, who define administrative tasks with their choices, act with limited understanding of administrative organizations and without attaching high priority to anticipating the consequences of their choices for the agencies' performance.[4]

Of course, this is not true for all programs. Some programs, like garbage collection in San Diego and processing of traditional Social Security checks, work very well indeed. Fire departments operate as models of efficiency. Police and prosecutors perform well; they arrest suspects in almost two thirds of all murders, and most of those arrested—72 percent—are convicted.[5] The problems that Derthick so deftly identifies tend to emerge when government officials create new programs to solve nonroutine problems and then apply the vending-machine model to manage them. When programmatic goals and administrative strategies are out of sync, problems—often failures—follow.

That, in fact, was the central problem in the government's response to Katrina. In a 2006 congressional hearing, Senator Joseph Lieberman excoriated Department of Homeland Security Secretary Michael Chertoff:

> How could you have left us with so many of those agencies so unprepared that when Katrina struck, too many of them ran around like Keystone Kops [aficionados spell it both ways], uncertain about what they were supposed to do or unable to do it? Why, in the days immediately before Katrina made landfall, as the National Hurricane Service and agencies within your own department warned over and over that this was the long-feared hurricane that would break the levees and drown the city of New Orleans, did you not mobilize more of the resources of the federal government to protect this great American city and its people? With all the information coming in to your department's operation center on the day that Katrina struck New Orleans that the city was flooding and people were trapped or drowning, how could you, as secretary of Homeland Security, go to bed that night not knowing what was happening in New Orleans and get up the next morning and proceed, not to New Orleans to oversee the response, but to Atlanta, for a conference?[6]

The real problem was not just that top officials "ran around like Keystone Cops," as Senator Lieberman suggested—applying routine solutions ineffectively to nonroutine problems. It was that DHS officials—indeed, most of the government officials involved in the Katrina response—were operating with a hierarchical, vending-machine model in addressing a highly nonroutine problem. Everyone was following the book, but they failed to rewrite the old book to fit new problems.

Unfortunately, it is a far too common mistake. In February 2007, a nasty storm hit central Pennsylvania. For days, weather forecasters had warned that winter weather was on the way. That part of the state is certainly no stranger to storms, and Mother Nature frequently strikes in the middle of February. But this storm turned ugly, especially in east-central Pennsylvania. Instead of a typical storm that dropped snow and moved through, this one turned from snow to sleet and freezing rain at 4:00 AM on February 14 and continued for hours, sometimes slipping from snow to sleet, then back to snow and on to freezing rain. Roads became ice rinks. A member of the governor's cabinet noticed that one of the major interstates through the area, I-78, had not been plowed. Officials at the Pennsylvania Department of Transportation (PennDOT) told him that the department had instructed plow operators not to plow the roads, "so that the snow could 'absorb' freezing rain." PennDOT later denied there was such a policy, but the roads went unplowed and tractor trailers began jackknifing on I-78, as well as on two other main highways, I-80 and I-81.[7]

The state police told emergency management officials that there were problems, but that they were handling them. In fact, problems were quickly escalating. Traffic was backing up, drivers were becoming stuck, accumulating ice was knocking out electric power to some of the state police barracks. At least 150 miles of interstate highway had become clogged and hundreds of drivers were marooned in freezing weather, some for almost an entire day. The emergency management system broke down, and no one knew how many people were stuck. The state police did not coordinate with traffic officials to close the highways, so more drivers continued to enter the roadway only to discover they could neither move nor exit. PennDOT failed to plow, and clogged traffic prevented equipment from getting in to clear the roads. The National Guard was eight hours late in distributing emergency supplies. Communities along the way found themselves suddenly swamped by clusters of drivers who had managed to turn around or get off the roads.

At first, Governor Rendell said that the problem was due to Mother Nature's mischief. But as the scope of the problem later became clear, he issued an unusual public apology on behalf of his state government. He said that motorists had become stuck because of an "almost total breakdown in communication" among state agencies. He hired former FEMA director James Lee Witt to head an investigation into the problem, including why it took more than twenty-four hours to close the ramps onto I-78 and prevent more drivers from getting stuck. The situation, he said, was "totally unacceptable."[8]

Witt and his colleagues found that the state's response had been handicapped by insufficient communication and coordination, the lack of any central gathering point for information, the lack of an understanding by key state officials of their emergency responsibilities, and inadequate interagency planning. In an eerie echo of the problems after Katrina struck, Witt found "a lack of overall situational awareness among local and state officials" and a "lack of communication among state and local authorities."[9] The report concluded, "There is a remarkable lack of awareness and understanding of Pennsylvania's emergency management system, including the emergency alert levels, even amongst senior agency leaders."[10] There was no common language, including what it meant to "officially" close a road. Information went up the chain of command without verification, so officials sometimes were making decisions on the wrong information and often on incomplete information.

Perhaps worst of all, the vertical hierarchies inside some agencies, including the state police, meant that "commanders did not communicate horizontally to each other."[11] Top officials were not aware of what was happening on the roads. When they spoke with colleagues, they sometimes were not heard because words meant different things to different officials. They tried to apply their standard routines to a very nonroutine storm—and the system catastrophically failed.

Despite their experience with previous storms, Pennsylvania officials were caught flat-footed. Moreover, even though September 11 and Katrina had provided abundant evidence of the consequences for failing to solve these problems, the state had not updated its policies. Mothers were stuck on the highway without formula or diapers for their babies. People were marooned without their medications. And thousands of people were very, very cold and hungry until they could be evacuated.

ADAPTIVE SOLUTIONS FOR NONROUTINE PROBLEMS

Catastrophe is not the inevitable product of nonroutine puzzles, as Mildred's case makes abundantly clear. Every one of the residents on her floor in the nursing home was at a different point, following a different course of illness and requiring a different pattern of care. The challenge for those who cared for her was understanding where she was today, where she was likely to be tomorrow, how she differed from her neighbors, and how to provide her with specialized care within the overall framework of the nursing home's facilities, staff, and, most important, budget. When things worked well, which was most of the time, it was because the existing hierarchies—public, private, and nonprofit—worked in an integrated fashion, with all the elements supporting each other without duplicating service or care. The problem raised by Mildred's case was not the quality of her care. The puzzle is how to make routine the high level of nonroutine care that she received from so many staffers.

The same lesson holds for results in environmental policy. In a 2007 study on protecting the Chesapeake Bay's waters, the National Academy of Public Administration (NAPA) found that the bay was at risk. NAPA concluded that "a lot of progress has been made in reducing pollution," but "the Bay remains unhealthy." NAPA believed that this finding revealed a basic paradox, in which individual programs worked well but "the environmental outcome continues to be unacceptable." The reason was that "knowing what needs to be done and getting it done are two very different things."[12] Two key water pollution control programs—managing wastewater and storm water—worked well. However, pollution from runoff (from both agricultural and urban terrain) threatened the bay. The wastewater and storm water programs both deal with point-source pollution (pollution that comes from specifically identifiable places). Runoff pollution, however, is non-point-source pollution (that is, the source was generalized and did not come from a specific source).

Put differently, the programs that focused on specific sites, with standard routines and manageable boundaries, tended to work relatively well. Problems without clear boundaries, like the non-point-source pollution program and Pennsylvania's struggle with the Valentine's Day storm, proved far more difficult to solve. The gap between knowing what we want to do and how to get it done too often undermines our efforts. Even if individual programs work well, the effort can fail if the programs don't work well together.

The Mismatch of Problems and Governance

Many of these problems stem from the perspective that Americans have on government and its services. Most citizens—and even many reporters and some government officials—see government as a vending machine. They tend to view government as vertical and hierarchical, with a line stretching down from members of Congress and the president through cabinet secretaries and front-line bureaucrats. Indeed, some of the most thoughtful scholarly analysis on the emerging shape of governance views the system as a string of hierarchical interactions.[13] Government policy makers enact new legislation and assign it to a government agency for its implementation. They seek to make a government bureaucrat responsible for everything government does.

The model builds on the best of classical bureaucratic theory, which dates from the Progressive Era and explains how we can make government bureaucrats powerful enough to do their jobs while not making them so powerful that they are unaccountable. It is a system focused on effectiveness, built on hierarchy and authority, and bounded by law.[14] The Progressives worked to develop a model of American politics and policy, with hierarchical control of an enclosed service system. For the Progressives, the issue began with Americans' historic distrust of government power. When the founders met in Philadelphia, in fact, their greatest accomplishment was creating a government powerful enough to deliver goods and services while reining in its power enough to satisfy wary citizens. As private power grew in the nineteenth century, government reformers worried about the rise of monopolies and the quality of citizens' lives. The Progressives sought to expand government power as a counterbalance, but they faced again the challenge of the founders: how to expand government's power without risking tyranny.

This time, led by thinkers like Woodrow Wilson, they relied

extensively on borrowing the best management technologies from other countries and from the private sector. Those management approaches built on hierarchy, which at once created and controlled bureaucratic power. Government officials gained more power to spend money and regulate private interest, but they could exercise that power only within the narrowly circumscribed boundaries of their position and they could not do anything except what the legislature specifically authorized. From the private-sector innovators shaping the industrial revolution, they sought the "one best way" to do government's work.[15] Government's job was to be powerful enough to trump private power, when necessary—to prevent monopolists from imposing punishing costs on citizens, and to ensure that citizens received services that the private sector could not or would not provide.

The Progressives often took a mechanistic view of government agencies, where the goal was translating public goals, efficiently and responsibly, into public services. Wilson saw no problem in borrowing ideas from anywhere, provided that government created the mechanisms to hold the exercise of power accountable. As he wrote in 1887,

> If I see a murderous fellow sharpening a knife cleverly, I can borrow his way of sharpening the knife without borrowing his probable intention to commit murder with it; and so, if I see a monarchist dyed in the wool managing a public bureau well, I can learn his business methods without changing one of my republican spots.[16]

Wilson and the Progressives believed that they could borrow the best devices for empowering government without creating tyranny. They believed they could separate the instruments of government power from the way government used them, and they believed that they could create political institutions strong enough to hold the use of these tools accountable. Over the years, the approach was labeled the *politics–administration dichotomy*. In fact, their approach did not so much argue for the separation of politics from administration but for their confidence that America could—and must—build a strong and energetic government that could also be held in check.[17]

The Progressives built heavily on the thinking that lay at the heart of the rise of industrialization. America's private institutions worked to adapt to a new world, in which changes came quickly and complex machines created the promise of better lives at lower costs. In the decades bridging the dawn of the twentieth century, American government did the same. Policy makers created the large regulatory commissions (to restrain monopolies) and the Federal Reserve (to fuel economic growth). They created the income tax and the federal budget and the civil service, as well as cabinet departments to promote commerce and labor. They sought to borrow the best ideas to promote efficiency and then, as Wilson argued, they worked to strengthen government's power to pursue a broader array of public goals.

This approach led to a mechanistic view of government's tools. The industrial age brought new manufacturing processes to the private sector, which vastly expanded the efficiency of business operations. The Progressives believed they could borrow private-sector lessons to improve government's efficiency as well. Moreover, they believed that the mechanistic approach could also prevent the abuse of government power. Government's operations could be fine-tuned to enhance bureaucratic power while constraining its use. That view created a vending-machine approach to government, in which policy makers created programs, provided money, and relied on best bureaucratic practices to translate policies into results. Policy makers did not need to worry about how the bureaucratic machine worked. The mechanistic model, furthermore, not only promoted efficiency but also made the system more predictable. Critics sometimes complained about how industrial-age management sometimes reduced workers to cogs in a wheel, but it also made the system more robust. It told managers how best to structure the system, how best to train workers, and how to make sure it could repeat the job predictably. This approach, in turn, insulated the system from dependence on the special (and perhaps not replicable) skills of any individual employee. The Progressives' approach to government thus provided the foundation, in both theory and practice, for the vast increase in government's power during the twentieth century. The vending-machine model was the natural product.

The model also provided the strategy for fixing government when it failed to work well: crawl inside the machine and tinker with the parts—restructure, reorganize, reconfigure. If that did not work, the system's designers, in the White House and Congress, could simply build a new machine. There was something both reassuring and practical about a model that could simultaneously make government strong and protect its users—citizens—from the consequences of too much power in government's hands.

Reinforcing the approach is the widespread assumption, often at great variance with reality, that private corporations operate this way as well. The approach had dual roots. Government, after all, had borrowed the "one best way" approach from the industrial revolution. Relying on the private sector's model for improving government's operations was easy. In addition, the private sector's presumed efficiency provided a way for policy makers to talk to Americans about government, an institution that they had never much liked and even less often trusted. Borrowing a model from the private sector, which was often presumed more efficient than government, provided Americans with great comfort. It provided a scheme for building programs, making them work, holding them accountable. It also spared citizens and policy makers from having to take too close a look at government's inner workings. The model allowed them to content themselves with approaching government in the same way that consumers encounter vending machines: insert a coin in the slot and wait for the product to arrive.

From the very beginning, the model was more useful rhetorically than practically. As contracts and other indirect tools of government grew to dominate government's operations, as government moved from the industrial to the postindustrial age, the model fell further out of sync with government's operating realities. The cases of Mildred and Katrina are signature elements of this broader revolution—programs that appear on the outside as traditional forms of service delivery but that, because of the Mildred paradox and its corollary, operate in very different ways. The mismatch of the model and reality disguises important complexities and variations in government programs. Inside the machine was a complex and networked world, mostly invisible to citizens and policy makers alike. Mildred received government-funded medical care without ever encountering a government employee. Katrina's survivors suffered because government agencies could not link their programs. The 9/11 Commission criticized government's failure to "connect the dots" before the terrorist attacks. In the space shuttle program, private contractors spend 90 percent of the budget. In 2008, there was one support contractor employee for every soldier in Iraq. Analysts have called the phenomenon "indirect government," "government by proxy," "hollow government," and the "shadow government," but the simple fact is that most federal programs, as well as a rapidly rising share of state and local programs, spend government money but are administered through contracts, tax incentives, regulations, loans, and other third-party arrangements with for-profit and nonprofit organizations.[18]

Policy makers have had almost a willful aversion to looking

inside the machine. Members of Congress focus more on design-
ing policy and on creating symbols than on making sure the system
works. The president as chief executive has time for only limited
attention to the realities of executing the law. Tinkering with the
innards of government is far more difficult than talking about what
we want government to do, but that disconnect has often created
multiple problems. We expect government to solve big problems
but we fail to build a system that can do so reliably, we build systems so complicated that it's hard to get their machines to work
well, and when systems break we kick them instead of trying to
figure out what went wrong.

When it comes to fixing problems, the traditional approach
of redesigning the machine has proved flawed, sometimes fatally.
The vending-machine model has very often led reformers to an
instinct for structural fixes, to repair the machine in a hierarchically mechanical way. After the September 11 terrorist attacks, that
approach led to the creation of the new federal Department of
Homeland Security. When the department fumbled its first challenge, Hurricane Katrina, the uproar led to a host of proposals to
restructure FEMA, including pulling it back out of the department into which it had just been placed. Cooler heads prevailed,
but the eternal reflex—when in doubt, reorganize—has been an
inextricable part of the American political instinct. Because Americans have always looked to political and organizational structure
as the best mechanism for creating, balancing, and controlling
political power, the hold of the vending-machine model has been
tremendously strong.

The vending-machine model leads to a view of most problems
as technical issues that require internal tinkering. When reformers
use the vending-machine mind-set to diagnose and fix problems
that stem, in reality, from how parts of the policy machine inter-
connect, problems cascade: they typically fix the wrong problem,

fail to fix the right problem, and magnify government's performance problems. We end up with a mismatch of strategies and tactics. Performance suffers, public confidence in government erodes, efficiency weakens, and everyone ends up unhappy. We tend to look for an individual to fire, when responsibility is shared across a broad network of players. We try to reorganize a single agency, when relationships actually stretch across multiple organizations and multiple sectors. We try to write new rules, when leaders need flexibility to respond. And when all of these steps predictably fail, we throw up our arms in disgust at government's incompetence.

In short, we pull prescriptions from the traditional world of vertical hierarchies, based on authority, and try to use them for new, interconnected public–private–nonprofit (and often global) networks that are based on bargaining as well as authority and other management mechanisms. We then wonder why programs so often fail to work and why our remedies too often fail to stick. In reality, for a large number of government's performance problems (and virtually all of the programs on GAO's high-risk list), the problem is not the failure of a single agency. Rather, it is very often a *system* failure, typically at the critical points of friction.

More and more of our public problems—and, as we saw earlier in the book, most of our important problems—fail to fit the model. They require a great deal of adaptive energy and instinct, to fit existing strategies to new problems and to put government's existing assets together in new, creative ways. Ronald A. Heifetz and Marty Linsky conducted an extensive survey of organizational successes and failures in all sectors. They concluded that "the single most common source of leadership failure we've been able to identify—in politics, community life, business, or the nonprofit sector—is that people, especially those in positions of authority, treat adaptive challenges like technical problems."[19] That instinct, all too often, has meant misdiagnosing the problem and applying the wrong remedy, frequently making things worse and rarely solving the problem.

Compounding the problem is the fact that citizens have come to expect more from government. In the 1950s we wanted high-speed highways. In the 1960s we wanted a war on poverty. In the 1970s we wanted clean air and water. In the 1980s we wanted all of that—and lower taxes. Citizens expect government to protect them from terrorists and to provide quick aid when disasters strike, even if they build their homes on shorelines, in floodplains, or atop fault lines. No one says that citizen demands have to be reasonable and no one wants to tell citizens they are making unwise decisions, from lighting up cigarettes to failing to save for retirement, that pose big long-run costs to the system. Citizens want government to solve their problems.

Media attention only underscores that instinct. "Can you believe how your government screwed up this problem?" is a regular staple on television news magazine shows. One such show reported the sad story of a young boy who had died after eating a contaminated fast-food hamburger. The question? Why the government had failed to prevent this from happening, even though the problem was that a beef producer had shipped meat containing dangerous bacteria and the fast-food company had had inadequate quality control over its product. In the end, we expect government to protect us from problems, and the list of problems from which we expect to be protected is constantly growing.

Once upon a time not long ago, spinach was a bitter green that came in two equally unpalatable forms: frozen or canned. The cartoon character Popeye loved it, but "eat your spinach" was the universal code for trying to get children to do the most unpleasant thing imaginable. But California farmers figured out how to grow it, gather it, wash it, pack it, and ship it so that it stays fresh and crisp from coast to coast and for days on the supermarket shelf.

Spinach changed from a bitter vegetable to a vitamin-filled salad staple, and business exploded.

In 2006, however, spinach contaminated with *E. coli* bacteria found its way into the nation's food supply. The outbreak killed three people and sickened hundreds. Investigators traced the problem back to manure contamination in a California field. Citizens called on government to step in. Even worried growers asked for more government regulation. "Anyone who ignores this," said one industry spokesman, "will be out of business."[20] People expect government to protect them from a large and growing collection of risks and dangers.

Public goals have become far more entangled with the behavior of private individuals and organizations outside of government. There could never be a large enough government to ensure that all spinach is safe, that no cars pollute, that all hospitals provide high-quality and error-free care, and that no household cabinets emit carcinogens. This is a quiet deal that America has made with itself. The growing appetite for government is balanced with the fears of what a larger government might bring. We never stop to ask explicitly where to set the balance. In fact, we rarely stop even to consider that we are setting such a balance. We do so, in the accumulation of uncounted decisions, and we almost never stop to think about how these decisions build into significant consequences for governance.

Our public policies increasingly blur the boundaries between the public and private sectors. More of our programs also confound the boundaries of federalism. Medicaid, which kept Mildred alive, is a premier case, with the program's governance responsibilities shared between federal and state governments. The program therefore is different in every state. Many of the efforts to respond to Katrina foundered on the jagged edges between levels of government. Local officials did not work well with the Louisiana state government, and federal officials struggled to connect with them.

The administration of Social Security's core programs and of garbage collection succeed because both fit the vending-machine model. Government's efforts to deal with Katrina and the I-78 ice storm failed because the bureaucratic and programmatic strategies to attack them did not fit the model or the problem. When the problems, programs, and bureaucracies fall out of sync, we face yet again the recurring problem of government performance. It is little wonder, therefore, that the effort to make government work better has created so much conflict. The incentives in the system, from the very top, tend to push reformers and managers increasingly out of sync with the problems they have to solve.

There is tremendous cynicism about the ability of government to perform. But even government's most curmudgeonly critics must grudgingly admit that much of government works well most of the time. How can we account for this pattern of success? In part, the explanation lies in the development of polished routines for routine problems. In part, it lies in the development of new approaches for solving nonroutine problems, especially in leveraging complex public–private partnerships. Sometimes, as in Mildred's case, they work well. Too often, as in Katrina and I-78, they work poorly. Sometimes the best we can do is struggle with the combination of environmental programs that converge on a single spot like the Chesapeake Bay, with some big successes, some significant failures, some problems uncovered—and the public goal, as a result, poorly served. At the core, however, solutions based in routine for problems that are nonroutine are prescriptions for failure.

The central strategy for leveraging these partnerships is managing the boundaries between organizations, public and private. When we face problems that do not fit the boundaries of our governance organizations, we can force the problems to change to fit the organizations (which rarely works) or adapt the organizations to fit the problems. The issue comes down to managing boundaries. Give a two-year-old a coloring book and a box of crayons, and the result is art that adorns the refrigerator doors of the child's grandparents—sometimes dogs with purple fur and skies of brilliant green. Grandparents find the art irresistible, even though the artist's crayons rarely stay within the lines. The result is not always so positive when we apply the same approach to a growing set of public problems. We tend to design our programs like shapes in a coloring book, but like the child's crayons, our problems rarely stay within these lines.

Sometimes we solve this problem remarkably well. Mildred is a stirring example of our success. Too often we do not, and when we fail, we typically do not understand that the performance problem flows from the mismatch of goals and governance. In particular, the recurring instinct to apply routine strategies to nonroutine problems explains why performance problems are so common. They also suggest how to do better, by adapting new strategies for nontraditional problems. The answer is to make Mildred's story the solution for the new generation of interconnected problems that require networked solutions.

Getting Results for Nonroutine Problems

The stunning spread of SARS in 2003 makes the case that effective solutions for wicked, nonroutine problems are critical. Short for *severe acute respiratory syndrome*, an especially nasty respiratory disease, SARS began as an unusual form of pneumonia in China's Guangdong Province.[21] Over the next few months, doctors could determine only that SARS seemed highly contagious and had an unusually high death rate. Communications were sparse, but the

Beijing office of the UN World Health Organization (WHO) received e-mail reports of a hundred deaths from the disease within a week. Residents panicked, clearing drugstore shelves of anything they thought might possibly protect them from the illness. Lab tests found that the illness was not the flu, but investigators did not know what they faced. Chinese health authorities, however, assured WHO that they had the situation under control.

In February 2003, one of the doctors treating patients in Guangdong traveled to Hong Kong to attend his nephew's wedding. The sixty-four-year-old physician checked into Room 911 of the Metropole Hotel, near Kowloon's famous shopping district. He was feeling a bit under the weather, but his respiratory symptoms did not keep him from sightseeing and shopping with his fifty-three-year-old brother-in-law. The next day, however, he was feeling much worse and checked himself into the Kwong Wah Hospital in Hong Kong. He told doctors he was worried that he had contracted a "very virulent disease" in Guangdong. Concerned physicians admitted him into intensive care. Ten days later, pneumonia killed him. His brother-in-law soon arrived at the same hospital complaining of respiratory symptoms. The doctors treated and discharged him. Within a week, he was back in the hospital and soon he was dead as well.

Mysterious reports of virulent pneumonia began surfacing around the world. A seventy-eight-year-old woman from Toronto, who had been touring Hong Kong, fell ill. A twenty-six-year-old Hong Kong man developed a serious respiratory tract infection. A forty-eight-year-old Chinese American businessman traveling through Vietnam was admitted to a Hanoi hospital, and a twenty-six-year-old woman was treated in Singapore. Public health experts later tracked all of these patients, suffering from the same disease in such disparate places, back to the ninth floor of the Metropole, where they had either stayed or visited friends. Except for the brother-in-law, none of them knew the Guangdong doctor. But all seemed to have contracted the illness from him—some, perhaps, from doorknobs or elevators, without ever having laid eyes on him.

Health care workers who had treated the patients themselves started to fall ill. A WHO doctor cared for the businessman in Hanoi and ended up in a Bangkok hospital. Pneumonia began spreading through health care workers in Hong Kong and Hanoi. Meanwhile, the son of the Toronto tourist died. A doctor who had treated the first cases in Singapore headed off to a conference. He complained of respiratory symptoms not long before boarding a plane back to Singapore. Health authorities in Frankfurt took him, along with his pregnant wife and her mother, off the plane during a stop there. A month after the Guangdong doctor had checked himself into the Hong Kong hospital, the mysterious disease— later christened "SARS"—had spread across three continents and thirteen countries to at least 386 persons, and had caused 11 deaths. It continued to spread, to passengers and flight attendants on a flight from Hong Kong to Beijing and, especially, in Toronto. A few days later, Carlo Urbani, the WHO doctor who had first identified the new disease in Hanoi, died as well.

Within two months, the disease not only had spread furiously but also had caused enormous economic damage. Analysts estimated that the Chinese economy alone had taken a $2.2 billion hit, along with $1.7 billion in Hong Kong. Losses totaled $15 billion, they believed, in part because worried tourists stayed away from the region, fewer people went out to restaurants, and retail sales plummeted.

Outside Asia, Toronto took the brunt.[22] The tourist had unknowingly brought the disease back and developed muscle aches and a dry cough. No one recognized her condition as being related to the Hong Kong illness, and when she died quietly at home, the coroner listed "heart attack" as the cause. But then her son fell ill and went to Toronto's busy Scarborough Hospital. The hospital was so crowded that he spent nearly a day in a busy emergency department, separated from other patients and health care workers by only a curtain, before being admitted to a room. At first, doctors suspected tuberculosis. Word about the strange disease in China had not yet reached them, and not until after skillful sleuthing revealed the common link back to the Metropole—after the tourist's son had died as well—did the picture emerge. Two of the patients sharing the emergency department with him developed the disease. The doctor who had inserted a breathing tube became infected as well, even though he had worn a gown, gloves, and goggles. Three nurses attending the procedure became ill as well.

Public health officials realized they had a major, vicious disease on their hands. They identified everyone who had been in the hospital after the illness struck and ordered them to stay isolated at home for at least ten days. Medical workers treated those who fell ill in negative-pressure rooms, which were specially designed to prevent the disease from seeping out. They quickly faced a shortage of the special rooms and then struggled to find enough health professionals to staff a newly opened satellite facility. Ontario Premier Ernie Eves declared a provincewide emergency and the hospitals went into "Code Orange" mode, suspending nonemergency services. Spread of the disease began to slow, but new cases continued to pop up, including the child of a school nurse and family members who had begun developing symptoms after attending a funeral. Another thirty-one cases developed among members of a tightly knit religious community and some of the health care professionals who had cared for them. In all, Toronto's public health agency investigated 1,907 separate reports, in addition to 220 probable or suspected SARS cases.

Canadian authorities were stunned by how rapidly the disease spread and by how hard it was to control. They recognized that cooperation across the usual boundaries was essential, but most of the collaboration depended on voluntary partnerships. The law proved a weak tool. Indeed, as a national advisory committee concluded, "The lack of formal terms of cooperation impedes rapid responses to emergency situations." Governments, at all levels, had not asked in advance about how they would coordinate their work in a crisis, and the committee warned that "what happened with SARS could happen with a natural disaster"—or an assault from bioterrorism or an even more vicious pandemic.[23] Ordinary routines, which worked satisfactorily on normal problems, failed in the crisis. Canadian government officials worried, moreover, that such a crisis might well occur again.

No one knew for sure just how the Guangdong illness had started. Public health experts suspected, but could not prove, that civet cats—weasel-like mammals sometimes served in restaurants—were at the root. They thought that perhaps a disease organism had mutated and the cats had carried it; that it had jumped into the human food chain in rural China; and that once humans had become infected, normal antibodies had been quickly overwhelmed, with the disease often proving fatal and its spread hard to stop. A single doctor treating patients in the region had left for a short break in Hong Kong and unwittingly passed the syndrome to about a dozen people staying in his hotel (see Figure 4.2). They, in turn, had infected more than 8,000 others in two dozen countries across North America, South America, Europe, and Asia. A total of 774 people had died, from an epidemic that had rippled out from just a single case in Hong Kong.[24]

The Challenge of Public Value

Government is not just a service delivery system, and citizenship is not simply a transaction in which individuals exchange cash for goods and services. As Mark Moore reminds us, public programs

FIGURE 4.2   Transmission of SARS–2003

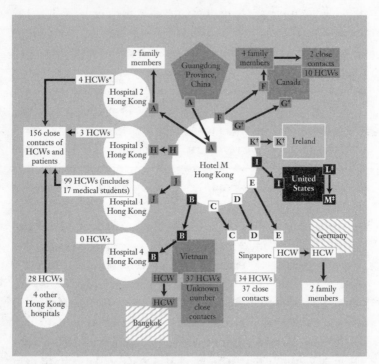

Source: Centers for Disease Control, "Update: Outbreak of Severe Acute Respiratory Syndrome— Worldwide, 2003," *Morbidity and Mortality Weekly Report* 52 no. 12 (March 28, 2003), 241–248, at http:// www.cdc.gov/MMWR/preview/mmwrhtml/mm5212a1.htm. "HCW" is an acronym for "health care worker."

are about creating public value.[25] Moreover, citizenship is not a spectator sport. The *Federalist Papers* are full of discussion about the "rights of citizenship." The nation's founders, in fact, worked so hard to declare independence and frame a constitution because they believed that citizens could—and should—interact with government, through free discourse, debate, and voting. The Bill of Rights is an extremely activist document. It contains substantial protections against the misuse of government power, but most of it seeks to empower an active citizenry that will be practicing religion, engaging in free speech, peaceably assembling to debate and protest, petitioning the government for redress of grievances, keeping and bearing arms, and engaging in due process of law. The founders clearly believed that citizens would be connecting intensely with each other and with their government, and they wanted to make sure to protect their right to do so.

Louisiana Governor Kathleen Blanco tried to make this point following intense criticism of her government's preparation for Katrina, especially in failing to evacuate vulnerable residents from nursing homes. She argued that government can do only so much. She said that government had sounded the alarm and asked citizens to evacuate, but government ultimately had to rely on the "individual responsibility" of citizens to respond.[26] Fixing the balance of government responsibility and personal responsibility is difficult indeed, and Blanco reaped enormous public criticism for her role. Ultimately, however, she was right: the core issues come down to citizens. But that point is also the source of the breakdown. The fact that no one ultimately is in charge of anything means that it is impossible to pinpoint accountability. It also means that it is easy for citizens to skirt their responsibility, to expect government to drift more deeply into a passive vending-machine approach to government that serves them, and to escape the active role in citizenship that the founders imagined.

Following the September 11 terrorist attacks, Washington-area officials tried to reconsider citizens' roles as they thought the unthinkable: how, if necessary, they could evacuate the region. A 2006 study found existing plans "not sufficient." Local officials said that highways, strained under ordinary traffic, might become gridlocked in a major disaster; and that the Metro subway system could become overwhelmed. David Snyder, a Falls Church, Virginia, city council member who also serves on the region's

Emergency Preparedness Council, said simply, "There's no one in charge." Snyder pointed to great progress over the years. But he also acknowledged the fundamental problem. "What's lacking," he said, "is an overall decisional framework."[27] Citizens typically pay little attention to what level of government is responsible for which problems. They often do not even fully understand which programs are government programs and which are not—hence the plaintive call to keep government's hands off Medicare. They often tend to understand even less about the responsibilities of different levels of government—hence the quiet comments of many state legislators' staffs about dealing subtly with citizens' requests for help with Social Security problems, even though Social Security is a completely federal program.

The driving truth is that citizens just want their problems solved. They do not want to have to spend time trying to figure out whose job it is to do so. They simply want to insert their money, if grudgingly, and receive their services. But they are increasingly disconnected from their citizenship responsibilities.

Consider the E-ZPass system, an exquisitely elegant solution (developed and managed through the private sector) to the problem of carrying pockets of change to negotiate highway tollbooths. Entrepreneurs developed a small plastic box containing an electronic chip and installed detectors at the toll stations. When drivers pass through a station, the detector identifies the car's owner and deducts the toll from a computer account, which can be automatically restocked with charges against the car owner's credit card. Some newer E-ZPass toll centers even have separate lanes with overhead detectors. Drivers with E-ZPass can fly through toll plazas at sixty miles per hour while drivers without E-ZPass back up in long lines to pass along their quarters. The system has become hugely popular, especially in the Northeast, where the small white box affixed to the windshield is even more a mark of the committed road warrior than is a radar detector.

Analysts have studied the effect of the E-ZPass system on tolls and have found that the tolls on roads and bridges with E-ZPass have risen more quickly than on those without it. The fact that the transaction is relatively invisible—drivers notice only that the toll-gate rises or a light changes to a satisfying green—disconnects citizens from the cost of their decisions.[28] That detachment, in turn, makes it easier for governments to raise tolls, because the cost is relatively invisible to drivers. Checking one's E-ZPass transactions is possible, but it requires a multistep trip through a special Web site, and for most drivers, the thrill of zipping past backed-up non-E-ZPass vehicles is all they need to know. E-ZPass creates a different kind of vending machine in which citizens neither directly insert money nor play an active role as citizens. That arrangement weakens citizen oversight of government programs, to the point that tolls rise faster than might otherwise have been the case.

Beyond the thrill of beating the toll plaza backups is the more fundamental paradox illustrated by E-ZPass. Citizens are increasingly involved in government in more of what they do, both in their jobs as part of the provider networks and in their lives as service recipients. Even as they have become more part of government, however, they have come to feel less connected to it. Sometimes they have been more alienated by it.

A bigger government with more shared responsibility has created a system in which no one is fully accountable for anything government does. No program fits within any single government agency, and it would be impossible to redraw the boundaries to sort out the responsibility. More problems slop over boundaries between levels of government, between sectors of society, and between nations.

It is little wonder that citizens feel alienated. They see demonstrable performance problems, from inept government response during the Katrina crisis to problems with garbage pickup in their neighborhood. They see that poor performance often has few consequences because no one seems to be in charge. They hear confusing explanations about divided responsibility. They know their taxes are too high. Cynicism is the logical result.

The vending-machine model itself is a paradox. Citizens do not need to know how complex government programs work. Indeed, many programs are so complex that, for most citizens, trying to probe the details would prove impossible. We hire experts, in fact, precisely so that we do not have to understand the complexity. Listening to air traffic control radio transmissions around busy airports like Chicago O'Hare and Atlanta Hartsfield would befuddle all but the most experienced ears. Passengers simply care about getting safely to their airport gates. On the other hand, the abstraction of the vending-machine model also disconnects citizens from their government. The disconnection of policy making from its implementation makes it far too easy to set expectations that government must struggle to meet, and it confuses individuals about their obligations as citizens. The issues of organization, complexity, and accountability that we saw in Chapter 3 only compound the problem.

Government is facing a growing class of wicked problems that pose especially difficult puzzles. The failure to solve them brings especially severe consequences. And they echo the challenges that the cases of Mildred and Katrina help frame: how to deal with important problems for which government's existing programs and structures prove a poor fit. Trying to deal with such twenty-first-century problems with twentieth-century approaches is a prescription for disaster.

Can we do better? Are the challenges of twenty-first-century government represented by the deep muck of Katrina, which threatens to clog the workings of government beyond repair? Will long-established routines prevent us from adapting to new challenges? Or is the future the more positive face of Mildred, where skillful administrators adapt organizations to fit new, complex, shifting problems? We turn to that difficult puzzle in the next chapter.

5

TECTONIC NATION

On the morning of September 12, 2001, the *New York Times* surveyed the crushing damage of the previous day's terrorist attacks. "It was, in fact, one of those moments in which history splits, and we define the world as 'before' and 'after,'" the editors sadly wrote. "We look back at sunrise yesterday through pillars of smoke and dust, down streets snowed under with the atomized debris of the skyline, and we understand that everything has changed."[1] Chris Patten, foreign affairs commissioner for the European Union, added, "This is one of the few days in life that one can actually say will change everything."[2] In the somber days after those horrendous attacks, that seemed the universal conclusion. From top government officials to ordinary citizens on the street, the consensus was that everything had changed. But that judgment was wrong. The September 11 attacks were wrenching, but deeper forces had already profoundly transformed American government. Things had fundamentally shifted long before September 11—we just had not yet recognized it.

Throughout its history, American government has periodically undergone wrenching transformations. September 11 was one of those moments. Like previous shifts, however, there were advance clues, often missed, of a buildup of intense forces. To understand the underlying message of September 11, we need to look at the forces that both shaped that day and revealed important underlying challenges. Those are the clues for the lasting meaning of September 11, for its links to other big policy puzzles, and for the kind of government we need for the future.

A close look at the crisis shows surprising connections to the tales of Mildred and Katrina, and to the other cases we have examined as well. On a wide range of issues, fundamental forces had built up to require wrenching changes in American governance. In each case, deep pressures long went unnoticed until they burst onto the scene—sometimes violently or abruptly, as in the cases of September 11 and Katrina; sometimes far more quietly, as in Mildred's case. All three cases mark punctuations in the evolution of American government.[3] They grew from forces buried deep in the political geology of American politics.

The Triple Junction

German geologist Alfred Wegener observed early in the twentieth century that the continents, if cut out and slid around, would fit neatly together like pieces of a jigsaw puzzle. He concluded that the continents had once been joined and gradually, over a very long time, drifted apart. Geologists later proved him right. They embraced a notion that the continents float on vast tectonic plates, driven by motions that rearrange their landscapes and their relations to each other. Most of the time, this movement is slow and imperceptible. Sometimes it occurs in a jolting, violent earthquake that transforms the land around it.

The biggest transformations occur where the plates grind against each other. The most wrenching of these happen in the rare places where three plates converge—a phenomenon called a *triple junction*. Just off California's coastline, near Eureka, is one of these triple convergences, christened the Mendocino Triple Junction. The Pacific Plate is slowly creeping north at about two inches a year, and it is thrusting under the southern edge of the Gorda Plate. Meanwhile, an 800-mile segment of the Gorda Plate is sliding underneath the continental North American Plate. Although geologists argue among themselves about precisely which pieces of which plates are thrusting where, they do agree that the forces of these three plates have transformed the region in the past by creating new topographical formations—from the volcanoes that dot the Northwest to spectacular attractions like Half Dome and El Capitan in Yosemite National Park—and that the future will bring more shifts.

Along the West Coast, the landscape is deceptively stable. The ground is firm enough to support skyscrapers, large bridges, and complicated highway systems. The relics of earlier volcanic eruptions, produced by the same forces, have become tourist attractions of uncommon beauty. San Francisco's rapid transit system includes a subway that tunnels through rock under the bay, near the very heart of the San Andreas Fault. People go about their daily lives paying little attention to the powerful forces beneath them. Every once in a while, however, the tectonic forces build, the plates slip past each other with wrenching friction, and the resulting earthquakes reshape the landscape and transform the lives of citizens living along the snaking fault lines.

Just as tectonic action transforms the Earth's surface, big changes periodically transform American government. The nation's governance rests on different political traditions and, like the geological plates, the patterns of governance prove remarkably stable for long periods of time. Now and then, however, these patterns are disrupted by dramatic change. The key to understanding the history of American government lies in understanding how the tectonic plates of government work. And the key to understanding America's future is to understand that forces are building again that will force fundamental changes in what government is and how it works.

When tensions surface, Americans go back to the basic principles framed by the founders. We comfort ourselves that our enduring political institutions protect us against the actions of individual politicians and administrators. When our political institutions, especially Congress and the presidency, strain under the weight of tough problems, we remind ourselves of the strength of our ideals. When new policy problems test our ideals, we find strength in telling ourselves that our Constitution is alive and has shown remarkable ability to adapt.

That is surely all true. But celebrating the stability of American politics is like driving across San Francisco's Golden Gate Bridge, admiring the city's skyline, and enjoying the lapping waves and the barking seals on Fisherman's Wharf. The durable beauty is striking. We know, however, that lurking underground is a powerful fault driven by the forces at the Mendocino Triple Junction, that this fault has changed the city in the past, and that it surely will do so again. In fact, early in 2001, FEMA planners identified the three biggest disasters facing the nation: a terrorist attack on New York, a major hurricane strike in New Orleans, and a big earthquake in California. Within four years, two of the three occurred, and geologists warned that the third disaster was inevitable.

Like the forces that build along the fault lines of the West Coast, pressures have regularly built up along the tectonic plates of American government, and Americans have tended to approach the tensions in three ways. One is to think about American politics as an evolutionary process, built atop the stable bedrock of constitutional boundaries and changing gradually. Charles E. Lindblom's notion of "incrementalism" describes, more powerfully than any other single idea, how the nation inches along a path of steady, but frequent, small changes.[4] To be sure, big forces like the New Deal and World War II sometimes intervene to produce big changes. But for the most part, Lindblom argues, American government steadily evolves through incremental change.

However, although incrementalism might describe most of American government, most of the time, it does not capture the most important events in defining and transforming government. The fact that politics moves incrementally most of the time is as true as the fact that the geological plates do not shake all the time. Far more important, for the Earth as well as for politics, are the events that periodically redefine the geology of the land and the politics of the nation. Knowing how things work most of the time is important and useful, but it is not as important as understanding the big transforming events that reshape the core realities.

We can also think about American government as a pendulum swinging between extremes: between centralized power (in the hands of the national government) and decentralized action (dominated by state and local governments); between big government (empowered to solve our problems) and small government (restrained to avoid interference with our freedoms); between government power (to do what citizens want done) and individual freedom (to prevent government power from intruding excessively in their lives).[5] The balance between centralization and decentralization, for example, comes from "a continuous and imperfect process, not one to be realized once and for all," according to James W. Fesler in 1949.[6]

The result, Paul C. Light argues, is that government—and especially government reform—tends to wash back and forth between conflicting values. Light explains, "Reformers have no overarching theory of when government and its employees can or cannot be trusted to do their jobs well. Lacking such a theory, government lurches back and forth from trust to distrust, from liberation to war on waste, scientific management to watchful eye." As a result, "Just as surely as high tide follows low, today's effort to liberate government from endless rules and structure will surely be followed by an effort to enslave government once again."[7] Much of American government builds on fundamental but conflicting, irreconcilable values. Much of American history has, in fact, swung back and forth between them. Just as important, however, is whether the to-and-fro has a long-term direction.

That puzzle leads to a final alternative, premised on the need for periodic reinventions of what government is and how it works. The nation's framers loved the language of change. Thomas Jefferson argued the advantages of periodic revolution, and ever since, reformers have typically urged large, sweeping changes on American government to cure its ills. In the public sector, David Osborne and Ted Gaebler argued in the early 1990s for a need to "reinvent" government and concluded, "The kind of governments that developed during the industrial era, with their sluggish, centralized bureaucracies, their preoccupation with rules and regulations, and their hierarchical chains of command, no longer work very well." In response, "new kinds of public institutions are taking their place," they argued, in a movement that drove the Clinton administration.[8] Newt Gingrich countered with a Republican revolution advanced in his "Contract with America."

American government has been formed by how the nation's enduring traditions—its political plates—have shifted against each other. Sometimes those political transformations have been gentle, like the slip of the tectonic plates past each other when fluids deep underground reduce the friction. Sometimes the transformations have been wrenching, with as deep an impact on the body politic as the great 1907 San Francisco earthquake had on the Bay Area. Sometimes the transformations have resulted from the slipping of just one plate. Sometimes all three plates have combined to form larger changes.

With great skill and unusual luck, geologists have occasionally been able to predict where the next earthquake will occur. A careful look at the plates on which America's enduring political traditions rest shows that, for the first time in American history, all three plates shifted at once at the end of the twentieth century. This shift set the stage for governance for the century to come.

Shifting Political Plates

American government as we know it today is the product of transformations that have occurred throughout the nation's political life. It is no secret that twenty-first-century government bears little resemblance to the constitutional system created in 1787. "Father of the Constitution" James Madison and his colleagues would scarcely recognize government management of airport screeners, the air traffic control system, Social Security, or Medicaid. But they would unquestionably recognize the basic questions at the core of modern government. What should be government's relationship with the rest of society and the economy? How should government sort out the power relationships between the federal government and the states? And how should the United States fit into the rest of the world? From the time of the founders, these have been the great questions about the role and structure of American government. The history of American government has been built on the ongoing search for answers.

American government rests on three plates, defined (as is the case at the Mendocino Triple Junction) by what occurs at their boundaries:

1. *Privatization*: the role of government—the relationship between public institutions and the private and nonprofit sectors
2. *Federalism*: the role of federalism—the relationship between the national, state, and local governments.
3. *Globalization*: the role of the United States in the world—the relationship between America and the other forces (political, economic, and social) that shape global life

Throughout American history, these plates have periodically shifted, but usually they have shifted one at a time. At the turn of the twenty-first century, however, they all shifted at the same time, which the awful spectacle of the September 11 terrorist attacks underscored. Simultaneous shifts of all three plates that make up the political triple junction have been relatively rare in American history. Only once before 2001, with the rise of the Progressives at the end of the nineteenth century, had all three plates shifted at once (and, as we shall see, the shift of the globalization plate had been unsteady, as Americans for a generation resisted the burdens that come with global power).

Early political struggles set the stage for these periodic shifts. For example, early in the first president's first term, Treasury Secretary Alexander Hamilton advanced his plan for the federal government to assume responsibility for the debt of the states. Hamilton saw it as the essential foundation of the new republic. Strong public credit, he believed, would both fuel the private economy and strengthen the political integrity of the new nation, by tying the interests of the American elite to robust and successful political institutions.[9] It subtly pulled power to government from the private sector and to the national government from the states. That strategy, however, collided directly with the agrarian ideals that Jefferson and his colleagues had promoted. They wanted a small government that would allow private industry to flourish and a national government that would not trample upon state power. Hamilton, however, saw a strong national government as the indispensable step for forging the nation's economic future—and for discouraging foreign governments from seizing the raw, young nation. That temptation was very real among the Spanish, French, and even the English. Hamilton believed that building a strong national government—one that promoted and regulated commerce, had supremacy over the states, and reinforced America's role in the world—was the most important step toward creating a truly modern state.

As George Washington settled into the President's House just down the street from Philadelphia's Independence Hall, the three tectonic plates were in motion. Just how far should government go in trying to steer the private economy? For Hamilton and at least some of the Federalists, the Constitution's commerce clause provided the license and the nation's great potential provided the motivation. Any federal step, of course, would come at the expense of the power of state governments. Given the wide variation in the debt burdens carried by individual states, some states stood to benefit far more than others from Hamilton's plan. His "Report on Credit" was a plan to make America a great world power; without it, he warned, the young nation would inevitably fail to achieve its destiny.[10] The answer, Hamilton concluded, was robust federal power coupled with a strong executive branch.

Debates among the nation's "founding brothers" were sometimes friendly, often sharp, and clearly focused on these big issues.[11] The founders resolved some of them. The federal government did indeed absorb the states' debts, thereby helping to establish the new national government's preeminent position in the emerging economy. The founders engaged in bitter fights about other issues, including a combination of personal and policy battles that led to Hamilton's death at the point of Vice President Aaron Burr's dueling pistol. But perhaps most important, they came to consensus that, at the least, these were the truly important questions, and that shedding blood to resolve such problems would make for bad policy and worse politics. Some of the founders were horrified when disputes about how to address these questions led to schisms that produced two political parties, but the parties became the institutionalized manner in which Americans fought, debated, and resolved (at least temporarily) the big issues they faced. Hamilton's plan for a strong national bank—a question of government's role in shaping the economy—took until 1913 to resolve, with the creation of the Federal Reserve, after bitter battles led to the closing of the First and Second banks of the United States. But the first plate settled into a place beyond which it would not slide: government asserted its power—indeed, its obligation—to manage the economy.

Although many states' rights advocates feared the shift of power that federal assumption of state debts would bring, they framed a compromise: yielding some power to the federal government in exchange for shedding the burdens of state debt. On most other issues, especially slavery, the states retained the upper hand, although the federal government asserted power in deciding how far slavery could extend beyond the original colonies. The most fractious issue remained whether the federal or state government was paramount when they conflicted, and the Civil War confirmed that the nation would remain the more or less *united* states. The federal and state governments continued to operate within the framework of this delicate compromise. Following the War of 1812, the nation settled into a period of relative international calm bred from introspection.

In the waning decades of the nineteenth century, the transition from an agrarian to an industrial economy brought huge challenges for government. Could steamship riders expect safe passage without the boilers blowing up? Was electricity's new and puzzling technology safe, and could citizens get reliable electric and telephone service to their homes without encountering a thicket of wires running down their streets? Did the rise of large political machines threaten to weave corruption throughout local government? Did the rise of enormous corporate monopolies threaten to cripple national government and undermine the public interest?

The Progressive movement sought to solve all these problems by taking on big issues, along all three plates over the course of a generation. W. E. B. Du Bois took on racism. Upton Sinclair's *The Jungle* brought attention to the harsh life of immigrants near the Chicago stockyards. John Dewey made the case for progressive education and Frederick W. Taylor sought the "one best way" to improve factory production. Lincoln Steffens decried "the shame of the cities." William Jennings Bryan told Americans they did not need to be subjected to commercial interest. Woodrow Wilson, first as a professor and then as president, championed the Progressive cause of bringing new goals and new institutions to American government. Reformers created the great regulatory commissions, including the Interstate Commerce Commission and the Food and Drug Administration. They established the income tax to make tax collections fairer and they vastly expanded the scope of government power. Wilson himself ultimately led the nation through World War I.

The Progressives concluded that the nation needed a stronger government. Their challenge was how to enhance government's power without threatening liberty. They wanted a government that could effectively regulate private power and efficiently deliver public services, but they did not want to create a socialist state. Their genius lay in creating an administrative state that could borrow tools from the private sector and even from other countries but insisting that public officials use them in an accountable way. That combination of private resources and public accountability, in fact, was the foundation of the vending-machine model. The model identified the members of the machine, defined the role of each member, trained each one in the skills required to do the job, and coordinated their work so that hard things could be done in a predictable way. Its mechanistic approach grew from the industrial age, which gave it persuasive power. It also had great political value, for the machine limited the power of unelected bureaucrats. All power flows from the votes of the people to the officials they elect. Elected officials, in turn, delegate power to administrators but hold them responsible for how they use it, within a hierarchy that tightly defines each person's role and limits that person's power to what is required to exercise that role. The hierarchy provides not only a strategy for efficient management but also a road map for democratic responsiveness.

This vending-machine model grew out of the rule of law. To make the case for expanding government's power while holding it accountable, the Progressives argued that the law—what it empowered bureaucrats to do, and how it held them responsible— was the essential bulkhead between industrial-age government and tyranny.[12] The Progressives' approach built on an explicit strategy: Government agencies would administer government programs. Government's power would be expanded to do so. The rule of law would shape and govern the exercise of government power within public bureaucracies and thus hold it accountable.

The rise of Mildred- and Katrina-style problems a century later, however, fractured the Progressives' strategy. The Progressive movement grew from a powerful commitment to use public institutions to rein in private power, but the key players in that movement had not counted on the rising importance of private partners in providing public services. The government needed private contractors to fight World War II and to run the space program. The federal government needed state and local governments to rebuild cities and construct the interstate highway system. Medicare was politically impossible without complex public–private partnerships. Medicaid added federal–state partnerships to the Medicare governance brew. But by sharing power across government boundaries and with private contractors who exercised substantial power on government's behalf, these strategies shifted away from the hierarchical model on which the Progressives had relied to expand public power and to hold unelected bureaucrats accountable. That power sharing, in turn, produced big challenges for the programs' performance and responsiveness.

Government continued to rely on agents to exercise its power, but more of the agents were in different government agencies and many of the agents were in the private and nonprofit sectors. The pragmatic development of practical government tools profoundly challenged the system that the Progressives had developed to ensure effective and accountable government because it strained the rule of law that they had devised.

Theodore Lowi warned in 1969 that these strains were weakening America's political institutions. As the legal bulkhead weakened, interest groups gamed the system to enhance their own position. Lowi's case was really a brief for reassertion of the Progressive spirit, for restrengthening the accountability of bureaucrats and politicians, and for rerooting policy implementation in a legal structure devoted to pursuit of the common good.[13] Lowi had difficulty selling his prescription because the policy system had expanded far beyond the boundaries that the Progressives had created. But Lowi's argument underscored the basic point: government's shifting policy strategies had severely strained the mechanisms that had been created a century earlier to enhance public power while holding it accountable.

The rise of the new generation of public tools has not made the rule of law any less important. Indeed, within public bureaucracies, the Progressives' basic model remains robust. Rather, as the system relies on more tools (including grants and contracts) through multiple organizations (including federal, state, local, public, private, and nonprofit agencies), there are multiple rules, each covering individual elements of the system. The traditional model does not provide a mechanism for holding the system as a whole accountable, and no alternative has emerged. That, in fact, was Michael Brown's central defense for his actions during the Katrina crisis: he had managed his agency well, he argued, but he could not control others beyond his own hierarchy.

The retreat to this narrow view of accountability did not convince policy makers or the public, and it failed to solve the problem. In one sense, Brown was right. He had a clear and straightforward system for managing his agency. That system, however, had proven a profound mismatch for the problems he was charged with solving. Critics showed Brown no mercy when he claimed he had done his job as well as he could, because it was demonstrably clear that people had suffered as a result. His vending-machine model became clogged by the problems he was trying to solve. The same troubling scenario has rippled through countless other public programs as well. Consider the following policy puzzles, which illustrate the big challenges that echo FEMA's Katrina problems and the issues that flow from shifting tectonic plates.

PRIVATIZATION: TRANSPORTATION CONGESTION

The first fault line was along government's boundary with the private sector. In the early 2000s, the nation's transportation system was becoming increasingly clogged and congested. Air traffic congestion was becoming so bad, the *Philadelphia Inquirer*'s Dave

Boyer joked with his readers, that "you're in no danger of going anywhere else." In fact, he said, Philadelphia residents will find vacations "much less frustrating if you think of Philly airport as your final destination." He urged his readers to enjoy "the delightful charade of boarding a plane to nowhere." In fact, he wrote, there are even padded benches where visitors can "crack open a good book while you await confirmation that you're not going anywhere."[14]

For Boyer and his many fellow summer travelers, the joke was not very funny. Air traffic, especially during the summer construction and thunderstorm season, limped along, with disruptions near key hubs disrupting traffic everywhere. Frustrated fliers sometimes waited hours to board the plane, only to have the flight canceled. Sometimes delays caused them to miss a connection or to arrive at the destination but not be able to get off the plane. In one especially bad episode in August 2007, a computer failure left 17,000 inbound passengers stuck on planes arriving from international destinations, some for as long as eight hours. The snafu occurred because one Ethernet card, an internal component that allows computers to connect to the Internet and that can be purchased for as little as fifteen dollars, had failed. Usually, when such small components go bad, they simply stop working. But this one proved especially devilish, sending out repeated cries for help and creating a data storm that crashed the network. US Customs and Border Protection, which processes 46,000 people an hour through the customs lanes, ground to a halt because without the computers, federal agents could not check incoming passengers against the terrorist watch list. The agency's contractor spent several hours tracking down the problem, until it finally located the single misbehaving computer circuit.[15]

These problems are just part of a far larger transportation issue. As former US Secretary of Transportation Norman Y. Mineta explained, "Congestion is one of the single largest threats to our economic prosperity and way of life." All together, planes circling airports, trucks stuck in traffic, and cargo backed up at seaports cost the nation about $200 billion a year. Americans lose 3.7 billion hours a year stuck in traffic. They burn 2.3 billion gallons of fuel going nowhere. "Congestion kills time, wastes fuel, and costs money," he concluded. "But we don't have to let traffic delays put our lives on hold any longer."[16]

The Department of Transportation (DOT) developed an extensive strategy to reduce the congestion of roads, ports, railroads, and airways. The plan was ambitious, ranging from new technologies for air traffic control and new collaboration with the Department of Homeland Security for reducing delays at border crossings, to congestion pricing (charging more for access to roadways during peak periods) and innovative state partnerships with the private sector. For DOT, one fact was inescapable: although no one could dispute (or escape) the looming congestion problem, the department could not single-handedly solve it. After accounting for the 43,500 air traffic controllers who worked the nation's air routes, the federal department had just 12,000 employees to handle the rest of the system. Its $61 billion budget (in fiscal year 2006) was a tiny fraction of transportation spending for the country, and less than a third of what its experts estimated that congestion was costing Americans every year.

How could a relatively tiny department hope to solve such a huge problem? It could create new programs and use its budget to reshape government policy. And although the department certainly had planned to do that, its top officials recognized that their leverage was far too small to move the entire system. Instead, they concluded that they needed to use their public resources—spending, regulations, and rhetorical power—to leverage the private system. They did not view this as a problem they could solve, as much as an issue to which they needed to recruit others. Undersecretary of Transportation for Policy Jeffery N. Shane told a House subcommittee that the department planned to encourage "States to tap private sector resources" and to reshape economic forces to change the incentives for consumers and manufacturers alike.[17]

In short, DOT officials understood instinctively that they were riding a plate defining the relationship between government and the private sector. Dealing with the frictions that congestion produced required a strategy of building partnerships—with state and local governments (along the federalism plate), with other nations to deal with trade and security (along the globalization plate), as well as with the private sector (along the privatization plate). DOT officials worked to create new partnerships with partners in the private-sector transportation community to ease congestion's tectonic tensions.

To the degree that public programs are administered across public–private boundaries, policy makers have to rely on the law of contracts and the power of economic incentives. Government's private partners are not politically accountable through the lines of hierarchical authority that shape government units. This is not to say that these private partners are unaccountable. Rather, they are accountable in a different way. A well-established body of contract law replaces the system of political accountability. The buyer and seller negotiate over what good or service to produce and how much it will cost. They agree on standards for measuring compliance and remedies for nonperformance. The challenge for government is to simultaneously juggle both traditional and market-based accountability systems and match the right system to the job at hand. This juggling act does not render accountability impossible, but it does vastly complicate the task.

Government's capacity for acting as a smart buyer in this marketplace—defining what it wants to buy, determining what it ought to pay, and assessing whether it has gotten its money's worth—has eroded over time.[18] The capacity of public managers to fill these critical roles has declined as the importance of these tools has grown. Contract management is critical, but it is often not viewed by government employees as a prestigious area of advancement. In addition, many government employees hired for their functional expertise, whether in environmental protection or human services, often end up as contract managers overseeing third parties who do much of the work. That role can prove doubly troublesome, for they often find themselves doing unfamiliar work far from the frontlines.

Moreover, the form of government's relationship with the private sector has gradually changed. In the Medicare and Medicaid programs, private service providers work through a separate system of private financial management organizations to control and distribute public funds. To be sure, government regulations and contracts define how this system ought to work. But with a tiny handful of government officials sitting astride a system managed principally by private organizations, government's capacity for managing accountability is weak at best. The job is hard enough for programs that rely heavily on contracts. It is even harder for the new breed of "lead systems integrator" contracting relationships on which NASA, Homeland Security, the Pentagon, and many local-government social-service agencies have all relied. This does not mean that the rule of law is inconsequential. But it does mean that applying it has become far more difficult because the supply chain has become far longer and the links in it have become more intricate.

FEDERALISM: FEMA'S PROJECT IMPACT

A second fault line was the separation between the federal government and state and local governments. These tensions pre-dated the creation of the federal government: small states like Delaware were afraid their big neighbors (such as Pennsylvania) would push them aside, and all the states worried about surrendering their power to the federal government. Without the delicate balancing act enshrined in the Constitution's grand compromise, the American states might never have become united. The boundaries between the federal government and the states, however, have never been clearly fixed. Instead, they defined where conflict was most likely to develop.

That conflict almost destroyed the union during the Civil War. It took a century to settle many legal questions, including whether "separate but equal" facilities for different races was constitutional, but the Civil War, once and for all, established the supremacy of the federal government. The Great Depression reinforced that role, when Roosevelt launched the federal New Deal after the states proved ineffective in responding to the economic collapse. The Great Society's policy revolution of the 1960s, which helped create the Medicare and Medicaid programs from which Mildred benefited, reinforced the point.

These complex intergovernmental strategies lay at the core of FEMA's remarkable remediation work during the 1990s. The agency used national power not to assert supremacy, but to leverage action. The strategy emerged from a series of vicious storms, which had demonstrated to agency officials that it was far better to prevent the damage than to fix it after the fact. Mary Klotsche of Freeport, New York, was glad for the plan. She had lived in her home for more than thirty-five years, but a series of hurricanes and nor'easters had repeatedly soaked her basement and garden. "I'm getting too old to be sweeping water out of the house," she told a *New York Times* reporter.[19] While bailing out her home from Hurricane Gloria's damage in 1985, Mary had suffered a heart attack from which she fortunately recovered. The continued flooding along Long Island's south shore, not far from Coney Island, was not doing her health or her home any good. Another of the town's residents, Richard Carvell, went to bed during a nor'easter forecasted to be relatively mild. Instead, the cries of his Labrador retriever woke him early in the morning and he found a foot of chilly water in his house, with thousands of dollars of carpeting and furniture ruined.

In 1998, FEMA stepped in to help the town. "We have to stop the damage–repair, damage–repair cycle," explained director James Lee Witt. Freeport was to become one of the first communities in Project Impact, FEMA's new program to reduce the risk of disaster damage by working with state and local governments, private and nonprofit partners like the American Red Cross and Home Depot, and individual citizens. FEMA and its partners focused on mitigation: taking steps in advance to lessen the impact of disasters on property and lives. Better to prevent or minimize the damage, FEMA's top officials concluded, than to work after the fact to repair it, often at far higher costs.

FEMA's struggles with a series of big natural disasters in the 1990s led Witt to undertake a fundamental restructuring of FEMA and its programs. He put FEMA to work analyzing the risks that disasters, such as the 1989 Loma Prieta earthquake in California and Hurricane Andrew's devastation of southern Florida in 1992, could bring. His strategy was not for FEMA to take charge but to use the agency's leverage to build broad partnerships—as he put it, to "empower all Americans to fulfill their responsibility for ensuring safer communities."[20] It was a bottom-up strategy; FEMA did not tell communities what to do. Rather, it provided grants to communities willing to take on the job of deciding for themselves what steps would prove most effective in building those partnerships, identifying hazards, prioritizing risk reduction steps, and developing communication strategies to broaden the partnerships.

In Freeport, FEMA launched one of the first partnerships in

1998. The agency brought together twenty-one different players, who committed to a broad-based and integrated strategy. They identified bulkheads that needed to be replaced or repaired. They worked with home owners to identify structures that were especially flood-prone and prepared key items of infrastructure whose loss would put the community at risk. FEMA put up $300,000, while Freeport supplied a $100,000 match. They built an emergency siren system, to warn residents to place sandbags to keep out rising waters, and helped home owners protect appliances and other items subject to water damage in the lower floors. In all, analysts estimated that the project would save the community more than twelve dollars for every dollar invested.[21] Because of the programs' efforts, storms that hit Freeport early in the summer of 2007 did relatively little damage.[22]

Witt's FEMA took the same strategy to Florida, to develop new designs for hurricane-resistant homes. In Deerfield Beach, Florida, FEMA partnered with State Farm Fire and Casualty Company to build a next-generation home, just two miles from the beach, that could resist winds up to 156 miles per hour. It cost just 10 percent more than the cost of a conventionally built home and, analysts believed, would be far more effective in reducing damage and injury in a major storm. Special roof trusses helped to keep the roof from blowing off. Steel bracing supported garage doors, and doors opened outward to reduce the chances that storm winds would blow them open. Specially designed windows would not break when hit with a baseball bat, and a low-profile roof design lessened exposure to winds.

In a careful study of FEMA's efforts, William L. Waugh Jr. found that FEMA had to invest much more up-front effort, spend far more time building relationships, and share more control over its programs. Waugh concluded that a long-term investment in building personal relationships was critical to building trust and that such relationships "provide the glue that holds the network together."[23] The partnerships, he found, can significantly reduce damage. When Witt left FEMA in 2001, however, the agency moved away from those long-term relationship–building strategies. That shift in focus, in turn, weakened FEMA's capacity to respond to Katrina. FEMA had not invested in the relationship-building partnerships required to bring state and local partners together, and when the storm struck, they had to begin virtually from scratch.

Moreover, individuals continued to insist on living in storm-prone areas and did not do enough to mitigate damages. Insurance companies began pulling back from these areas or dramatically increased the cost of coverage. Everyone looked to the federal government as the insurer of last resort. All these forces conspired to undermine the lesson that Witt's leadership of FEMA had taught: it was much cheaper and more effective to build partnerships in advance to mitigate damage than to try to build partnerships of trust in the middle of a disaster and then write large checks for seriously damaged buildings. The federalism fault line proved an enduring place of conflict that was hard for often-warring parties to bridge.

Programs administered through the intergovernmental system were not so much stripped of the rule of law as they were subjected to rules that multiplied in each government agency charged with administrative responsibility. FEMA's response to Katrina was different in each jurisdiction. Relations with both the city of New Orleans and the state of Louisiana were troubled, but in different ways because of the different administrative capacities and political motivations. Relations were different with Alabama and Mississippi. FEMA had multiple faces in responding to Katrina—a fact that played itself out just as richly in Medicaid, with the millions of Mildreds around the nation facing different programs. Each of these programs was legally accountable, but the proliferation of government units created a vastly complex legal environment that confounded the effort to bring a tight system of accountability to it.

GLOBALIZATION: PET FOOD AND TOYS

After the young United States broke with England, the third plate—America's relationship with the rest of the world—remained relatively undisturbed for a very long time. The British returned in 1812 to burn part of Washington, but after that Americans settled into a paradox. They sought to conquer the continent but they also had a powerful instinct for global isolation.

In the twentieth century, however, two world wars and a long cold war changed that. World War I pulled the nation into European affairs, but most Americans believed it truly was the "war to end all wars." With World War II, the nation became enmeshed in even fiercer warfare, and the war ended with the United States as one of the world's great powers. From that point forward—through the cold war, the gasoline crisis of the 1970s, the Gulf wars of the 1990s and 2000s—tensions along this tectonic plate proved some of the most profoundly jolting. The globalization of trade and commerce toward the end of the twentieth century made it clear that every American had to navigate the complex boundaries of globalization—the "flat world" described by Thomas Friedman, where the international fault line proved the site of increasing friction.[24]

That was the lesson for Jacqueline Johnson and her gray tabby, Gumbie. When, early in 2007, the cat seemed lethargic and would not eat, Johnson took it to the vet, who found that Gumbie was suffering from acute renal failure. It took intensive injection of intravenous fluids, both at the vet's office and later by Johnson at home—along with bills of more than $3,000—to bring Gumbie around. "Thankfully we got her to the vet in time," she said later.[25] But hundreds of other pet owners were not so lucky. Their dogs and cats died of kidney failure following contamination of their food.

As reports of sick pets multiplied across the country, investigators struggled to find something the animals shared. More digging identified a common source: Menu Foods, a Canadian company that manufactured pet food for companies ranging from high-end specialty foods to supermarket-brand chow. In all, the investigators identified more than 100 dog and cat foods that could have been contaminated, mostly wet "cuts and gravy"–style food packaged in pouches and cans, but some dry food and dog biscuits as well. The foods had been manufactured at the company's plants in Kansas and New Jersey. The most likely source of the problem? Wheat gluten, the part of flour that Menu Foods had purchased from ChemNutra, a Las Vegas company. But ChemNutra had not grown the wheat or processed the flour. The company had bought it from Chinese manufacturers, who had mixed melamine into the gluten.[26] Melamine is a chemical rich in nitrogen and often used as a fertilizer. Manufacturers also found that they could mold melamine into almost unbreakable plastics, and many baby boomers remember it as brightly colored plates and bowls that could survive hard bounces off kitchen floors.

Although melamine has important industrial uses, it is unsafe as a food additive. Investigators, however, found that two companies—the Xuzhou Anying Biologic Technology Development Company and the Binzhou Futian Biology Technology Company—had slipped it into additives for the pet food. Investigators suspected that the companies had adulterated wheat gluten with melamine to increase their profits. Menu Foods had then unknowingly used the adulterated gluten in its manufacturing process for more than 100 pet foods, and pets across the country had died.

Worried pet owners demanded to know how government had allowed this to happen. The answer was that government regulation of the pet food industry was relatively light because tight resources required focusing attention on human food. The US Food and Drug Administration (FDA) had written tough rules to ensure the safety of pet food, principally in labeling and ingredients, but it had too few inspectors to visit most manufacturers or to test many pet food samples. State departments of agriculture regulate animal feed. The industry is mostly self-regulating, through standards set by the Association of American Feed Control Officials, an alliance of federal and state regulators.[27]

Store owners emptied their shelves of the recalled products, and panicked pet owners searched for recipes for home-cooked pet meals. At the bottom of the story was a case of colliding tectonic plates. A Canadian company that manufactured its product in two American states was forced to recall pet food because two Chinese companies had adulterated a food additive. The FDA had regulatory responsibility but shared its work with state officials and a voluntary association. Defining where private responsibility ended and government work began was impossible. So, too, was allocating government responsibility between federal and state officials. Ultimately, it became a case study of the forces of globalization. Gumbie's owner might not have realized it, but she was riding the shift of these tectonic plates.

The case continued to reverberate for months. Investigators found that the Taixing Glycerin Factory had mislabeled glycol, a chemical used to manufacture antifreeze, and had sold it as a sweetener. The product ended up in cold medicine that killed more than 100 people in Panama. Glycol also ended up in toothpaste, and a Florida company was forced to recall several products. Seafood full of banned antibiotics made its way to the United States. Meanwhile, the FDA banned the import of Chinese catfish, eels, shrimp, and other seafood because investigators had found banned chemicals in the products.

Chinese government officials quickly realized that the global publicity was undermining their efforts to expand the nation's enormous export industry. They drew international attention to the trial of Zheng Xiaoyu, the nation's former chief food and drug regulator. Chinese officials charged him with accepting $850,000 in bribes, in exchange for approving hundreds of medicines. Among the fraudulent applications were 137 drugs without proper applications and another 6 that were phony.[28] "Zheng's dereliction of duty has undermined the efficiency of China's drug monitoring and supervision, endangered public life and health and has had a very negative social impact," the Chinese Supreme People's Court concluded.[29] The court turned down Zheng's appeal, and he was soon executed.

As the scandals rippled around the world, Americans counted themselves lucky that products for humans had been spared. But that feeling of relief changed with the recall of 19 million toys by Mattel, which had been manufactured by its Chinese partners. Mattel removed from the market 436,000 die-cast toy cars representing the character Sarge from the popular 2006 movie *Cars*. The manufacturers had used lead paint, which can prove toxic to young children. It also recalled 18.2 million other toys, including Batman action figures, Doggie Day Care play sets, and a pooper-scooper accessory for the perennially popular Barbie doll. These toys all had magnets that could come lose and be ingested or become stuck in children's ears.

Mattel's decision followed a New York company's recall of 1.5 million wooden railroad toys modeled after Thomas the Tank Engine. Retailing giant Toys "R" Us removed vinyl baby bibs from its shelves because tests showed that some contained lead. The recalls complicated the Marine Corps's annual "Toys for Tots" drive, when volunteers had to check each donated toy against a thirteen-page recall list. "You don't want any lawsuits," explained Marine Sergeant Carlos Rivas, who headed the effort in Chicago. "You want to be one of Santa's elves."[30]

In each of these cases, investigators found that Chinese companies had violated safety standards in manufacturing the products. The Consumer Product Safety Commission worked with the companies to recall the products, but the impact rippled throughout the world. The head of one of the companies implicated in the toy scandal, Zhang Shuhong, committed suicide. The federal government indicted two Chinese companies and the American importer that had distributed the tainted dog food. Florida retiree William Howell, whose Japanese Chin had been euthanized after eating some of the food, said simply, "Somebody should be held responsible . . . I don't know if it's Menu Foods or their distributor in China who put the ingredient in, but somebody should be held responsible."[31] But the rise of issues along the globalization plate magnified the Mildred paradox: no one was ultimately responsible for the safety of these products. Buyers of another recalled product, Thomas & Friends Wooden Railway toys that contained lead paint, got some relief. In a $30 million settlement, the company offered worried families refunds or replacements, along with a bonus toy and a promise of better quality control.

The recurring question in each case was how government could have allowed the problem to happen and what government should do to prevent it from recurring. Democratic Illinois Senator Dick Durbin worried that the pet food scandal suggested bigger problems with the human food chain because it revealed gaping holes in the government's regulatory system. "It appears that there is a light federal presence in this area and instead we rely on a patchwork of state inspection systems and voluntary guidance," said Durbin, who launched a congressional hearing into the issue.[32] The US Government Accountability Office agreed. "Any food contamination could undermine consumer confidence in the government's ability to ensure the safety of the U.S. food supply, as well as cause severe economic consequences," the GAO concluded. The agency found the regulatory system "fragmented," which "has caused inconsistent oversight, ineffective coordination, and inefficient use of resources."[33]

Worries grew when, early in 2008, investigators found that at least nineteen people had died from contaminants in heparin, a blood thinner that reduces the risk of clots following heart attacks, embolisms, and surgery. Contaminants had found their way into substances manufactured in China, causing the deaths and producing serious allergic reactions in hundreds of other patients. The FDA struggled to catch up because it did not have a strong regulatory presence in China, and Chinese drug safety regulations proved inadequate. "Just focusing on the borders of the United States does not work," explained Deputy FDA Commissioner Murray Lumpkin. "In order for us to do our job better domestically, we have to work better internationally."[34]

Americans wanted strong rules to ensure that the products they bought were safe, regardless of where they were manufactured. The system involved both the federal and state governments. It involved regulation of American companies by American government, as well as efforts by American regulators to reach into the legal systems of foreign companies selling their products in the United States. There was not a single legal framework but an intricate patchwork, and no one ultimately was in charge of a system that stretched across the ocean and deep into the industrial supply chains of other nations. Law ruled, but there was no coherent rule-of-law framework.

The Challenges to American Governance

When observers after September 11 suggested that "everything had changed," they were right, but not in the way they thought. For the first time since the framers had constructed American government by finding ways to bridge the new nation's fault lines, all three plates had shifted simultaneously. On the global-relations fault line, the pressure buildup was obvious. The end of the cold war had removed major tensions with the Soviet Union, but it had left behind great uncertainty about the new world order. It was clear that the United States was the globe's only superpower; it was far less clear what that meant.

While most Americans, including analysts and policy makers, were preoccupied with analyzing that question, al-Qaeda cells were quietly plotting a fiendishly clever attack. On a single morning, America's relationships with the rest of the world explosively shifted, with new enemies who had previously been unknown to (almost) everyone launching asymmetric attacks, with pointed jabs aimed at weaknesses in the government's muscular system. Government faced the challenge of developing new strategies of "soft power"—diplomacy and persuasion—and a "war on terror" supplementing, and in some ways replacing, the traditional muscle of American military force in dealing with a new breed of asymmetric warfare.

However, the forces shaping September 11 were in motion long before that day. That terrible morning was the earthquake that revealed the deep changes in the fault lines of America's role in the world. The plate had already shifted. It took the terrorist attacks to bring the fissure to the surface. Moreover, a close look at Mildred and Katrina reveals that they were part of a far quieter, but no less important, shift of the other two tectonic plates.

Mildred, of course, was the beneficiary of vastly expanded public programs. But she never saw public officials. The service system for her was part of a universe of mostly private and nonprofit organizations: frontline organizations that supplied her care, other organizations that served as intermediaries between government payers and frontline providers. In the programs' first forty years, the privatization plate had slowly, almost imperceptibly slipped, with private organizations moving into a commanding role in the service delivery system. Tectonic motion can sometimes be gradual, with plates sliding by inches into vastly new positions. That is just what happened to Medicare and Medicaid.

Katrina sat on the uneasy federalism fault line. Most media attention centered on why the federal government had not responded more quickly, but of course emergency response to natural disasters was an area where state and local governments had long had primacy. Federal, state, and local officials fought for years afterward about who was at fault and where to draw the line separating federal responsibilities from those of state and local governments.

The tectonic plates of government collided as they shifted. September 11 was a quintessential reminder of the importance of globalization. But it was also a puzzle in federalism, as local first responders found themselves working side by side with agents from across the federal government. In the months that followed, the drumbeat of "connect the dots" led to new debates about what role local governments should play in national homeland security policy and how much national security information federal officials should share with local officials.

September 11 raised privatization issues as well. Within weeks of the attacks, the nation was debating whether to nationalize airport security guards (yes) and whether to have federal officials take over baggage screening (no).[35] The attacks proved a seminal event, not only because at their core they demonstrated the huge and unacceptable cost of a government service system out of sync with the problems it was trying to solve. Later, Katrina framed a similar debate: whether to nationalize emergency response (no) and whether to make it easier for the national government to intervene (yes); whether to rely more on voluntary organizations and private contractors in aid efforts (yes) and to exercise strong government control on where private citizens could rebuild their homes (no).

Most of the earlier policy debates had focused on one of the big fault lines: globalization (foreign strategies dealing with the Soviets or establishing new trade patterns with the Chinese), federalism (strategies for renewing inner cities or fighting poverty), or privatization (contracting out weapons systems or garbage collection). With the turn of the twenty-first century, more policy problems tended to involve all three tectonic plates, in strategies that covered over the fault lines along them. September 11 thrust forward "homeland security" as an issue. At once, it became a combination of globalization, federalism, and privatization pressures. So, too, did climate change, immigration policy, tax policy, and many of the other big issues that framed the debates in the first years of the twenty-first century. Indeed, as Figure 5.1 shows, many of the most difficult issues of American policy lie at the intersection of two plates. Important and even more difficult issues occur at the collision of all three, from the growing congestion of the nation's transportation system to the difficulty of managing the health and safety of products imported from abroad.

The German geologist Wegener had observed that the continents seemed to have once fit together and then drifted apart. He might likewise have observed that the three tectonic plates of American political life had once been apart and then drifted together. As the shifting forces of public policy brought the plates closer together, the points of friction multiplied and pressures increased, sometimes to a wrenching political quake. These tensions at the boundaries along the plates—the interactions of global,

FIGURE 5.1   Issues at the Triple Junction

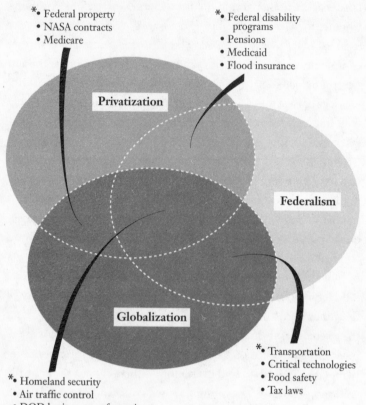

*• Federal property
• NASA contracts
• Medicare

*• Federal disability
  programs
• Pensions
• Medicaid
• Flood insurance

Privatization

Federalism

Globalization

*• Transportation
• Critical technologies
• Food safety
• Tax laws

*• Homeland security
• Air traffic control
• DOD business transformation
• DOD contract management
• DOE contract management
• IRS system modernization

*Agencies in overlapping government sectors.

federal, and privatization pressures—increasingly have come to define the critical issues of American government.

Throughout American history, the nation has undergone periodic, sometimes wrenching change along the tectonic rifts of privatization, federalism, and globalization. The most basic problems predictably depend on these lines, and the tensions just as predictably occur along the points of friction between the tectonic plates of governance. Moreover, each transformation sets the stage for the next. That is the case for shifting geological plates: earthquakes simultaneously release built-up stress and begin to create the stress points for the next temblor. The same is true for the tectonic pressures in American government, which has faced these challenges before.

The tectonic shift at the end of the twentieth century had four notable characteristics. First, all three tectonic plates shifted, with government asserting greater control of the economy, the federal government beginning the broad shift to greater power over state and local governments, and everyone recognizing that the industrial era had brought a fundamental shift in the global economy.

Second, for the first time since the nation's founding, tensions had mounted along all three fault lines of American government. A series of shifts—from the preindustrial to the industrial era and then to the information age—had also brought fresh challenges for government on all fronts.

Third, the consequences for failing to act quickly and effectively were often large indeed. Problems anywhere could ripple everywhere in very short order. The rising tide of globalization made the whole system far more susceptible to the smallest shocks.

Finally, unlike the Progressive era, the reservoir of intellectual capital for understanding and solving these problems was low. The Progressives had provided a clear diagnosis of the situation and a forthright prescription for solving it. For the most complex and important issues that the shifting plates brought at the dawn of the twenty-first century, however, the stock of intellectual capital was dangerously low.

In the Progressive era, the triple junction of pressures that came from the transition to the industrial age met the triple junction of responses, framed by problems, reforms, and intellectual capital. These changes, in turn, set the stage for what came to be known as the American century. Toward the close of that century, major pressures began building yet again, this time without the intellectual capital to understand the forces or to prescribe how to manage them. Indeed, September 11 focused a harsh, inescapable spotlight on major shifts of the privatization, federalism, and globalization plates that had already taken place. How strong must government be to protect the ability of ordinary citizens to go about their daily lives? How much government power must rest at the federal level to prevent the vast array of subnational governments from creating uncoordinated confusion? How can American government ensure the nation's role in the world without becoming either a bully or an isolationist? Each new issue, from the safety of the food supply to the stability of the banking system, raises these basic issues in fresh ways—and in forms that present tough challenges for the nation's governance system.

The Progressives approached the issues of their day with a robust stock of intellectual capital, in a large collection of ideas developed by cutting-edge thinkers. As the nation struggles to cope with the realities of twenty-first-century government, it finds itself with far less understanding and shared appreciation of the basic problems and their implications. As a result, many of government's best managers feel alone, cobbling together pragmatic solutions to big problems but without intellectual support to validate their efforts or to protect them from sniping. They risk either trying to do the wrong things more and more efficiently, or trying to do new things with precious little support. That makes the transformation from industrial to postindustrial government even more difficult because it has proven even riskier, professionally and personally, for public officials on the frontlines trying to manage it.

It is tempting to look back a century and impose more order than the Progressives would themselves have recognized. The Progressive reforms stretched over several decades, proved highly contentious, and never won unanimous support. Their lasting importance took more years to become clear. So it is too easy to suggest that the Progressives had an easier time with the reforms they struggled to bring to American government. But with the dawn of the twenty-first century, the nation faces challenges just as fundamental as those facing Progressive reformers a century earlier.

The Progressives made a powerful intellectual case for the challenges they faced and developed a coherent plan for solving them. At the start of the twenty-first century, there is no consensus on either the challenges or the plan. Moreover, the Progressives aggressively marketed their reforms because they knew that, without them, cherished American values were at risk. The dawn of the twenty-first century has not brought the same widespread recognition about the need for big changes—or about the costs for failing to act. The Progressives implicitly made a tectonic argument: the shift of large, fundamental forces required deep, fundamental change. They explicitly argued that slow, incremental change would put the country at risk because rising problems threatened to swamp the government's ability to govern. With the opening of the twenty-first century, we have a queasy sense of big problems but no strong intellectual movement to guide us.

Elected officials find themselves increasingly called on to get results from systems they do not control. Bureaucrats find that the results they are responsible for producing depend on building strong working relationships with a wide-ranging host of players. Citizens, tired of paying taxes, increasingly insist that government do more with less, so government faces tough resource constraints at every turn. Governance has transformed itself from process and structure to an approach that puts a high premium on individual leadership and organizational leverage.

That transformation, in turn, makes it harder for policy makers to find the levers for effective action. We had tried to shrink the number of government employees and agencies, but September 11 prompted the creation of a mammoth new department supported by 170,000 new employees. We have vastly increased the amount of government contracting to restrain the growth of government, but government does not feel much smaller. Rather than limiting government's reach, these strategies extended it. Toy manufacturers and spinach growers alike called for more government regulation to protect their businesses. Instead of privatizing the public sector, we have governmentalized the private sector. Because people want more of their problems solved and the system is so complex, policy makers have acted in ways that increasingly blur the boundaries. Policy makers often dream of rolling back time, clarifying the responsibilities of the players, or reverting to the old "size of government" questions. However, government's size and power is increasingly defined by its leverage over the economy and private organizations, and successful governance requires a very different approach.

The pace of public action has changed fundamentally as well. Twentieth-century government faced big crises but, with notable exceptions (like Pearl Harbor), the crises often built slowly and provided officials the opportunity to frame a considered response. Many of the twenty-first century's problems have emerged quickly with little warning, have swamped government's capacity to respond, and have produced irresistible demands from citizens for solutions. The combination of the twenty-four-hour news cycle, the existence of multiple news networks devoted to filling that airtime, and the rise of blogs and other forms of viral electronic communication have made it possible for problems to explode out of nowhere. Katrina was an undeniable tragedy, but the story was all the bigger because television anchors slogged through the floodwater to broadcast the story live. Indeed, there was the sense that they were more in tune with the story—and therefore so were Americans—than was the Bush administration, which seemed sluggish and distant.

We rely on government agencies to solve problems, but no single government agency can possibly hope to manage or solve any big problem that matters. The pace with which big problems emerge now demands quicker solutions, and citizens have new ways of creating and feeding a community of outrage when government's response is slow or ineffective. The result is a growing imperative for effective responses to inescapable problems. Too often, government is unprepared for the speed with which new problems emerge, the need to launch quick solutions, the capacity required to make those solutions work, and the ability to create transparent and accountable governance.

Turning Points

To deal with these problems, for more than a century, Congress and the president have periodically launched big changes to strengthen government management. There have been regular and recurring cycles in which new problems demanded new reforms, before new problems pushed the old reforms aside and readied the ground for a new round of efforts.[36] These cycles are the result of the tectonic plates rubbing together: big forces build up, erupt onto the policy scene (sometimes with explosive power), and demand dramatic change. A new equilibrium emerges, until the next buildup forces yet another shift in the fabric of American government. These periodic turning points are invariably times of wrenching political turmoil and major policy change. They have also been times of great intellectual debate, full of big stresses and big ideas. Moreover, these cycles have been remarkably regular. Five such eruptions have occurred since the 1880s along the tectonic plates—privatization, federalism, and globalization—to remake the federal government.

REFORM 1.0: THE PROGRESSIVES (1881–1913)

In 1881, Chester Arthur came into office following James Garfield's assassination by Charles Guiteau, who was furious at the president for spurning his demands for a federal job. Arthur took up the cause of civil service reform, a centerpiece of the Progressive movement, and the 1883 Civil Service Reform Act became the foundation for the modern governmental era. Before the reforms, the spoils system dominated government hiring: getting a job depended on who you knew, not what you knew. The Progressives were convinced that modern government needed the most skilled managers. Hiring became based on standardized tests, promotions depended on performance, and salaries were determined by the requirements of the job. Reform 1.0 sought to empower the government to tackle the challenges of the industrial age without creating government administrators so powerful that they could threaten individual liberty. It brought skilled bureaucrats into the government but limited their power, through the creation of new government agencies that simultaneously expanded and bounded government's power. Reform 1.0 also established new budgeting and accounting procedures aimed at making government more efficient and more transparent. It was a tectonic shift of the privatization plate, for it moved the government significantly into issues that previously had been the private sector's domain.

Reform 1.0 continued until the first decade of the twentieth century, when banking crises and farmers' problems in getting credit suggested to reformers that government needed to be even broader in scope and more muscular in power to prevent swings in the private sector's economic activity from harming the public welfare.

REFORM 2.0: SUPER-PROGRESSIVES (1913-33)

These economic problems built the foundation for Reform 2.0, which extended and expanded the foothold that the Progressives established with Reform 1.0 through aggressive changes aimed at further increasing the government's efficiency. Congress and the president joined to create new cabinet departments, including Labor, and to establish the Federal Reserve (both in 1913), as a continuation of the movement to create new structures to promote more government efficiency. In 1921, the budget process was transformed from the ad hoc process that had previously dominated—the budget being whatever accumulated spending decisions added up to—into a new process in which the president formally proposed a spending plan to Congress.

Reform 2.0 was a further advance along the privatization plate, in the tradition that Reform 1.0 had helped establish. It made the government far more powerful, but when the Great Depression crippled the economy, the federal government found itself hamstrung. New agencies created to promote steady economic growth, including the Federal Reserve, struggled to stop the economy's freefall. Reformers concluded that they needed a radical new strategy.

REFORM 3.0: THE FDR ERA (1933-53)

That crisis set the stage for Franklin D. Roosevelt's New Deal, which was a double tectonic shift: an earthquake along the privatization plate, as the government intervened far deeper into the private sector, and along the federalism plate, as power flowed significantly to Washington from the states. Roosevelt reformed the banking system, strengthened the Federal Reserve, created new bank insurance agencies, and tightened their ties to the White House. As the alphabet soup of New Deal agencies grew, reformers sought to give the president more leverage over the expanding executive establishment. The Brownlow Committee, a three-member board established to advise him on how the presidency could meet the crisis, famously concluded that "the president needs help." During World War II, Roosevelt followed its advice to strengthen the White House staff.[37] The strategy for Reform 3.0 focused on dramatically increasing the power of the presidency. Indeed, Roosevelt's reforms defined the modern White House. Crises, both economic and international, led to a stronger presidency, but as the war wound down, even the biggest fans of Reform 3.0 knew that they needed to rethink the strategy. Responding to each new crisis by establishing more administrative agencies and bureaucratic processes, they realized, was creating a government that could prove sluggish and unresponsive in the long run. They knew they needed to institutionalize the best ideas of past reformers with a long-term plan that would make the system sustainable as the war effort wound down. They knew that the nation could not sustain the increase in spending that had advanced the New Deal and then World War II.

REFORM 4.0: BUDGET REFORMS (1953–81)

As America emerged from World War II, Congress and Harry Truman focused on transforming the large wartime government into a sleek peacetime establishment. There was little appetite for shrinking government's role, but there was keen awareness that the government's operations needed streamlining, on both the defense and domestic fronts. The globalization plate had shifted and America's role in the world had forever changed. The challenge for Truman was how to define this new role—and how to help the government effectively pursue it. Former president Herbert Hoover was appointed to chair a commission and conduct an efficiency scrub of the government's operations. The commission prescribed steps ranging from the restructuring of government agencies to new management processes, to improve the government's operations.[38] The efficiency theme continued through the Eisenhower administration, when a second Hoover Commission produced a new round of recommendations.

For a generation, each president further refined this pursuit of administrative efficiency. John F. Kennedy brought in his "whiz kids" from the private sector to improve government management, especially in the Pentagon.[39] Lyndon B. Johnson advanced the Planning Programming Budgeting System, which sought to identify and control the costs of a program throughout its life, instead of just making a series of annual decisions.[40] Richard M. Nixon and then Gerald Ford upped Johnson's ante with Management by Objectives, which promoted the identification of an agency's objectives, the alignment of agency activities from top to bottom to pursue those objectives, and the support of those activities with budget decisions.[41] As Georgia governor, Jimmy Carter championed Zero-Base Budgeting, which tried to force program advocates to make a fresh case for each new infusion of money instead of taking for granted that a program, once funded, would last forever.[42]

Reform 4.0, in short, focused on increasing the budget's leverage over the federal government's work. Reformers concluded that they had pushed the benefits of government reorganization as far as possible. Faced with rising opposition from citizens to everhigher taxes, they worked to improve the budgetary process, to force policy makers to wring the most from each tax dollar. In the late 1970s, however, growing pressures pushed the movement off track. Congress resented the Nixon administration's efforts to use the budgetary process to pull more power into the White House. That shifted the efficiency debate into a balance-of-powers battle. Mandatory spending programs—entitlements—occupied a growing share of the federal budget, so there was less money left to fight over. More broadly, citizens fiercely contested the growing size of government and demanded strategies to reduce government spending instead of simply trying to increase efficiency. The budget strategies of Reform 4.0 offered little traction on these big questions.

REFORM 5.0: PRIVATIZATION, REINVENTION, AND PERFORMANCE (1981–2009)

The Watergate of the 1970s had fed public distrust of government. The stagflation of the 1970s—low economic growth coupled with high inflation—had strained the pocketbooks of many citizens. This was an economic phenomenon driven by another shift in the globalization plate, as a major international oil crisis rippled through the global economy. These twin pressures bubbled over with tax-limitation votes, especially California's Proposition 13, which in 1978 capped property tax revenues. Many citizens simply decided that government was inefficient and unresponsive, and they concluded that the market incentives of the private sector made it inherently more efficient. Ronald Reagan harnessed this theme to win the presidency. On taking office, he significantly expanded the privatization of government programs. A special commission identified a host of new public activities that could be contracted out, and the federal government embarked on a sweeping effort to turn public activities over to private companies.[43] As we have seen in earlier chapters, this movement was a shift in the privatization plate. It appeared on the surface as an effort to push government power back to the private sector. In reality, it was a wrenching, grinding change that governmentalized more of the private sector even as the government sought to privatize more of its operations.

Democrats fiercely opposed the effort on both ideological and political grounds. The privatization movement aimed at shrinking Democratic programs and attacking Democratic constituencies, especially public employee unions that had reliably supported the party. Caught in the party's New Deal and Great Society legacies, the Democrats struggled to find a way to respond to the spending limits movement without undermining their core constituencies.

Bill Clinton cleverly counterpunched. He embraced the need to shrink government and make it work better while serving the party's traditional bases of support. The model proposed by David Osborne and Ted Gaebler's best-selling *Reinventing Government* offered a plan: government could do better and cost less if its workers were freed from inflexible governmental rules. With his "reinventing government" movement, Clinton believed he could make government more effective and responsive without slashing traditional governmental programs. Under the leadership of Vice President Al Gore, the movement slashed rules and streamlined government processes, like the complex procurement system. The administration also aggressively downsized the workforce.

The downsizing proved the administration was serious about cutting government, but because it did not determine what its right size ought to be, the movement also left the government short of the skilled managers it needed. Since then, the Government Accountability Office has named workforce management as one of the government's high-risk areas, the issues that most expose the government to waste and mismanagement. The Clinton reinvention effort thus has a mixed legacy: a fresh focus on empowering workers to produce results, but a mismatch between the workforce and the problems it is trying to solve.[44]

George W. Bush built on the Clinton effort with a new strategy, the President's Management Agenda (PMA), which forced all federal agencies to define the objectives of their programs and to measure their activities in pursuing those goals using the Performance Assessment Rating Tool (PART). The goal was to give management reform genuine teeth by harnessing it to the budget process.

The PART process, however, had several important problems. First, analytical measures were combined with ideological objectives, especially a focus on contracting out government work. In some other nations that have pursued management reform, the goal was to discover the management tool that produces the best results at the lowest cost, whether the work was done by private contractors or government officials. The PART, however, set more contracting out as a goal in itself. It thus combined a *process* with the *results* that the process was designed to achieve, which stirred conflict around its ideological focus and hurt the more straightforward, broadly supported effort to analyze results.

Second, the PART focused primarily on activity measures. That is, the PART tended to assess internal agency processes, such as the number of applications processed or the number of individuals placed following experience in a federal training program. This discouraged agency managers from setting broad outcome goals, which depend on complex partnerships among many players and are less directly controllable. That, in turn, limited the impact of the PART process.

Third, the PART process laid bare the limited analytical capacity in many federal agencies. The PART analysis often became a paperwork compliance exercise that did not penetrate to the agency's frontline operations. GAO found, in fact, that agencies were collecting much more information than in the past, but few of them had made progress in using the information to improve the way the agencies worked.[45]

Fourth, the Office of Management and Budget (OMB) never fully integrated the PART into the annual budget process, which had been the goal from the beginning. Did a low PART score suggest an agency in need of more resources—or were low scores a sign of an agency on whom additional resources would be wasted? The mingling of analytical and ideological PART elements, moreover, made it even harder for the OMB's examiners to assess what the PART ought to mean for the budget. Critics suggested that the PART sometimes was used selectively, singling out some programs for spending cuts while ignoring other programs where evidence might be mixed or more positive. The PART process thus triggered a typical dilemma of performance measurement: give the measures teeth, with big consequences, and managers will do everything possible to escape the target painted on their backs; make the measures more benign, and top officials will pay little attention to them.

Reform 5.0 was a spirited effort, characterized through both Republican and Democratic administrations by a strategy that first sought to streamline government structures and processes and then led agencies to assess their performance. Advocates of each approach would no doubt bristle at being grouped in the same era, but Reagan, Clinton, and Bush led reforms fundamentally of a piece: introducing new analytical processes aimed at improving government's performance while making government smaller.

But with the end of the George W. Bush administration came the natural end of yet another reform era. The September 11 terrorist attacks made clear that, despite the substantial progress that the reformers had made, Reagan-style privatization strategies did not help government identify its role and then perform it. Clinton-style downsizing and customer service did not provide the coordination that the crisis needed, and Bush-style performance measurement only tightened government's bureaucratic bottlenecks. In fact, these measures often kept agency officials from connecting with one another.

Hurricane Katrina put an exclamation point to the end of Reform 5.0. Congress and the Bush administration eyed the "connect-the-dots" problem of September 11 and created the new Department of Homeland Security to ensure coordination. Indeed, the response was precisely in the spirit of Reform 4.0 strategies dating back to the Hoover Commission of the 1940s: when confronted with a management problem, improve managerial efficiency by creating new structures and new procedures. When the new department spectacularly failed its first test following Katrina's strike, it was a devastating blow to the governance strategies that had dominated during both Reform 4.0 and 5.0. New problems highlighted the growing gap between government's capacity and the problems it faced.

As Reform 5.0 ended, the next step was not clear. The intellectual capital driving the reform movement had run out. Indeed, for the first time since Reform 1.0, there was no new road map, no new "big idea" to follow. Reforms 1.0 and 2.0 had the focused good-government agenda of the Progressives. Reform 3.0 had a presidential commission and a legion of public administration experts striving to empower the presidency. Reform 4.0 had smart private managers and budget innovators from all levels of government and the private sector. Reform 5.0 had ideologues from both the right and the left. But when Reform 5.0 staggered to an end with September 11 and Katrina, there was no natural next step. As successive crises made clear, the government needed Reform 6.0, but reformers found the shelves bare of new plans.

The challenge was even larger than the dearth of "big ideas." For the first time since these cycles of reforms had begun with the Progressives, America found all three tectonic plates in motion. The September 11 terrorist attacks were a potent sign of the shift of the globalization plate. Mildred's case captured the shift of both the federalism and the privatization plates. As observers noted after September 11, everything had in fact changed, but the scale and scope of the changes were far larger and more wrenching than even the post-attack commentaries suggested. The nation's governance system had been shaken to its very tectonic foundations—and the events pointed to the need for fundamental reform.

Together, these factors explain why traditional government strategies so often produce results that disappoint citizens and policy makers alike. They explain why the Progressives' reforms have proven lacking for twenty-first-century problems. The explanation lies in the rise of a tectonic nation, where the motion of the plates shaping American governance confounds the ability of America's institutions to respond effectively to inescapable problems. We need a Progressive-style response to problems that no longer fit the Progressives' model. In fact, attacking twenty-first-century problems with twentieth-century strategies is a prescription for both poor performance and disappointed citizens. Thus, the primary mission of the next government of the United States must be to marry the great traditions and ideals of American government with new strategies to fulfill the aspirations of the people. In the next chapter, we turn to the puzzle of how to accomplish this goal.

6

ROCKET SCIENCE

How can American government deal with the challenge of critical problems it cannot escape? Government manages many of its routine functions relatively well. But nonroutine functions, such as dealing with Mildred- and Katrina-style problems, increasingly pose grave challenges to America's government. Any solution will have to bridge the three shifting plates—privatization, federalism, and globalization. The puzzle is whether America's political institutions will be able to rise to the challenge.

Much of government continues to operate within the vending-machine model. Government still calculates and distributes monthly Social Security payments. It collects taxes and audits returns. It picks up garbage and mows parkland grass. It maintains national historic sites and runs mass transit. The vending-machine model is the great governance legacy of the nineteenth-century Progressives, and it tends to work reasonably well for programs that produce relatively routine services within hierarchies.

Mildred and Katrina, however, represent the new generation of problems. A growing array of services are nonroutine. Moreover, an increasing number of policies, especially those that pursue critical twenty-first-century public issues ranging from health care to homeland security, do not operate within hierarchies. Mildred and Katrina require a different kind of approach to governance, in both policy design and public management—one very different from the approach that shaped government for much of the twentieth century.

They need instead a *leveraged government* across complex networks: government leaders who can effectively align public, private, nonprofit, American, and global players across the messy boundaries of action. Indeed, leveraged government has become the primary form of government action. Government does not itself do most of what, on behalf of citizens, it sets out to accomplish. Rather, it relies on a vast collection of tools, from grants and contracts to regulations and incentives, for public purposes.[1] Government uses these tools to enlist others—in other levels of government, in the private sector, in the public sector, in nonprofit organizations, and in organizations around the world—to pursue its goals.

These tools have vastly expanded government's reach and its ability to attack Mildred- and Katrina-style problems. They also embody an approach very different from the traditional vending-machine model, in which government seeks to design a machine by which it produces government services itself. There lies the critical problem: government's ability to work effectively and to hold its agents accountable depends on its ability to leverage the way these other actors employ tools on its behalf. The right combination of effectiveness and accountability, in turn, requires great subtlety and skill. It also needs an approach to governance that relies on leverage instead of command, on building incentives instead of fine-tuning the vending machine. For those people, especially elected officials and reporters, who still think of government as a vending machine, the shift of strategy and tactics creates great frustration as they try to understand why programs so often work poorly and determine how best to make them work better. For everyone, the shift demands new strategies and tactics if government is to work.

This transformation, in turn, has created a deep pathology: a new generation of problems that require new approaches, coupled with an instinct by policy makers and citizens alike for relying on a vending machine that proves a poor match for the problems at hand. The results have been fundamental governance problems, which flow from the Mildred paradox (that she received core government services without encountering any government employees) and from the Mildred corollary (that in the complex service system responsible for her care, no one ultimately was in charge).

The system's enormous difficulty in solving these problems has created the two great governance problems of the day: One is how to manage traditional services in a reliable and efficient way. The other is how to govern the increasingly complex array of Mildred- and Katrina-style policies. The puzzle is how to put the vending-machine and leveraged-governance approaches side by side—to assign the right program to the right approach, to ensure that each works well, and to prevent one from interfering with the other. Past governance revolutions largely replaced one system with another. Even though it took time, the Progressive revolution swept through government from top to bottom.

The government that Mildred and Katrina require is not one that sweeps away the old and replaces it with the new but one that governs through two interconnected systems: one for routine policies managed through hierarchies, the other for nonroutine problems governed through networks. If we get this wrong, problems with accountability and performance are sure to follow. FEMA failed in the Katrina crisis because it used the vending-machine model in a leveraged-government situation. Repeating this mismatch in other cases is a prescription for policy failure and public cynicism.

Maintaining the vending-machine model is essential. It worked very well for more than a century, and it continues to work well for some kinds of problems. Its great virtue is the creation of robust routines to do difficult things efficiently and predictably. It also provides the bedrock of accountability, for, as the Progressives recognized, it creates a way of increasing government power while holding government accountable. Churning out tens of millions of monthly Social Security payments, accurately and on time, is no easy job. Periodic garbage strikes show how quickly a semifunctioning system can make a big city unlivable. What problems does the vending-machine model best fit? Those that recur in regular patterns (even if the patterns are complex); those best solved through routine strategies (even if the routines require high levels of training); and those whose most important pieces fit relatively well inside a single organization (even if some steps require coordination with other organizations). What problems does the model not fit? Those whose patterns make it hard to develop stable routines ("if you've met one Alzheimer's patient, you've met—one Alzheimer's patient"); those that require highly adaptive work by administrators (who use their expertise to match the right collection of solutions to rapidly evolving puzzles); and those that demand careful collaboration among multiple organizations across the seismic divides (including complex public–private, intergovernmental, interorganizational, and international partnerships).

For generations, the vending-machine model developed by the Progressives served the country well. However, blind faith in the Progressives' approach to government has increasingly failed us, as Mildred- and Katrina-style programs have increased in scope and scale. The model does not need to be abandoned, for it continues to work well for routine programs and it ought to be used where it fits. But for programs where new policy problems and administrative strategies strain the model, we need a new system that solves the Progressives' basic question for the new kinds of tools that are emerging: how to create a government powerful enough to get the job done but not so powerful that it strains accountability. How can government work well and how can democracy thrive? The answer, I suggest, is to make government managers into rocket scientists, to frame a new model of governance that can fit comfortably side by side with the traditional vending-machine model.

The Rocket Science Model

In 2000, two British researchers set out to determine which crime reduction strategies worked best. As they visited communities throughout the United Kingdom, they found some remarkable successes. From reducing fraud at a community college to preventing bullying and gang violence, the researchers found that the police officers they talked to had adapted their old routines to solve some of these new problems. As they surveyed the successful projects, many of the police officers they talked to explained their techniques modestly. "It's not rocket science," the researchers heard repeatedly. They concluded that the crucial contributions to success were "hard thinking, imagination, and determination."[2]

Rocket science (along with *brain surgery*) has become the universal catchphrase for the most difficult tasks in the universe—the things that mere mortals could not accomplish. But despite the enormous technical difficulty of launching rockets, the Russians staged a series of breakthroughs in the late 1950s. They had put the first satellite into Earth orbit and had sent a cosmonaut into space before the United States managed to launch a manned rocket. As the Americans struggled to catch up, a test rocket veered off course, and ground controllers were forced to hit the "destruct" button. A few days later, another rocket, this time with a capsule like the one astronaut Alan Shepard was preparing to ride, also went off course.

American rocket scientists were feeling the pressure and struggling to make their spacecraft perform. Not long afterward, as Shepard lay on his back inside his Mercury capsule, waiting for the launch, flight controllers noticed more problems, this time with a fuel pressure gauge that showed a high reading. They debated whether they ought to delay the countdown for safety's sake. "Why don't you fix your little problem," Shepard shot back, "and light this candle." They did. Shepard's Redstone rocket pushed him into a successful suborbital trip, higher and faster than any American had ever flown. Americans had finally mastered rocket science and gotten their man into space. It was the first step toward John Glenn's first American orbital flight and a moon landing in 1969. Shepard returned to space in 1971 in an Apollo mission, when he became famous for the longest golf shot on the moon.

Given this long struggle and occasional spectacular failures, it is little wonder that *rocket science* has become the label for anything extraordinarily difficult. Saying "it's not rocket science" has come to mean just the reverse: that solving a problem requires just a simple, straightforward approach that anyone can employ. The British law enforcement officials had discovered strategies that, they believed, represented straightforward, commonsense approaches that anyone could follow. What worked? Thinking strategically, defining problems, making evidence-driven decisions, building effective multiorganizational teams, involving the community, creating a system that rewarded success, and driving it with strong leadership.

The findings of the British study were impressive, and the

authors' analysis was right on target. The only problem lay in the title of their study: *Not Rocket Science?* In fact, the strategy they described *is* rocket science. The steps they outlined are precisely the ones that rocket scientists follow in successfully launching rockets. Rocket science is based on teamwork, with a carefully integrated network of experts from a wide range of disciplines, focused on a mission and driven by leadership.

The procedures for launching the space shuttle, for example, have long been a case of a carefully leveraged government program. The goal was getting the shuttle into orbit, accomplishing its mission and bringing the crew safely home. Since the beginning of America's manned space flight program, however, responsibility for key space flight decisions has been split: between the space center at Cape Canaveral, Florida, and Mission Control Center in Houston, Texas; and between government officials and private contractors. The key to successful rocket science has depended on successful management of the relationships between the centers and with the contractors who have built and, often, operated the complex systems.

Since the Truman administration, Cape Canaveral has been the prime rocket launch site.[3] Its location near the equator makes it easier to get rockets into orbit, nearby islands provide good sites for tracking stations, and the flight path over the ocean makes launching safer if a rocket blows up, as sometimes happened in the early days of the space program. For controlling operations after liftoff, NASA established its manned space flight center in Houston. Once the rocket is aloft, of course, the operations center can be anywhere. When the decision was made to locate Mission Control in Texas, it didn't hurt that it was the home state of Lyndon B. Johnson, who helped establish NASA and who, as vice president, chaired an advisory committee on the nation's space program.[4]

Having two space centers hundreds of miles apart responsible for managing one space vehicle accelerating at incredible speed toward orbit and burning some of the most powerful explosives known to man is obviously a huge challenge. How should NASA coordinate that two-center process, in which the slightest slip could incinerate the launch vehicle and kill the astronauts? For the Apollo moon launches, the handoff came at the moment the rocket rose above the launch tower—hence the phrase made famous on television and movies: "and the vehicle has cleared the tower!" For those anxiously watching on television, it was a moment of high drama, but for NASA officials managing the launch, it was the code to switch control from the cape to Houston.

For the space shuttle, NASA changed the switchover. The Cape Canaveral mission control center maintains control over the launch vehicle through ignition of the liquid-fueled engines on the shuttle (which can be turned off in an emergency) and passes control to Houston at the instant the solid rocket boosters are ignited (which, once lit, have to burn themselves out). Houston retains control of the vehicle until the shuttle has landed and the astronauts have exited the vehicle. At that point, control returns to the cape (even if weather has forced a landing at a strip across the country), and the launch team begins preparations for the next launch.[5]

At the cape's Launch Control Center, a launch director is in charge of coordinating the process. The launch director works with three teams. A prime launch team is composed of 200 to 300 experts in charge of the hardware and ground support equipment. Support staff includes Air Force officials who manage the launch range and provide weather information; a nearby station that provides voice and data transmission; the Goddard Space Flight Center in Maryland, which manages the transmissions; and officials in Houston. An engineering support team provides backup technical oversight and support. And a senior government and contract management team oversees any general technical or safety issues.

Together, they work through five volumes of instructions to deal with 25,000 separate instrument readings.

At twenty minutes before launch, launch managers lock the door of the firing room, and no one is allowed in or out. Should any problem arise on the pad after the launch teams load propellant into the external fuel tank, a special "red team" goes to work. In advance, shuttle managers train a large number of experts both in their specialty and in broad skills like fire and rescue techniques. In the event of a last-minute glitch, mission controllers do not rely on a preexisting organization. Instead, they put together an ad hoc team consisting of the experts they need to solve the problem at hand.

This is how rocket science works: a government agency is charged with an extraordinarily difficult and dangerous mission, where a misstep could lead to disaster; complex partnerships develop, often involving many private contractors, that make it difficult for the agency to manage and control all of the elements for which it is responsible; and a management system focuses on a well-defined mission that assigns clear responsibility to managers for producing results. It is a very risky system, diffusing responsibility through the large contractor network for mission-critical details; making it difficult for anyone to be fully in charge; and creating a program in which any flaw anywhere can ripple through to create large, important, expensive, even tragic consequences everywhere. This characterization describes NASA—and Mildred and Katrina as well. It is what put NASA on the US Government Accountability Office's high-risk list, along with the Medicare and Medicaid programs that served Mildred, a key FEMA program, and management of the nation's homeland security efforts.

In short, making twenty-first-century leveraged government work *is* rocket science. What makes rocket science work is the same thing that brings success to other important government programs. What sometimes causes problems is often the same thing that plagues other public programs: the inability to leverage a complex system, in which responsibility is broadly shared and no one can fully control anything, to achieve the mission. As it becomes increasingly impossible for any single organization to control any outcome that matters, making government work in the twenty-first century depends more and more on rocket science: institutionalizing leadership, management, and coordination mechanisms that are, by their very nature, not institutional.

Rocket Scientists

How can American government bring in more rocket scientists to solve the problems of leveraged government? Consider Admiral Thad Allen, who brought the rocket science model to the Coast Guard. Following the government's tragic stumbling in its Katrina relief and recovery efforts, DHS Secretary Michael Chertoff replaced FEMA Director Michael Brown, just days after President Bush had applauded him for "doing a heck of a job." In his place, Chertoff sent in Coast Guard Chief of Staff Thad Allen. Allen had a wide range of experience in the Coast Guard, including leading the service's response to September 11, which had required an unprecedented boat evacuation from Manhattan and intensive security screening to identify further terrorist risks. His no-nonsense demeanor and stocky build captured everyone's idea of a tough on-scene commander. He immediately took charge. In briefing reporters, Allen said his next step was "to hold a meeting with everyone in this building." He explained, "We'll have an open and frank conversation, and we'll move out."[6]

Within days, Allen and Army Lieutenant General Russell Honore had begun turning the operation around. Allen began by defusing the contentious relationship that had developed between the federal government and Louisiana state officials.[7] Louisiana Governor Blanco had been highly critical of federal officials, so Allen confronted the issue directly. He picked up the phone and asked the governor, "Have I done something to give you the impression that I'm interested in anything else but helping the people of Louisiana?" His message was clear: mission was all that mattered to him.

Allen pushed a reluctant Pentagon into sending mobile mortuary units to New Orleans, to help recover the bodies found floating in the fetid water. He sought out the New Orleans director of homeland security, Terry Ebbert, a former Marine colonel. Ebbert had suffered through the storm himself and found that the enormity of the challenge left him little time to eat or sleep. Allen brought Ebbert to the small aircraft carrier that had been brought in to supply power, air conditioning, showers, bunks, and food for the relief workers. Allen gave Ebbert a meal and asked him what he needed most. Ebbert's reply was short and elegant. "We need hope," he said.

Allen set to work on just that. He reached back to a maxim that had guided him for years: transparency breeds self-correcting behavior. He let in sunshine (and reporters), and he used the harsh light of public scrutiny to force the squabbling players into partnership. Allen was fond of pointing out that strategic plans became obsolete the minute anyone put a date on them (and was polite enough not to point out that some of the key players had not read the plans and were not following them). Instead, he focused on what he called *strategic intent*, to use the nature of the problem to define the partnerships required to get results and then to push everyone in the same direction.

Allen also saw the enormous project as a series of steps that had to begin with fulfilling the most basic needs (including providing food and water) in order to achieve longer-term economic recovery. Allen had earned a master's degree in public administration from George Washington University, and he reached back to Abraham Maslow's organization theory classic. In 1943, Maslow had written about a "hierarchy of needs," ranging from the most basic, tangible objective of subsistence through the highest and most abstract goal, self-actualization.[8] "If you are drowning, the first thing you want is dry land," Allen said, translating Maslow into the Coast Guard's perspective. "If you are on dry land, the next thing you want is something to eat and drink. Having eaten, you want a place to sleep, and then you want a better place to sleep. Then you want aid to start rebuilding and getting your life back in order." What drove Allen was the sense of overall strategy and the steps, from the most basic through the more complex, required to get there. He focused on bringing the right assets together to do the job, driving those partners with a focus on strategic intent, and holding them accountable for results through transparency. There was an unconscious irony in the strategy: Allen was a high-ranking admiral in a military organization, structured and controlled by hierarchy and authority. But he used his authority to build and drive a complex interorganizational network based on collaboration, with individual contributions supporting the shared mission.

Allen's strategy emerged from lessons that the Coast Guard painfully learned and then carefully tested. The key lessons had emerged from the 1989 *Exxon Valdez* disaster. On March 23, the huge tanker had left the Alyeska Marine Terminal in Valdez, Alaska, carrying 53 million gallons of crude oil from Alaska's North Slope.[9] It was a giant, state-of-the-art ship, longer than three football fields. Just after midnight on March 24, the Coast Guard learned that the *Valdez* had run aground and the crude was quickly leaking into Prince William Sound. The ship lost one fifth of its crude, which spread over 3,000 square miles and washed up on 350 miles of shoreline. It contaminated parks and four national wildlife refuges, a state game sanctuary, and four critical wildlife habitat areas. Scientists later estimated that the spill had killed 300 harbor seals, 2,800 sea otters, and 250,000 birds.

Since construction of the Trans-Alaska Pipeline, environmentalists had warned about the risks of a major spill, either on the delicate tundra or in the sound, which is one of the nation's most fragile ecosystems. The Alyeska Pipeline Service Company, owned jointly by a conglomerate of oil companies including Exxon, told government officials that they had put safeguards into place and that, if there ever was an oil spill, they had the capacity to contain and clean it. In fact, a month earlier a tanker at the terminal had developed a leak. The crew had stopped the leak, surrounded the crude with a boom, and cleaned the oil out of the water. The company pointed to this incident as evidence that it was ready to respond.

Then the *Valdez* ran aground. Trying to maneuver around ice, the ship left the navigation lanes and struck a shoal clearly marked on the charts. The company's response vessel was out of service; a replacement ship was on the way, but it was near Seattle when the accident happened. Experts disagreed over whether to use oil dispersants and no one seemed to be in charge. The Coast Guard's marine safety officer charged with coordinating the effort became enmeshed in backroom politicking and second-guessing, which undermined his ability to exercise frontline command. After continuing confusion and ineffectiveness in directing the operation, President George H. W. Bush finally sent in Alaska's most senior Coast Guard official to run the response: Coast Guard Rear Admiral Joel D. Sipes. As the admiral later recalled, "When asked about preparedness for this incident, Secretary of Transportation [Samuel K.] Skinner said that on a scale of 1 to 10, response was a zero."[10] Analysts later suspected that years of success had lured everyone into complacency.

The official federal investigation into the response to the disaster was scathing. As DOT Secretary Skinner and EPA Administrator William K. Reilly told the president,

> Government and industry plans, individually and collectively, proved to be wholly insufficient to control an oil spill of the magnitude of the *Exxon Valdez* incident. Initial industry efforts to get equipment on scene were unreasonably slow, and once deployed the equipment could not cope with the spill. Moreover, the various contingency plans did not refer to each other or establish a workable response command hierarchy. This resulted in confusion and delayed the cleanup.[11]

It was scarcely a case in which planners had not anticipated such a disaster. It was a big spill, but about thirty others have been bigger. It was, rather, a big problem that required a crosscutting and integrated solution, but the spill caught the system flat-footed. It was Katrina—just with colder water.

The *Exxon Valdez* case led the Coast Guard to a searching exploration of what had happened and what could be done better the next time. Preparations had fallen short. Command authority had been weak. Worse yet, the key players had struggled to coordinate their efforts. Top Coast Guard officials knew that similar disasters were likely but that their scope, location, and timing were unpredictable. They concluded that the Coast Guard needed new, flexible strategies to anticipate disasters, to put new capacity into place, and to be able to respond more effectively to a wider range of emergencies. From the top down, the service drilled and practiced to be better prepared the next time. Its motto, *Semper Paratus* ("always ready"), took on a fresh new meaning.

The Coast Guard's next *Exxon Valdez* turned out to be not an oil spill but the September 11 terrorist attacks. After the World Trade Center's first tower collapsed, there was mass confusion. All the bridges and tunnels were closed. Mass transit was crippled, and it was a long walk to escape the carnage. The Hudson and East rivers offered the quickest way out, but the thousands of people packed between the crumbling towers and the rivers began to panic. Ferries, barges, and other vessels rushed to help, and people tried to scramble aboard anything that floated. Emergency officials feared that a collision between would-be rescue ships was inevitable.

One *Exxon Valdez* lesson for the Coast Guard was the need for initiative in problem solving. As soon as he recognized the two airplane crashes into the World Trade towers as attacks, the Coast Guard's Kenneth Concepcion left his Staten Island station and headed for Manhattan's Pier 11, near Battery Park at the tip of the island. He reached the pier twenty minutes after the second tower collapsed. Concepcion organized the city police officers and transportation officials, and then got them to sort the crowds by destination. He took control over the vessels at the pier, made sure that injured firefighters were given evacuation priority, and coordinated the rescue workers streaming to the scene from the New Jersey side of the river. His job as chief of the US Flag Deepdraft Vessels and Plan Review had put him in touch with many of the boat operators in the area, so he already knew most of the key players in the boat lift. By 4:00 that afternoon, Concepcion had led the rescue of more than 70,000 people from southern Manhattan. One official later said that the scene reminded him of World War II's Dunkirk evacuation, in which a ragtag flotilla of ships plucked allied troops from the French coast in 1940, when they were on the verge of being destroyed by the advancing German army. Concepcion's heroism won him the 2002 Service to America Medal.[12] He was the model of leveraged government that the Coast Guard tried to build after the *Exxon Valdez*: a frontline commander who quickly took the initiative to solve a problem without waiting for a permission slip from top officials—an officer who quickly sized up the job to be done, built partnerships with the resources on hand, and used the problem to drive partnerships.

The other *Exxon Valdez* lesson was a powerful focus on "situational awareness"—a keen understanding of precisely what was happening, firmly grounded in the precise details of reality. Back at Coast Guard headquarters on September 11, Thad Allen had to shape the larger strategy. Simply sorting out the nature of the attacks took considerable time. Determining which problems most needed the Coast Guard's attention was even more difficult. Allen helped deploy the Coast Guard's fleet of cutters, which had guns, trained sailors, sensors to detect possible further attacks, and communications equipment to ensure he could stay in contact. Allen developed an integrated command structure to tie the pieces together. As he later described the Coast Guard's role, "We're an organizational chameleon. We can be whatever color anybody wants us to be for the mission at hand," for it was situational awareness—the instinct of how to couple organizational assets with the problem at hand—that drove the Coast Guard's work. Allen was modest about his own work. "I didn't act any different after 9/11 than I did before," he recalled later. "You know, I'm Popeye" (the famous spinach-eating cartoon character). "I am what I am"—Popeye's famous slogan. In fact, Allen was a leader who found a way to get from his people and his resources what was needed to effectively attack an enormous problem. "You surge to meet the event," he explained.

Allen took that initiative and situational awareness—born from the Coast Guard's rich history, reformed after the *Exxon Valdez* disaster, battle-tested on September 11—to the Gulf after Katrina. He arrived looking for officers who were "dogs that could hunt," he said, quoting his grandfather. He worked to knock down obstacles as they flared up. Allen and his coordinated team first got the basic operations of New Orleans under control, and then developed a plan for handing off responsibility to a joint federal–state recovery office that would take over from there a few months later. They struggled mightily with the problems they faced, but it was the arrival of rocket scientist Allen in New Orleans that turned the tide of recovery.

The Secrets of Rocket Science

As Thad Allen described his view of effective management, "the operational genius of the Coast Guard is still that we give our field commanders a mission, an area of responsibility, and their own resources and assets, such as cutters and aircraft, and then we leave it up to them."[13] The Coast Guard drew those basic lessons from its long history, stretching back to its creation in 1790 as a service to save lives and enforce the collection of customs revenue. The twin mission of service and enforcement has always proven a difficult one to balance. But it has also framed the Coast Guard culture.[14] Centuries ago, a cutter and its crew could be at sea facing everything from sailors washed overboard to smugglers trying to sneak contraband into the country. As Allen explained it later, "It takes [only] an inner tube and a pair of flippers to enter our world of work." That broad mission helped create a culture of flexible problem solving and a commitment to helping the organization learn to adapt to new problems, including some beyond the fears of disaster planners. The *Exxon Valdez* problems had prompted the Coast Guard to change what it did. The September 11 terrorist attacks had provided an operational test.

Thus, when Allen took over the Katrina operation, he had the backup of a powerful and robust force that had thought about how to adapt to problems never seen before. In fact, two important elements contributed to the Coast Guard's rocket science approach: nimble response and surge capacity. No one had ever encountered a problem quite like Katrina before—the force of a weapon of mass destruction on a whole American city. Allen faced a challenge that had already humbled Michael Brown, ruined FEMA's reputation, and undermined the bold pledges of the nation's readiness following the September 11 reforms. Allen led the response not only by deploying the Coast Guard's forces but also by leveraging other assets and bringing them together to where they were needed most. The GAO, in fact, later applauded the Coast Guard's response. Its advance training, the GAO concluded, "allowed the Coast Guard to respond with greater flexibility using a mix of personnel and assets from any operational unit."[15]

For Thad Allen, the Coast Guard's approach to Katrina was rocket science, guided by seven leadership principles:[16]

1. *Clear objectives.* Every operation has a clearly defined and attainable objective. Coast Guard personnel never moved into action until they knew what they were going to do; they then focused on how to get it done. Helicopter rescue teams plucked survivors off rooftops. Armed safety officers provided security for government officers when civil order almost completely disappeared and the Wild West ruled New Orleans' streets.

2. *Effective presence.* Commanders focus on bringing together "the right assets and capabilities at the right place at the right time."[17] The Coast Guard has always faced the dilemma of patrolling thousands of miles of coastline with a remarkably small force. When Alexander Hamilton created one of the Coast Guard's predecessors, the Revenue Marine, he argued that the "right place at the right time" approach was critical to the force's success. The Coast Guard brought helicopter repair specialists in from its Miami station and air rescue teams from Alaska to help in the effort.

3. *Unity of effort.* Operational officials know that, for most of the problems they face, they will not have sufficient assets on their own to solve them. Coordinating what is at hand—or can be gathered in—is hardwired into the Coast Guard's operations. Just as with the launch of a rocket, only one person can be in charge. In fact, Coast Guard doctrine holds that one person *must* be in charge. To do the job, however, this person must work to identify all the forces—perhaps in other federal agencies, at other levels of government, or in the private sector—that can help solve the problem. Leadership lies not just in command but in coordination. Allen focused on bringing together everyone who could lend a hand, and then ensured that they were all working in the same direction without tripping over each other.

4. *On-scene effort.* On-scene commanders who know the mission and know their training are encouraged to do what it takes to get the job done, without waiting for information to flow up and down the chain of command. The demands of the problems they face define the forces they bring and the way they lead them. In the first response to Katrina's devastation, a junior C-130 aircraft pilot arrived over New Orleans. Her assignment was to fly over and inspect the condition of the city. As soon as she arrived, however, she realized that the search and rescue helicopters frantically working below could not communicate with officials on the ground, especially at hospitals and those seeking safe landing areas. She abandoned her environmental overflight and created the first airborne communication system, so that the rescue pilots could avoid flying into each other and could get the victims they were carrying to care and safety as quickly as possible.[18] "Operational awareness" defines and drives leadership.

5. *Flexibility.* Leaders focus on using the limited resources at hand to solve the widest range of problems. On the Great Lakes,

where the water can often freeze for months during the winter, the Coast Guard has a small fleet of iceboats for rescue. These are specially designed craft that can move quickly over the top of ice instead of floating in the water. The Detroit station put together a team of boats and crews, which proved especially effective in navigating underwater New Orleans. They worked jointly with US Army personnel to find and rescue many victims who were stuck, thirsty, and hungry in the city's many narrow, flooded streets.

6. *Managed risk.* Commanders ensure that their units have the proper training, and they are careful to put the right forces in the right place, without subjecting them to unnecessary danger. Coast Guard commanders in the region had long anticipated the risks from hurricanes, and they had practiced plans to get their forces out of harm's way—and then bring them back quickly for rescue duty as soon as conditions warranted. They have a keen understanding of the capabilities and limits of their boats and planes because they know they will not be able to rescue others if they themselves need rescue. The Coast Guard thus avoided the failures that had dogged FEMA because that agency had put assets at risk at the beginning and failing to deploy them effectively after the storm.

7. *Restraint.* The Coast Guard has long recognized its power, and it trains its personnel to use that power responsibly. Cutters often patrol alone, far from shore, with powerful guns and vast law enforcement power. The challenge of balancing the twin service and enforcement missions has always focused on the principle of restraint in the use of this power. When Coast Guard personnel (or Coasties, as they call themselves) had to exercise force, they tried to be sensitive to the very human needs of their victims. Evacuees directed their anger over having been stranded so long at the first government representatives who arrived to

help them—the Coasties being lowered by hoist to rescue the trapped citizens—but the Coasties nevertheless worked hard to treat those evacuees with sensitivity. Even when divers jumped into tepid water to gather evacuees and it was sometimes logistically easier to collect smaller groups at a time, they tried to keep evacuated families together to lessen their stress. Remembering that those they were evacuating were people, and treating them with sensitivity, helped make them heroes to many stranded hurricane victims.

The Coast Guard's special history and mission, and its careful cultivation of its crew members, made it especially nimble in dealing with Katrina's daunting problems. Long before the storm struck, the service recognized that "few other organizations afford their members as much responsibility and authority at junior levels as does the Coast Guard." It is little wonder that the Coast Guard, and the other organizations in the Gulf that behaved like it, performed so much better than FEMA, and that Thad Allen succeeded where Michael Brown had failed. Allen and his Coast Guard colleagues were rocket scientists.

March of the Rocket Scientists

Is the Coast Guard unique? Is the kind of leadership that Thad Allen and his colleagues showed idiosyncratic, or is it replicable at other times and in other situations? The level of public dissatisfaction with the performance of public agencies is high and daunting, so it is clear that rocket science leadership has not extended as far as it needs to go. However, rocket scientists like Allen have turned up throughout government, often in the most unexpected places. The sheer variety of the problems with which they have struggled—and the remarkable resonance in their strategies and tactics—provides hope that government can replicate the rocket science approach. Consider the following cases.

THE OKLAHOMA CITY BOMBING

On the morning of Wednesday, April 19, 1995, LeAnn Jenkins was working at her desk in Oklahoma City. For a little less than a year, she had been executive director of the Federal Executive Board (FEB), a tiny organization designed to provide links among federal agencies in the region. Her office was in the old post office building, on the south side of the federal government's office complex that included the Murrah Federal Building. At 9:02 AM, she felt an enormous explosion. The 500-pound bookcase in her office nearly crushed her, and the lights fell out of the ceiling. When the dust cleared, a pile of rubble thirty-five feet high was all that was left of the Murrah Building's front.[19]

The explosion killed 168 persons—160 inside the Murrah Building, including 15 children in the first-floor day care center. It sent 426 people to area hospitals with brain injuries, lacerations from flying glass, and broken bones. Through good luck and good police work, a state trooper arrested prime suspect Timothy McVeigh within ninety minutes for driving without a license plate. The T-shirt he was wearing included a wanted poster for Abraham Lincoln and the phrase "sic semper tyrannis," which John Wilkes Booth had shouted after killing the president. (Following his conviction, McVeigh was executed in 2001.)

As McVeigh was speeding from the scene, Jenkins was scrambling to help with the rescue and to get key agencies running again. One of the most immediate problems was that the devastation in the front of the building was so complete that it was hard to know where to look for possible survivors—and how to identify some of the victims. The rescue workers did not know who was where: how many employees were likely to have been at their desks when the bomb went off, and where they were likely to be located.

Searchers looked to the Federal Executive Board for help. FEBs, scattered around the country in twenty-eight cities, help coordinate the federal government's field efforts and bring new management practices into federal agencies. The highest-ranking federal executives in each agency, who comprise the board, meet regularly to explore how best to streamline their efforts. When she started as the Oklahoma City FEB's executive director, Jenkins set out to identify what the FEB needed, starting by developing a map of who was where, what their phone numbers were, and how to reach them at home (since cell phones had then barely crept into the market). Jenkins' computer had been damaged, but she and her assistant managed to extract the list from the assistant's computer. This tool proved invaluable to rescue workers, who had only blueprints of the building but no sense of who worked where.

Over the following weeks, Jenkins worked with federal managers to help find new space for their employees so that the government agencies that had lost their offices (including the Secret Service, the Drug Enforcement Administration, and the Social Security Administration) could get back to work. Office managers also discovered that mail addressed to the Murrah Building was piling up at the post office. Much of it was from citizens trying to transact business with the government. Managers did not want the mail to be forwarded to the temporary spaces where they were working, because they did not want to have to invest even more energy trying to keep up with the mail trail. Jenkins worked with the post office to arrange a special pickup service, which allowed designated employees to drive to the post office, stop at the call window, show a government identification, and pick up the mail for their agency. All those steps required throwing out standard procedures to make things work after the emergency. "It was communication in a big way," she explained later. "The resources were scattered in a big way, off the grid," and the challenge was finding a way to pull things back together again.

Then there was the challenge of providing care to the employees and the families of those killed and injured. In addition to the victims and their families in the region, family members of those killed and missing flooded into the city from around the country, often without resources for a long-term stay. Local nonprofits, including the Red Cross, Salvation Army, Catholic Charities, among others—anyone who had money to distribute—joined to create an "unmet needs committee." Jenkins served as the committee's conduit for help to employees and their families. The committee members wanted to get aid out quickly, and they also wanted to avoid fraud. "We wanted to prevent someone from going to five different nonprofits to pay the May utility bill five times—and we wanted to make sure that no one had five months of utility bills piling up," she explained. President Clinton announced a scholarship fund to help pay the education expenses of children who had lost a parent in the blast, and Jenkins got the word out to the employees. Some employees found themselves hospitalized, without a way to get to the workers' compensation office to file for the benefits they were due for their injuries. Jenkins worked with the office to "reinvent they way they did business. They had case workers come into hospitals and adjudicate claims on the spot."

In short, Jenkins led a federal effort to help employees recover from the blast and to restore federal offices to normal functioning. Few of the rules or procedures they had on the books applied to the situation. Even the invaluable first step, the list of offices and employees, had been created to deal with weather emergencies, not domestic terrorism. Many problems required brand-new solutions. The key to the solutions, Jenkins recalled later, was the ability to adapt quickly. Rapid adaptation, in turn, depended on communication, and the communication was built on preexisting relationships of trust that had been nurtured long before the explosion. "The time to meet someone is not at a disaster," Jenkins said. "You don't waste time doing the introduction dance. The introduction dance is shaking hands, sizing them up, and determining what their motivations are. A lot of time is wasted," and the middle of a disaster, when big problems require an immediate response, is not the time for waltzing. Instead, the relationships that federal executives from different agencies had built before the attack helped them immeasurably that April. "You know who to trust and who has the strength in a particular area," she explained.

In fact, Jenkins emphasized, the importance of "communications and collaboration and relationships can never be overestimated." Moreover,

> the relationships we formed in 1995 still help us today. We have state and local government people who serve on our continuity of government committee, and they're all treated the same. Full membership. Full membership means you're greeted with, "Hi, Gail. How are you? How are the kids?" If you are a member of the group, you lean in and you participate fully.

The committee formed to respond to the Oklahoma City bombing became an ongoing unit. It brought together those with a stake in solving common problems, and it focused on what each member would contribute to the mission, not the organizations they represented. The committee established parity in participation and built relationships based on interpersonal connections and trust. These relationships were reciprocal, and everyone was expected to contribute. Finally, the committee built on the premise that everyone would "lean in," in ways that contributed to the mission at hand.

The result is a constant search to "know who to trust and who has the strength in a particular area." Jenkins concluded, "Learning from each other makes us all richer and makes us all better." Too often, managers receive their information only from headquarters in Washington or up the chain of command. But when managers get together with others "who deal with completely different issues, they can incubate creative solutions from different perspectives, because it's a safe place."

After the Oklahoma City bombing, Jenkins helped build that safe place because she, and her colleagues, focused first on the needs of people. She then created a node for communications, both in and out, designed to promote results in service to those people. The node became a hub for even more extended conversations, and the utility of the process for all the players helped institutionalize it. It was an extra investment of time and money for everyone, but they all continued to make that investment because it paid rich dividends. As Jenkins explained, for many of the participants, coming to the meetings not only means time away from the rest of their work but, in many cases, a long drive as well. "We want to make sure that the return on their investment is worth their getting in the car to drive in."

ARLINGTON COUNTY ON SEPTEMBER 11

Christopher Combs was monitoring the television like everyone else on the morning of September 11. But unlike most viewers, he knew that the terrorist attacks were going to totally dominate his life for some time. A lead agent in the FBI's Washington Field Office, he knew he would be going to New York to join the investigation and to help restore federal law enforcement agencies, many of which had lost their offices in the attacks. He hurried home to put some clothes through the laundry and, on the way back to the office, heard radio calls about another attack just across the river. His response to the terrorist attacks suddenly pulled him much closer to home.

Soon after takeoff from Washington's Dulles Airport, hijackers had seized American Airlines Flight 77. They had turned the plane around and crashed it into the Pentagon. The massive explosion precipitated by the crash penetrated three of the building's five concentric rings and killed 189 persons. The resulting fire further weakened the building, threatening additional collapses, and injured workers who had survived the initial explosion.[20]

Within minutes after the initial report of the explosion at the Pentagon, Combs was speeding to the scene to join Arlington County Fire Captain Chuck Gibbs in establishing a command post. Unlike the situation at the World Trade Center, where the police and fire emergency responders were not talking with each other, Combs and Gibbs began building an integrated incident command post. In short order, a wide-ranging team was in place, staffed by the Arlington County Fire Department, the Arlington County Police Department, the Metropolitan Washington Airports Authority, Fort Myer, the Fairfax County International Urban Search & Rescue Team, the FBI, the National Capital Response Squad, and emergency responders from neighboring communities working as part of mutual aid agreements. The team quickly determined that the firefighters ought to take the lead because subduing the fire and rescuing victims was clearly the first priority.

The scene was intense, but the team had a strong start. For decades, emergency managers in the capital area had known that they were a prime target—first for the Soviets and then for terrorists—so they had conducted regular drills to test their reaction to a wide range of threats. In fact, Combs recalled later, many of the team members who gathered on the morning of September 11 had just conducted a drill a couple days earlier. They did not have to start with introductions or with allocating jobs; they already knew each other and their capabilities well. They had not practiced a response to a terrorist attack on the Pentagon from a hijacked airplane, but they had worked through enough different scenarios that they knew just what each team member could contribute to the response. Those instincts saved valuable time in the first minutes after the attack and vastly improved the effectiveness of their work.

One group had not been part of that drill—the security forces and emergency workers at the Pentagon itself. The Pentagon security staff had suffered one of their worst nightmares—a large attack that inflicted massive damage and penetrated the nation's defense command—so they were understandably on edge and wary of everyone. They knew, for example, that a coordinated attack might include a second wave of terrorists disguised as emergency responders, who might be able to enter the breach to inflict even more damage, and they were reluctant to allow local firefighters into the building. The team members who had established pre-existing relationships of trust had a running start, but it took precious minutes for the response team to build on-the-spot partnerships with the Pentagon's own security and emergency details.

As Arlington County's own report on the response later concluded, "Leadership isn't learned in a day; it is learned every day."[21] The team responding to the attack on the Pentagon consisted of organizational leaders who led with an eye toward results, and their work provided a hidden but sterling case of coordinated effort on that awful day. Federal, state, and local officials worked together in close partnership, with none of the acrimony or communication gaps that plagued some of the other response efforts. They stopped the fire, rescued many employees who otherwise would have died, and prevented further structural damage. Then, when the shutdown of the nation's airspace made it impossible to transfer large quantities of emergency supplies, including artificial skin that badly burned victims needed, they helped coordinate a ground-based handoff system among local law enforcement officials on the East Coast to get the supplies to the hospitals treating the victims. Preexisting relationships of trust, fueled by strong interpersonal communication and focused squarely on the mission, helped cement the collaboration that response to those attacks demanded.

THE AL ANBAR POWERPOINT PRESENTATION

In 2007, sectarian and tribal conflicts threatened to shred America's hopes for even the most rudimentary stability in Iraq. Sunni Iraqis were killing Shiite Iraqis, Shiite Iraqis were killing Sunni leaders, and both were killing American troops. President Bush's "surge" poured in more troops and helped restore order. But a quiet yet critical part of the resulting decline in violence was leadership by midlevel American officers, who cobbled together delicate deals to separate the warring sects and restore a bit of order to the troubled land.[22]

One effort that stuck out was led by Travis Patriquin, a thirty-two-year-old Army captain who had developed his own strategy and illustrated it with Microsoft's PowerPoint presentation program. Patriquin was stationed in Al Anbar, the nation's deadliest province for Americans. The attacks there were so fierce that top commanders had considered the possibility in 2006 of pulling troops out to concentrate on stabilizing Baghdad. The Army sent Patriquin, who spoke Arabic along with several other languages, to help stabilize the region. From his computer in Ramadi, he crafted an ultrasimple eighteen-page presentation, with messages at the bottom of each page written at the fourth-grade level and simple stick figures telling a story.[23] "This is an American Soldier," the presentation begins. "We'll call him Joe. Joe wants to win in Al Anbar. But sometimes it seems like other people don't share that idea." Through his slides, Patriquin explained the strategy he had developed—drinking tea with local leaders and building trust with the leaders' militias.

Patriquin's subtle argument, woven through his stick figure art (see Figure 6.1), was that local Iraqis could far better distinguish insurgents from citizens and that partnerships with local leaders were the key to bringing the militias to the American side. Joe discovers that the key to success is building relationships with the sheik and his colleagues, and that "if he'd done this three years ago, maybe his wife would be happier, and he'd have been home more." Joe grows a moustache to connect better with Iraqis, who "like people with moustaches and have a hard time trusting people without one." In the end, "Everyone wins! Except terrorists."

Patriquin's strategy came from his own experience about what worked and what did not. But it coincided almost perfectly with the findings of the Iraq Study Group, a special commission created by Congress and cochaired by James A. Baker III and Lee H. Hamilton. In its 2006 report, the study group recommended, among other things, that "the Iraqi Police Service should be given greater responsibility to conduct criminal investigations."[24] Patriquin's frontline experience led him to the strategy of creating personal relationships with local leaders and using those relationships to identify and drive out terrorists. Defense Secretary Robert Gates singled out the approach as an example of how the Army was shifting the course of Iraqi events. "At this young captain's direction," he told an audience in 2007, "the brigade courted local sheiks over cigarettes and endless cups of tea—outreach that, combined with Al Qaeda's barbarism, helped spark the 'Anbar Awakening' that has garnered so much attention and praise in the past months."[25]

A keystone of the strategy was shifting American troops away

FIGURE 6.1 A Slide from Captain Patriquin's PowerPoint Presentation

That terrorist is sad... he just got caught. Joe is happy. The normal Iraqi is happy. The Iraqi Policeman is happy. The Sheik is happy.

from remote megabases into neighborhoods. As Lieutenant Colonel Steve Miska told a reporter following his second tour of duty in Iraq, "We were trying to drive a wedge between the people and the insurgents. We couldn't do it if we were pulling away from them."[26] It required building personal relationships with the Iraqis whose trust the Americans were trying to win.

Patriquin's PowerPoint presentation swept by e-mail through the military command. He convinced countless officers of his approach, because of both the novel presentation and the sheer power of the message. The strategy made sense to commanders because it worked. They realized all too well that the relationships were extremely fragile, but the mission-driven improvisation had an unshakable power and made Patriquin a hero. Sadly, the strategy did not take root fast enough. On December 6, 2006, Patriquin was on patrol when an improvised explosive device killed him, leaving his wife a widow and their three children fatherless. Still, Patriquin's "How to Win the War in Al Anbar" PowerPoint presentation bounced around the Internet to hammer home his message.

RESTORING THE SCHOOLS IN NEW ORLEANS

Like many students around the country, Ramsey Green was horrified by the devastation he saw in the Gulf after Katrina. A graduate student in government administration, he had found a summer internship in 2006 with the Louisiana Recovery Authority (LRA), a multifocused consortium created to coordinate government efforts at helping Louisiana recover from the storm. The internship grew into a full-time job for Green, as an official in the LRA and later with the school district, working first as budget director and then within two years becoming deputy superintendent of schools. One of Green's biggest challenges in the post-Katrina days was negotiating with FEMA over how much aid the agency would provide. As Green explained, "We had in our schools $80 million worth of building contents, from paper and pencils all the way up to chalkboards and furniture. Much of it was destroyed or ended up in Lake Pontchartrain."[27]

FEMA agreed to pay for the damage, but officials on both sides found themselves hamstrung by the rules, which came from the Stafford Act.[28] The act and the rules flowing from it had been written to respond to relatively small-scale disasters with short-term responses, like tornadoes in Kansas or floods in North Carolina. The program provided for storm damage payments on a case-by-case basis to replace what had been lost. In New Orleans, however, the rules produced an enormous headache. If the storm ruined 1,000 books in a school, FEMA would pay to replace the books, but the school district would have to itemize each one and then replace each ruined book with another just like it. The school district also had lost 2,907 puppets in the flooding, but district officials decided that the cost of making a case for $94,469.05 in FEMA reimbursement just wasn't worth it.[29]

The district needed every penny, but the administrative chores were huge. How could the city's schools collect what FEMA had pledged without becoming hopelessly trapped in red tape? "They were asking us to account for the 5,000 different things we would put into our facilities," Green said, "and match the line items to 183 project worksheets." It made little sense for the school district to replace each item with literally the one that had been damaged or destroyed. FEMA countered that its rules required item-for-item replacement. "For 18 months, the school district and FEMA just beat the hell out of each other on this," Green explained, in an ongoing battle that prevented the flow of money. The question soon shifted to a war between accountants: FEMA consolidated its 5,000 budget codes down to 500. New Orleans officials said they wanted just four.

"You would think it would be very simple," Green explained, "but it was anything but." They had a series of what New Orleans officials called "where's my damn money" meetings. Green and his colleagues adjourned to a coffee shop to hammer out a new plan, with just four broad categories (furniture, publications, school supplies, and information technology). Each category had a commodity code that provided FEMA officials with an audit trail. New Orleans officials had a manageable number of categories into which to sort the money, and they got flexibility on what they could buy within each category. The coffee shop plan ultimately produced an agreement and a $50 million check, which Green proudly hung on his wall.

The bargaining was tough and nerves were often frayed. Sometimes, Green explained later, "there's a lot of comedy to it." Continuing pressure with an eye on the goal got the city its money and provided FEMA its accountability. In the process, Green learned an important lesson. "When we get a breakthrough, we vehemently share the credit," he said. The city's creativity built a new partnership with FEMA and got the money flowing.

The Skills of the Rocket Scientist

Coast Guard Admiral Thad Allen's leadership following Katrina might be unusual, but as the preceding four case studies show, it is not unique. The case studies are tales of rocket scientists—LeAnn Jenkins, Chris Combs, Travis Patriquin, and Ramsey Green—who worked out of instinct in the search for answers to the basic question of how best to solve the inescapable problem at hand. The vending machines around them had failed, and they knew they needed something different. So in LeAnn Jenkins' words, they "leaned in," worked to solve the problem, and created new partnerships. Facing challenges that required leveraged government, they developed rocket science strategies. Their experiences, born of individual action, define the common tenets of the modern-day rocket scientist:

1. *Focus on results.* Procedures and structures are important, but nothing matters if the job does not get done. Rocket science requires building rockets that fly. It requires ensuring that the mission drives behavior.
2. *Seek results through interrelated partnerships.* No single individual or organization can control any problem that truly matters. Any

successful attack on an important problem requires interorganizational partnerships. Rocket science requires creating teams
that draw together the forces required, and then leading them
toward results.

3. *Use information to fuel communication.* At the core of each of
these cases is the realization that communication is the critical tool for building partnerships, and that good information is
central to that communication. It is a truism that the postindustrial society is defined by the rise of information as the central
organizing force. In each of these cases, communication was the
most important mechanism for defining the strategic direction
and coordinating action to reach the goal.

4. *Rely on bureaucracies, as holding companies for expertise.* It is tempting to push traditional organizations out of the way, to argue
the end of bureaucracy with the rise of the postindustrial era. In
fact, of course, each of these rocket scientists used their existing
bureaucracies, with their structures, processes, and routines, as
repositories of essential resources. Just as the rise of leveraged
policies does not also mean the end of vending-machine processes, the rise of rocket science does not mean sweeping away
the great bureaucratic tradition. Rather, leveraged government
requires recrafting bureaucracies into holding companies of
expertise—where critical resources can be built and nurtured,
and then assembled as needed to solve the shifting and often
unpredictable problems at hand.

5. *Create relationships of trust before the relationships are needed.* Partnerships are crucial, but the middle of a serious crisis is not
the time to start building them. The key lies in exercises and
training, not so much to practice what to do in the event of
future disasters (since the real thing in the future rarely matches
practice in the past) but to build relationships among the people who will need to collaborate. A county emergency man-

ager once told me that one of the most valuable things she got from a joint exercise was the cell phone number of the local FBI field agent. In the event of an emergency, she would know how to reach him; when the phone rang, he would want to take her call. FEMA, by contrast, was crippled in the Gulf because many of its key officials had no preexisting relationships and trust ran deeper into deficit as problems grew worse. Rocket science involves very complex interorganizational partnerships, but these partnerships depend critically on interpersonal relationships.

6. *Steer resources.* Especially in very complex partnerships, it can be hard to identify who is involved in which partnerships or how to apply leverage. But the flow of money—where it goes and who spends it—creates an invaluable road map. It defines who does what, and how. Leverage over these partnerships comes from nudging resources—money, information, and people—in ways that strengthen the incentives for collaboration. Rocket science depends on focusing the right resources in the right places at the right time.

7. *Lead by making the public interest drive complex partnerships.* Partnerships are critical, but the government is not just one partner among many. The primary task of government leaders is to ensure that the public interest remains paramount. That focus is especially important for the pursuit of public goals that require complex relationships with private partners. Not all players in a partnership are equal. In these contracting, regulatory, and incentive-based partnerships, the government has to find a way to ensure that the public's goals come first. In intergovernmental programs, the challenge is to balance federal, state, and local power, where there can easily be competing visions of the public interest, as the New Orleans schools case illustrates. And in issues that stretch across international borders, like Patriquin's

delicate relationships with the Iraqis, an insistence on sovereignty can destroy the partnership. In each case, the core is making sure that the partnerships serve the public interest. The complexity of the partnerships means that it is often difficult to determine how best to accomplish this goal—and that a strategy that works well for one issue might stumble badly on the next. Rocket science requires leaders to keep their eyes focused on the ultimate goal.

These are the skills of the rocket scientist, and they are the keys to the next government of the United States. Those who cared for Mildred showed the same instincts. The many professionals in Mildred's case focused on providing her with the highest quality of life and searched constantly for strategies that worked (the emphasis on results). When new problems bubbled up, they looked for fresh ideas and new resources—from nutritionists to physical therapists and, eventually, hospice—to buttress her care (the creation of interrelated partnerships). Shared information, as they charted her condition and shared notes between shifts, was the key (the centrality of communication). They deployed a wide array of resources but worked hard to keep Mildred from being pigeonholed into standard operating routines (because the bureaucracies were holding companies for the expertise they needed). Mildred's caregivers were able to do this because they relied on experts they knew (as a result of preexisting relationships of trust). When emergency rooms were jammed, they were able to arrange for her to be treated anyway; and when nurses suggested a change in medication, her physicians knew they could trust the nurses' instincts. The staff worked to steer resources to the things that would help her most. And most of all, they pushed the system hard to make sure that Mildred's well-being drove the very complex partnerships involved in caring for her.

Both Mildred and Katrina produced rocket scientists who solved the problems at hand by using the problems to drive the action. These examples are reassuring because, in each of them, the leveraged-government instinct triumphed over the vending-machine model to produce the adaptive responses that the problems needed. In other cases, rocket scientists, driven by the same results-based culture, have used the same tools. Rocket science, fortunately, is not a rare event. The Coast Guard has tried to build this style of leadership into its organizational culture, but many practitioners of the approach have not only had to devise their tactics from scratch (requiring extra time for trial and error) but also had to fight against the prevailing vending-machine culture (exposing them to political and career risks).

When the vending-machine model fits, it often works well, although its mechanisms can always be fine-tuned. With the rise of wicked problems that demand creative rocket science solutions, however, government faces a twin challenge: (1) helping to breed rocket scientists and (2) creating a governance system, focused on results, that supports their work. Officials can work the easy way or the hard way. Too often, when rocket science is needed, rocket scientists have to do their work the hard way: alone and with little guidance, having to reinvent the wheel in an atmosphere where others either do not know they need a wheel to begin with or put obstacles in their path. With problems ever more wicked, governance does not have the luxury of long learning curves, false steps, and rearguard actions that get in the way of rocket science. When rocket science is needed, governments need to find a way to do it the easy way, with intellectual capital charting the path and a governance system that streamlines the course. That is the key to the next government of the United States. In the final chapter, we will examine how to make it work.

7

THE POLITICAL FUTURE

T he next government of the United States faces two central
challenges: One is matching the right governance style to
the right policy strategy, using vending-machine governance
for routine problems and leveraged governance for rocket science problems. The second, more difficult challenge is developing
rocket science leadership and making it stick. Too often such leadership has not been ready when needed and, when rocket scientists
have tried to use it, they have often struggled to build it from
scratch with little political support. American government cannot
afford haphazard solutions for big, inescapable problems. Smart
solutions will require a different political future.

The problem is that the development of rocket science solutions
has too often been ad hoc. The high quality of care that Mildred
received depended heavily on the skill of her nurses and on their
instincts about how to connect the parts of the system to solve
her problems. Thad Allen's success in New Orleans depended on
his personal leadership skills and his ability to marshal the Coast

Guard's emerging competencies to help Katrina's victims. For neither Mildred nor Katrina was good leadership a strong bet. In fact, the media regularly report on nursing-home residents who do not receive good care, and the federal government fumbled its first effort to respond to Katrina. And in both cases, the Government Accountability Office identified the programs' management as high-risk, subject to a high chance of waste and mismanagement. Such policy problems have become too frequent and the costs of failure too large to accept random chances that the right problems will find the right solutions.

Governance and Accountability

Long and complex chains of policy implementation have bedeviled public policy for generations. In their 1973 classic *Implementation*, Jeffrey Pressman and Aaron Wildavsky argued that translating big ideas into productive results often bogs down in "the complexity of joint action."[1] What is fundamentally different about the wicked problems that require leveraged solutions—about a shift of government's role from managing how its own organizations yield solutions to steering complex multiorganizational partnerships that produce results?

First, there are many more of these problems and they stretch into many more areas. Contracting out, for example, is nothing new; George Washington had problems with defense contractors that would have kept the Government Accountability Office busy, had it been in business during the American Revolution. However, the breadth and depth of government's private partners have increased significantly since World War II. Contracting out, along with other forms of public–private partnerships, has crept into almost every corner of public activity at all levels of government, from the space program to the delivery of social services. Such "blended power," Jody Freeman writes, is "now more the norm than the exception," with "deep public–private interpenetration."[2] Moreover, the rise of these blended tools of government has made the public and private sectors far more interdependent.[3] In the eyes of some analysts, it has produced "the shadow of hierarchy," in which government increasingly plays the role of "enabler and regulator of the provision of public services by private actors."[4]

Second, more of these policy chains are more complex. The role of contract integrators, to whom the government has contracted out the contracting process, has significantly increased. At the federal level, agencies have contracted out not only the production of goods and services but also policy and management analysis. NASA has contracted out much of the scientific work that supports the space program, to the point that the agency often does not have sufficient internal capacity to assess the advice its contractors are providing. The Medicare and Medicaid programs have become so interwoven into networks of public, private, and nonprofit organizations that tracking the money itself has become a tough problem. At the local level, nonprofit organizations have become integral to the delivery of social services and to welfare reform. Pressman and Wildavsky might have identified the "complexity of joint action" in the 1970s, but the joint actions have become far more complex since.

Third, these complex governance chains have produced mixed accountability systems, which muddy the task of holding anyone accountable for a program's outcomes.[5] Who is responsible for what, and how would we know? The First Amendment to the Constitution promises citizens the right to "redress of grievances." Accountability is the process of ensuring that grievances are redressed. The rise of these complex partnerships has made accountability far more difficult. For example, when members of Congress asked CIA Director Michael V. Hayden whether contractors had performed waterboarding (an interrogation technique designed to simulate the sense of drowning) on al-Qaeda prisoners, Hayden replied, "I'm not sure of the specifics. I'll give you a tentative answer: I believe so."[6] At best, it was a prime example of what Paul R. Verkuil calls "outsourcing sovereignty," in which the government shared important elements of its power with private partners.[7] At worst, it was a case of blurred accountability, in which the chain of action made it impossible to determine who was responsible for what—and perhaps for the CIA director to track who had done what. To compound the issue, everyone understood the question, but top officials, on Capitol Hill and in the CIA, did not know the answer.

This issue lies at the core of the Mildred paradox and its corollary: the growing role of nongovernment players providing public services and the inability of any single player to control the system and hold it accountable. In an effort to bring more precision to the study of American governance, scholars have sought to apply the principal–agent model to public policy, derived from the tradition of bureaucratic authority.[8] The rising importance of complex, interdependent tools of public action has made it ever more difficult to apply this model. Agents remain responsible to their principals for the implementation of public decisions, but more programs have multiple principals, more principals have multiple agents, and more agents have multiple principals.

It is not the case that there is no accountability. Rather, with so many principal–agent connections, *multiple mechanisms of accountability* are operating simultaneously in the same arena. They sometimes complicate, sometimes tangle, and occasionally break the chain from policy makers to service recipients. With so many problems having become so wickedly entangled, failures anywhere can become problems everywhere. Solutions anywhere can become problems elsewhere in the system, because one person's solution can become another person's problem. The levees around New Orleans are a perfect metaphor: relatively small breaks flooded much of the city and, in the process, relieved water pressure elsewhere in the levee system. For some, the levees were salvation; for others, breaches brought disaster.

Moreover, a win in one round does not guarantee success in the next. Each challenge in Mildred's care had to be fought and won on its own terms. As Mildred moved from nursing-home bed to doctor's office to hospital emergency room and back again, different professionals came in and out of her life, making decisions in a semicoordinated way. Each medical and social-work discipline advanced its own plan of care as each professional believed was most effective. Mildred's overall care was the product of this constellation of decisions that were weakly linked, without a single point of coordination or control. Government's role and, ultimately, its cost was the by-product of the decisions of individual professionals.

Much the same was true of Katrina. Federal, state, local, private, and nonprofit actors all weighed into the recovery process. Most of them operated within the framework of their own organizational goals, politics, and procedures. In Mildred's case, her overall quality of care was good because the linkages worked effectively most of the time. In Katrina's case, the early stages of performance were not good, because the countervailing pressures pulled players in different directions. In all these cases, the battle was the constant struggle to prevent wicked problems from occurring and to learn how successes against these efforts could help the entire policy system become more lithe and nimble.

The central issue, Laurence Lynn reminds us, is the "constitutional legitimacy of state action"—the use of government's power to achieve public ends and the mechanisms by which the use of that power is controlled.[9] The dilemma, as we have seen in this book, is that the vending machine's long legacy of hierarchical authority is comfortable but it often fails to control the postmodern strategies of public action. Once reality pushes policy makers and citizens away from that model into leveraged policy, "there is no handy alternative," Jody Freeman argues.[10] Consequently, American governance is left with a tough dilemma: comfortable strategies that do not work or new strategies whose novelty offers little comfort.

In fact, despite their success, the rocket scientists profiled in Chapter 6 had precious little political support and built on very little intellectual foundation. Their experience exemplifies the burden of the dilemma that Freeman describes: comfort with a model that often does not fit, and no handy alternative for building and replicating the model that does. The challenge is finding the right model for the right problem and doing so predictably. Applying the wrong model to a problem not only creates performance hurdles but also fails us in our search for constitutionally legitimate state action, which Lynn rightly points to as the cornerstone of democratic governance.

The great advantage of the vending-machine model is that it creates standard procedures to deal with repeated problems. The vending-machine model focuses on programs and agencies as the basic unit of analysis; rocket science focuses on building collaborations among multiple players with an eye on results. The vending-machine model searches for standard processes that can be applied in predictable patterns; rocket science builds flexible capacity for dealing with a variety of unpredictable issues. The vending-machine model seeks to insulate the system's performance from the vagaries of individuals; rocket science builds on individual insight and leadership, so the system's performance depends even more critically on the quality of individuals in key positions. Mildred's happiness depended completely on the insights of a handful of professionals who watched her carefully and made the right judgments about the care she needed. Recovery from Katrina fundamentally changed when the adept crisis manager Thad Allen took over from Michael Brown.

Rocket science might be the "handy alternative" that Freeman seeks, but producing it reliably where and when it is needed remains a fundamental challenge for American governance. When it works, it works well. When it is needed but is absent, performance often suffers terribly. The central challenge of twenty-first-century government is finding a way to match the governance needed for the problems at hand, to produce high-quality results in an accountable way—one that ensures the constitutional legitimacy of state action.

A New Strategy for Accountability

The Progressives' century, when accountability depended on hierarchy, helped unleash government's energy while harnessing its power. We have been relying on this model for so long that it is hard to imagine alternatives. Can we devise an accountability model that works in blended systems? And can the political system be transformed in ways that support this new model of accountability? Information-age society will need information-age accountability, but determining how best to achieve an effective and responsive system is an enormous challenge for governance. The entire system is flooded with information, but figuring out what the information really tells us—how we move from vast quantities of unorganized information to genuinely actionable knowledge— is a central dilemma for government in the twenty-first century.

Governance functions increasingly through a blended system, which requires "aggregate accountability," Freeman argues—a system capable of assembling the various accountability tactics into an approach that serves the public interest.[11] This is the defining foundation of government's shift from the industrial to the information age. As Table 7.1 illustrates, governance is undergoing fundamental change in the transition to the twenty-first century. In the industrial-age approach that flowed from the Progressives, policy makers relied on hierarchy to hold the administrative system accountable. This vending-machine approach continued to dominate how policy makers *thought* about policy implementation, but as nonhierarchical strategies became more important, the old public-management model became less useful. It did not evaporate—many routine parts of the system continued to work hierarchically—but it increasingly failed to match the emerging realities of governance.

As the information age emerged, reformers created a new public-management approach in the 1980s. They focused on measuring outputs—the activities in which government engaged—and they developed a host of new marketlike strategies aimed at creating incentives for efficiency that were driven by information about results, coupled with consequences for poor performance. But public managers complained about being held accountable for results that they could not control. And as policy systems became even more complex and less connected to existing hierarchies and relationships between principals and the agents who did their work, the new public-management approach increasingly encountered problems.[12] This effort sought to move beyond the vending-machine model by creating a new approach to governance.

Mildred and Katrina revealed the problem of relying on a single approach of any kind. As the policy system increasingly relied on networks, in which multiple players balanced multiple and often competing incentives, no single accountability strategy would work. The system, instead, required blended accountability, to harmonize all players' contributions to outcomes they jointly produced. The challenge of this approach is to create an agile, dynamic, and

TABLE 7.1   The Evolution of Governance Models

	Old Public Management	New Public Management	Leveraged Governance
Era	Industrial age	Information age	Networked age
Accountability Strategy	Hierarchy	Output	Blended contributions to shared outcomes
Challenge	Rise of non-hierarchical strategies, tactics	Inability of managers to control outcomes for which they are not responsible	Mixed systems of accountability: agile, dynamic, effective

effective system of accountability—and to balance the traditional hierarchical system with the mixed systems on which intricately interlaced networks rely.

Redefining information-driven accountability for complex, blended systems while retaining authority-based accountability for routine problems is a huge challenge for elected officials. It requires them to shift their thinking for some programs, retain their deeply rooted approaches for others, know when to use which approach, and devise a scheme for presenting this new system sensibly to the public through media always in search of gotcha headlines.

This task is a special challenge for Congress, which institutionally is more input based, process driven, and prone to highly fractured perspectives on policy through the committee and subcommittee system. Some members of Congress have focused on results over structure. The Senate Committee on Homeland Security and Governmental Affairs, in its investigations of FEMA's failure with Katrina, resisted the restructuring reflex and concentrated instead on how to force FEMA to focus more on outcomes. Some members of Congress have also demonstrated a taste for the performance information that the Clinton and Bush administrations began producing through their government reform initiatives— Clinton's "reinventing government" and Bush's "presidential management agenda."

Still, those steps did not come instinctively for members of Congress, and their difficulty in rising to the challenges of oversight only accelerated the slide of power to the executive branch.[13] Congress likes to create new programs and agencies, and then rearrange the old ones. But efforts to make government work in an era of growing fiscal restraint are likely to be much more successful if we focus on improving the function of existing programs and agencies instead of creating more new ones—and on ensuring that problems do not proliferate because citizens slip through the cracks between the loosely connected programs and agencies that have accumulated over time. One 2008 survey showed just how far government has to go in satisfying citizens' demands. A Harris Interactive poll revealed that 73 percent of Americans believe that "it is very important for the federal government to be open and honest in its spending practices," but only 5 percent of those surveyed believe that the government meets that standard. The problem, the poll showed, further undermines the public's trust in government.[14]

As we saw in Chapter 3, presidents often have demonstrated scant interest in the results that government actually produces. They tend to be drawn into governance issues only when demonstrable failures allow them no escape. However, the rise of the truly wicked problems of blended governance is increasingly likely to draw them into these issues. Chief executives who oversee a government that works well can expect little political gain but, as Katrina underlined, presidents who seem disconnected or ineffective in big, inescapable problems can suffer political punishment. As more problems become government problems, as more government problems become more complex, as many American problems become global (and vice versa), and as failures in solving these problems impose larger consequences, presidents might well find themselves with little recourse but to increase their focus on the executive function. The courts could fill in the gap, but since the judiciary is reactive—the courts hear cases brought before them and do not initiate proceedings on their own—the chances that the courts will play a significant role in redefining accountability are slim.

These dilemmas create a difficult calculus of accountability, in which elected officials have little incentive to make the extra investment necessary for gaining the leverage that real accountability requires but they can suffer serious political costs if problems occur as a result. Elected officials and citizens do not know—indeed, cannot know—about the details of policy. Without a trigger, they often do not track what happens; when big problems provide that trigger, they seek to exact political revenge. The challenge is how to create enough political support to make policy work and to organize an effective system of accountability.

As we saw in Chapter 2, the American public has traditionally been deeply cynical about government and fundamentally suspicious about government's ability to perform. But that cynicism scarcely has restrained Americans' taste for public programs, even as they complain about the public bureaucrats who run them. As nations, levels of government, and sectors become more intertwined—as globalization spreads; as federal, state, and local governments share more joint responsibility for domestic programs; as the government becomes more dependent on nonprofit and for-profit organizations for service delivery (and many of them become more dependent on government for their business)—the quest for accountability is likely to become even more magnified because the chains are likely to become even more tangled. The rise of the rocket scientists described in Chapter 6 offers hope, but creating a political system that is able to create incentives and systems for producing and supporting rocket scientists in the long run, to help them do what must be done the easy way instead of the hard way, is a daunting problem.

Local governments have experimented with information-based innovations to attack this dilemma. From San Antonio to New York, cities have deployed call centers that let citizens dial 311 to get help with nonemergency problems and questions, from reporting a pothole to finding out the operating hours of a neighborhood park.[15] Baltimore's 311 system feeds information into its pathbreaking CitiStat system, which tracks the performance of everything from its "rat rubout" program to graffiti removal.[16] The system saves taxpayers money and has significantly improved the quality of services.[17]

At the core, 311 and the performance-stat programs, which have spread to local governments around the country, seek to improve results by increasing transparency. The systems show what local governments are doing well and what they are not, often with Web sites that highlight performance. They also provide multiple channels for citizens to access government: dialing 311 on the phone, entering complaints on the Web, walking up to a service counter, or calling their councilperson. In addition, they provide a "360-degree feedback" mechanism. When citizens contact the government with a complaint, they receive a complaint number that enables them to track results and allows local officials to notify them when the problem is resolved.

The system enables top managers to assess the performance of supervisors in different regions (do some supervisors prove more effective than others in filling potholes?) and to compare the performance of different programs (does the response time of fire-fighters match that of police officers and EMT drivers?). Although evidence on the 311 and performance statistic systems remains rudimentary, anecdotal accounts suggest that the systems have not only improved results but also have connected citizens better to their governments—and have helped drive the reforms to a growing number of cities around the nation.

The new policy systems with mixed policy tools require a mixed system of accountability. In this system, two things seem certain: it is impossible to use traditional authority-based accountability as the single accountability mechanism for these mixed systems, and it is impossible to replace authority with a single alternative. Surely these constraints do not mean that we should abandon authority and hierarchy. We will continue to need them for the routine problems that the vending-machine approach addresses well, and we will use it for the basic scaffolding to hold other tools accountable. Because they rely on different mechanisms, however, different tools will require different systems of accountability.[18] Government's job is to blend these tools to ensure that the public interest is served. The blend comes from the following menu of accountability mechanisms:[19]

1. *Authority.* The ability to control through command is no less important in the new accountability regime. Thad Allen was able to bring together a substantial array of government assets in New Orleans because President Bush named him "principal federal officer," a designation that gave him substantial authority to issue commands. Allen's leadership style was highly collaborative, but his formal position and presidential authority buttressed the teamwork he created.

2. *Contracts.* All contracts build on a basic legal understanding in which the contractor agrees to provide a good or service in

exchange for the government's money. A vast range of issues might flow from the government's decision to contract out public services, including which services are appropriate for contracting and how the government can be a "smart buyer" for the things it buys, but everything flows from the legal foundation of contracts. The courts and a detailed legal structure for these agreements provide remedies for holding contractors accountable for their performance.

3. *Regulation.* The federal and state governments have written extensive regulations governing nursing-home care. The issues covered by these rules range from food handling and preparation to the kinds of restraints that staff members can use on residents. The federal government counts 150 standards that nursing homes must meet. State governments impose their own standards. State government inspectors regularly review the quality of care in each nursing home, both for compliance with their own rules and on behalf of the federal government. This is a highly blended system: state governments are responsible for ensuring the private nursing home's compliance with federal regulations. Nursing homes that are found to be out of compliance with these rules can lose their government payments, have a government manager be temporarily appointed to run the home, or be shut down.

4. *Private standard-setting.* Private associations often impose industry standards, frequently in concert with government administrators, to ensure high-quality services. The American Health Care Association, for example, developed a program of excellence in nursing-home care, with voluntary standards for quality-of-life issues ranging from pressure ulcers caused by extended bed stays to pain management. As the association's president told Congress, "The provision of skilled nursing facility care truly is a partnership between the federal government

and the profession that employs more than two million direct care workers caring for the nation's most vulnerable population."[20] The association not only imposes standards on nursing homes but certifies the training of individuals who work in them. The interconnection of these federal, state, and industry monitors creates an interlocking system of standards—part regulatory and part voluntary.

5. *Voluntary self-regulation.* The International Organization for Standardization (abbreviated internationally as ISO), a trade organization, has developed guidelines for a wide range of goals, including environmental protection and customer service. The ISO 14000 standard lays out steps for companies to manage their environmental impact, develop continuous improvement strategies for environmental performance, and demonstrate the environmental progress they have made. Companies that meet these standards can receive ISO certification, which then becomes a powerful marketing tool. Some companies, for example, will buy only from other companies that have received ISO 14000 certification. In addition, the organization's ISO 9000 program has set customer service standards, and many local governments have pursued certification of their quality improvement processes through the ISO 9000 process. Meanwhile, other governments have competed in the private sector's Baldrige National Quality Program; and several governments, ranging from the city of Coral Springs, Florida, to the Jenks, Oklahoma, public schools, have won recognition. As food safety regulation around the world became more enmeshed in controversy in 2007, European companies adopted their own safety standards and many private companies agreed to buy only from other companies accredited by private inspection offices. Major American companies, including Wal-Mart and McDonald's, soon followed suit.[21] Private certification of public-sector

performance has become an important motivator for quality improvement.

6. *Negotiated rule-making.* Especially in the environmental arena, federal and state governments have pursued strategies of negotiated rule-making, or *reg-neg* for short. Rather than imposing public standards on business without ensuring that the rules would work or would provide the most efficient course to the desired public objective, regulators convened the affected parties to negotiate a standard that would achieve legislative goals while allowing business the most flexibility.[22] The process has been used as well for reallocating nursing-home beds in Texas and setting new standards in the wood furniture manufacturing business. Critics have long contended that such negotiated processes risk surrendering public authority to private interests, but proponents counter that effective partnerships are more likely to advance public goals and prevent hyperconflict from gumming up the system.

7. *Markets.* In a handful of areas, companies have established private markets to achieve government objectives. For example, in 1993 the Chicago Board of Trade (CBOT), a private commodities trading market, joined with the US Environmental Protection Agency to create a market for trading the rights to produce sulfur dioxide emissions. As part of a broad-scale effort to reduce acid rain, companies faced tough new standards for reducing these emissions. Those that found it cheapest to reduce their emissions could sell their pollution rights on the CBOT to other companies. Sulfur dioxide levels dropped, and the market allowed industry to reach the target at the lowest economic cost.[23] Emissions trading had spread to other areas, such as compliance with nitrous oxide standards to reduce ozone. Emissions-trading markets have become more widespread in Europe as well.

8. *Incentives.* As FEMA discovered in the 1990s, it is far cheaper and more effective to create incentives for individuals to build hurricane-resistant homes and to make their existing homes less susceptible to damage than for the government to pay for damage after the fact. Experts contend that creating financial incentives, through insurance programs and related tools, can encourage individuals to make these investments as protection against storms. Insurance incentives can even help reduce the nation's exposure to damage from terrorist attacks.[24]

9. *Competition.* The George W. Bush administration encouraged aggressive market-style competition to force service and accountability improvements, by providing consumers with choice in public services such as education and social services. The administration's No Child Left Behind program, for example, gave parents the opportunity to transfer their children to another school if their neighborhood school did not perform as well as they hoped. Many of the administration's critics condemned the approach as a matter of policy and disagreed with using choice as a mechanism of accountability, and the approach acquired substantial ideological baggage. However, the basic approach—providing citizens with information and empowering them to make decisions about who will provide their public services—has endured. Still, a lack of information has often crippled citizens in making service choices. When our family searched for a facility to provide Mildred's care, we had to rely on recommendations of friends. There was no consumer's guide to nursing-home care to rely on; government-provided information was rudimentary at best. If Mildred had encountered problems in her care (which fortunately she did not), the family would have had no recourse but to rely on a new round of contacts with friends and to hope for success. The federal government has sought to provide consumers better information

about the quality of health care in hospitals through its "Hospital Compare" Web site; and a consortium of public, private, and nonprofit health care funders and providers in California joined to produce CalHospitalCompare.[25] The systems are rudimentary, but they suggest how market-based competition that relies on consumer information might supplement the accountability system.

These tactics provide a broad menu of approaches for pursuing the accountability of public programs through complex blended partnerships. Each has produced success, but no single tactic has fully replaced traditional approaches; all of them combined still leave important questions unanswered. The sheer size and complexity of the menu is both daunting and troubling. Research on these tools is relatively scant, and it is hard to know which tactic to match with which tool and which ones are likely to prove most successful. Moreover, none of these tactics offer the comfortable security of traditional authority, which in theory promises strong control through government direction. These tactics introduce forces that are different from—and sometimes competing with—government-directed authority. Regulatory negotiation, for example, puts government and the sense of the public interest carried by its officials at the table with private companies, whose executives might well have different interests, and asks them to negotiate an acceptable outcome. Might this process produce private pressures that would lead government officials to compromise on public goals? Is the public interest only one interest among many at a conference table?

At the core of these tactics is a deeper transformation, which shifts accountability from controlling policy design to assessing policy results, from reliance on authority to reliance on information. The system's rising complexity is the product of a pragmatic search for fresh approaches; the new approaches to accountability focus on whether these systems produce results. Accountability moves from a focus on organizations inside the vending machine to an assessment of the system's results from the outside. It moves from fine-tuning the machine internally to ensuring transparency externally. As one senior OMB official put it, accountability increasingly requires a "line of sight" between the people and the managers responsible for producing results.[26] Transparency, of course, can also be enormously threatening. It can expose information that otherwise would have remained hidden, and this new information can expose players in the system to political attack that they otherwise would have dodged. The levee boards in Louisiana's bayou country simply had not looked very closely at the state of the pre-Katrina levees. Had they poked more deeply, the findings would have upset the political order. The subsequent flooding revealed problems that had existed all along. It is very easy to argue in retrospect that the levee boards should have been far more transparent about the condition of the levees. It is just as easy, however, to underestimate how more information would have disturbed existing political relationships.

Blended policy systems and wicked problems create huge information-age quagmires for government. The problems are especially challenging because solutions fly in the face of a century's tradition of the vending-machine model of government. Nevertheless, rocket scientists have developed a series of innovative tools to reinvent accountability. The approach can be frustrating because it does not present the straightforward prescription that authority offers. That lack of a prescription, in turn, often confounds elected officials, who either struggle to use authority to gain accountability—or move away from results for symbolic political turf on which they feel most comfortable. However, the cases in Chapter 6 show that success is possible through rocket science. In this chapter we have seen that it is possible to build an accountable governance system through aggregate accountability: reliance on tools that individually might prove lacking but that, together, offer a transparent window into governance and how it can better achieve results.

The Challenge of the Next Government

Accountability has always been a troublesome nut at the core of government power. After the Civil War, veterans roundly complained about the government's sluggishness in paying their pensions. Their fights with government bureaucrats often literally required cutting red tape—slicing the twill ribbons that tied up government documents (pieces of which, encased in plastic, the National Archives once sold as souvenirs). Rules and procedures accumulated over time, eventually making government ever more sluggish. In the first days of the government's response to Katrina, that sluggishness caused government to founder.

The problem flowed directly from a system that was built to seek accountability but, ironically, produced an unaccountable system and a failed policy. As we saw at the beginning of the book, accountability for Katrina was based on boundaries: empower government, but impose constraints that limit how government can exercise that power. The more our boundaries have fallen further out of sync with the problems we are trying to solve, the more policy problems have multiplied. By the 2000s, public satisfaction with government, in fact, had sunk to the level of airlines and cable television.[27] Struggling to fix the problem by insisting even more strongly on structure and process only made the problem worse. The more we have tried to force government in the postindustrial age to live by the standards created for another time, the more we have courted disaster.

Establishing the next government we need, however, poses enormous challenges. Few agencies have established doctrines like the Coast Guard's to define and shape such collaborative, results-based behavior. The domination of old-style accountability often drives out the quest for results. That outdated focus leaves many managers struggling on their own for practical solutions to the inescapable problems they face. Their pragmatism often produces remarkably similar strategies, but the managers frequently find themselves working alone. The situation is like an army moving through tall swamp grass, each soldier clearing an individual path through the weeds without realizing that a colleague is struggling just as hard, and just a few steps away, to move in the same direction. There are always both easy and hard ways to do important things. A system in which individual leaders have to carve their own paths is unquestionably the hard way.

In fact, a common refrain of results-driven rocket scientists is that their work is faith based. Many leaders I have talked to, from a vast array of different organizations with widely varying missions, have said the same thing: they struggle to achieve important results through complex partnerships; they adopt rocket science–style tactics and hope that their steps are in the right direction; but they find little reinforcement that their strategies are sound. Theorists have not yet developed a model for how high-performing organizations in the information age ought to work, and elected officials provide little support. For officials grounded in the vending-machine model, the tentative steps often feel like unnatural acts. Their pragmatic instincts tell them that the new blended model is likely the right course, but they often find very little support for their risks, except among their colleagues—and in the satisfaction of finding that the approach seems to work.

Perhaps most troubling of all, America's great political institutions—the executive, legislative, and judicial branches—all too often perversely conspire to undermine results-driven leadership and to promote the very forces that lead to continuing bureaucratic pathologies. FEMA failed in Katrina in part because Congress was looking backward at September 11, drawing the wrong lessons from the past and hamstringing the agency's ability to adapt to the future. Katrina blindsided executive branch officials, from President Bush on down, because they were so narrowly focused on the past that they failed to learn the lessons it was trying to teach. The reason FEMA failed its first big post-September 11 test was that the powerful forces in legislative and executive branch politics, rooted fundamentally in the Constitution, led the key players to focus on precisely the wrong set of problems. Compare that path through Katrina's daunting challenges with that of the Coast Guard. The Coasties looked at their failures in the *Exxon Valdez* disaster, sharpened their strategy and vision, and rose successfully to their next challenge—the distinctly non-*Valdez* crisis of September 11—and then built on the September 11 lessons to refashion the government's response in the Gulf.

The founders built a government of remarkable strength and vitality. They created a system that allowed conflict to bubble without fracturing the pot—a system that stretched and adapted, over more than two centuries, from thirteen ragtag colonies to the world's greatest superpower. As the nation's power has grown, pessimists have long predicted its downfall, but such pessimistic predictions need not be America's fate. America is a land of remarkable energy, vitality, and imagination. But the complexity of its policy strategies could cause the country to choke on its own ambitions by failing to build a government that can achieve them. As the future unfolds, it is clear that the country will need to move even faster, that its problems will be even more interconnected, and that the consequences for failing to deal nimbly with those problems will be ever more serious.

There lies the challenge for American government. It has many powerful and positive features, but nimbleness is not one of them. In fact, the founders deliberately created a government that was slow and sluggish because they did not want a government that could easily be swayed by what James Madison called "the mischiefs of faction" and the short-term swings of public opinion. Indeed, that worry is the foundation for the separation of powers—dividing government authority to prevent anyone from accumulating too much of it.

What, then, caused the problems that plagued Mildred and Katrina? One explanation is that they were the product of the perennial shifts in the pendulum balancing the political forces in American government. As the president and Congress, in particular, struggle over power, the performance of policy is sometimes a casualty. In this explanation, a new swing of the pendulum will transform political power. Another explanation is that there are historical cycles, and that the current cycle has created government interactions with civil society that challenge government's ability to perform. In this explanation, a new equilibrium of government, problems, and society will emerge and solve these issues. The third explanation is that the problems themselves have become more complex, as have the administrative strategies that we have used to try to solve them. In this explanation, the further that government institutions fall out of sync with the problems, the larger the problems will grow.

The first two explanations are fundamentally hopeful. They suggest that American government is undergoing one of its periodic readjustments that are never pretty to watch and always produce high tension and drama, but that tend over the long run to allow government to adapt. The last explanation frames a much bigger danger: the government is falling increasingly behind problems that will not go away, that demand solutions, and that, in the event of failure, impose punishing cost. It suggests that more of the same from government will produce more of the same in poor performance and, in fact, a broadening performance gap that will serve neither the interests of citizens nor the political needs of officials elected to govern them. The tales told in this book point to the third explanation—and to the very real costs that will surely come if we do not create a new government with the capacity to tackle these problems.

Alexander Hamilton foresaw some of these issues and argued powerfully for making the president stronger. Most other founders recoiled in horror at the idea, for the very reason that President George W. Bush's aggressive effort to enhance executive power met with fierce resistance on Capitol Hill and among many critics. An imperial executive is surely not the right answer to building a more nimble government. Indeed, the Bush administration proved remarkably clumsy, in both political and administrative terms, when Katrina struck. But Congress, with its instinct toward symbols, restructuring, and process, along with its aversion to addressing the consequences of its own actions, lies at the very core of the problem. The founders created Congress as the first branch of the new federal government, and Congress has singularly failed to rise to the challenges of leveraged government. Congress's institutional failure to rise to these challenges might further hasten the swing of power to the president, but neither Democratic nor Republican presidents have shown much taste for administrative issues or an instinct for finding effective leverage over these blended systems. That presidential lack of interest in governance issues haunted the Bush administration after Katrina, and the Katrina debacle did not seem to change the fundamental White House instincts afterward.

Coordination is essentially centralizing, since it implies a coordinator. Blended systems are essentially decentralizing, with power and action fragmenting across government agencies, levels of government, public and private sectors, and ultimately global boundaries as well. The rise of these blended systems is a reflection of the shift from the industrial to the information age, where information flows easily across boundaries (in ways that authority does not). The importance of boundary spanning, in turn, suggests a new approach for government—an approach that democratizes the process by spreading participation, privatizes government by relying more on nongovernment partners, governmentalizes the private sector by drawing its organizations more into strong public roles, and ultimately challenges the framework of American democratic institutions.

The pessimistic reading of this portrait is that of elected officials fiddling while the system slowly burns, with a preoccupation on short-term political wins driving out attention to what government does and how well it works. The optimistic reading is that the current American government is peculiarly well positioned to become the next American government: the fragmentation of political power can adjust itself to the pressures that the information age brings, and the fundamental pragmatism of the American people will force government to nurture rocket scientists (or at least look the other way as they develop their craft). The choice that American government takes will define not only its performance in the coming decades but, indeed, whether it will prosper—or go the way of those who have long predicted its downfall.

That is why we need the next government of the United States. Unless we take the steps to build the next government of the United Sates, we will be punished by a government whose results increasingly fall short of its performance. We will suffer the equivalent of pushing our government back to the 1950s when our rockets failed because we had not yet learned how to do rocket science. On the other hand, we have the experience of strong and effective leaders who, when faced with tough new problems, tore up the book and wrote a new one, with an approach focused squarely on making government work while holding it politically accountable. They recognized the traditional and important questions. Their genius, like the genius of the nation's founders and of the Progressives, was framing a new approach to governance. The great risk is that we will not build this government quickly enough, that big problems will continually buffet the system only to have the government fail to respond, that public disgust will weaken government institutions until they can no longer govern.

The great opportunity is that public officials can learn the lessons of Mildred. Here was a ninety-year-old woman presenting a constantly changing set of problems that required the most imaginative treatment her caregivers could manage. Had they simply resorted to standard procedures and pushed her into a preprogrammed pattern of care, her life would have proven miserable and certainly shorter. Instead, as agents of the government, even though they were not government employees themselves, they figured out how best to comfort her and enrich her life. They were rocket scientists who honed their craft by striving hard to make things work well. Their effort shines a beacon for the next government of the United States.

NOTES

Chapter 1. Mildred and Katrina

1. John L. Frisbee, "A Tale of Two Texans," *Air Force Magazine Online* 69 (March 1986), at www.afa.org/magazine/valor/0386valor.asp.

2. Claudia Williams, James Rosen, and Molly O'Malley, *Profiles of Nursing Home Residents on Medicaid* (Washington, DC: Kaiser Commission on Medicaid and the Uninsured, 2006), at www.kff.org/medicaid/upload/7510.pdf.

3. U.S. Government Accountability Office, *Nursing Homes: Federal Monitoring Surveys Demonstrate Continued Understatement of Serious Care Problems and CMS Oversight Weaknesses*, Report GAO-08-517 (May 2008), at http://www.gao.gov/new.items/d08517.pdf; General Accounting Office, *Nursing Homes: Quality of Care More Related to Staffing than Spending* (June 13, 2002), at www.gao.gov/new.items/d02431r.pdf.

4. Wan He, Manisha Sengupta, Victoria A. Velkoff, and Kimberly A. DeBarros, *65+ in the United States: 2005* (Washington, DC: US Census Bureau, 2005), at www.census.gov/prod/2006pubs/p23-209.pdf.

5. Jon Donley, "NOLA View: A Weblog," www.nola.com/weblogs/nola/index.ssf?/mtlogs/nola_nolaview/archives/2005_08.html#074694.

6. White House, "President Discusses Hurricane Relief in Address to the Nation" (September 15, 2005), at www.whitehouse.gov/news/releases/2005/09/20050915-8.html.

7. CBSNews.com, "On New Orleans, Not a Word from Bush" (January 24, 2007), at www.cbsnews.com/stories/2007/01/24/politics/main2393207.shtml.

8. Peirce Lewis, *New Orleans: The Making of an Urban Landscape*, 2nd edition (Santa Fe, NM: Center for American Places, 2003).

9. Greg Brouwer, "The Gathering Storm," *Civil Engineering Magazine* (June 2003), at www.pubs.asce.org/ceonline/ceonline03/0603feat.html.

10. *Frontline*, "The Storm" (November 24, 2005), at www.pbs.org/wgbh/pages/frontline/storm/etc/script.html.

11. Investigations included work by the National Academy of Sciences, *Third Report of the NAE/NRC Committee on New Orleans Regional Hurricane Protection Projects* (Washington, DC: National Academies Press, 2006), at http://newton.nap.edu/books/0309103568/html/1.html; the US Army Corps of Engineers, through its Interagency Performance Evaluation Task Force, *Performance Evaluation of the New Orleans and Southeast Louisiana Hurricane Protection System* (Washington, DC: USACE, 2006), at https://ipet.wes.army.mil; the American Society for Civil Engineers, *Hurricane Katrina: One Year Later—What Must We Must Do Next?* (Washington, DC: ASCE, 2006), at www.asce.org/files/pdf/Ch9_WhatMustWeDoNext.pdf; and Team Louisiana, *The Failure of the New Orleans Levee System during Hurricane Katrina* (2006), at www.publichealth.hurricane.lsu.edu/Adobe%20files%20for%20webpage/Team%20LA%20indiv/Team%20Louisiana%20-%20cov,%20toc,%20exec%20summ,%20intro.pdf.

12. US Army Corps of Engineers, *Performance Evaluation of the New Orleans and Southeast Louisiana Hurricane Protection System: Draft Final Report of the Interagency Performance Evaluation Task Force* (June 2006), I-3, at www.nytimes.com/packages/pdf/national/20060601_ARMYCORPS_SUMM.pdf.

13. National Research Council, Committee on New Orleans Regional Hurricane Protection Projects, *Structural Performance of the New Orleans Hurricane Protection System during Hurricane Katrina: Letter Report* (Washington, DC: National Academy of Sciences, 2006), 3, at www.nap.edu/catalog.php?record_id=11591.

14. MSNBC, "Nurse: 'It's Like Being in a Third World Country'" (August 31, 2005), at www.msnbc.msn.com/id/9139219.

15. CNN.com, "American Morning" (December 5, 2005), at http://transcript.cnn.com/TRANSCRIPTS/0512/05/ltm.02.html.

16. CNN.com, "'Can I Quit Now?' FEMA Chief Wrote as Katrina Raged" (November 4, 2005), at www.cnn.com/2005/US/11/03/brown.fema.emails.

17. White House, "President Arrives in Alabama, Briefed on Hurricane Katrina"(September 2, 2005), at www.whitehouse.gov/news/releases/2005/09/20050902-2 .html.

Chapter 2. Network Challenges

1. See Stephen Goldsmith and William Eggers, *Governing by Network: The New Shape of the Public Sector* (Washington, DC: Brookings Institution Press, 2004); Donald F. Kettl, *System under Stress: Homeland Security and American Politics*, 2nd ed. (Washington, DC: CQ Press, 2007); Robert Agranoff, *Managing within Networks: Adding Value to Public Organizations* (Washington, DC: Georgetown University Press, 2007); Philip J. Cooper, *Governing by Contract: Challenges and Opportunities for Public Managers* (Washington, DC: CQ Press, 2003); Lester M. Salamon, ed., *The Tools of Government: A Guide to the New Governance* (New York: Oxford University Press, 2002); H. Brinton Milward and Keith G. Provan, "Governing the Hollow State," *Journal of Public Administration Research and Theory* 10 (February 2000), 359–379; Laurence J. O'Toole Jr., "Treating Networks Seriously: Practical and Research-Based Agendas in Public Administration," *Public Administration Review* 57 (1997), 45–52.

2. See the special issue of *Public Administration Review* 66 (December 2006), 1–170.

3. Social Security Administration, *Annual Performance Plan for Fiscal Year 2008 and Revised Final Performance Plan for Fiscal Year 2007* (2007), at www.ssa.gov/ performance/2008/FY08PerfPlan_streamline.pdf.

4. Quoted by James Jay Carafano (Heritage Foundation), *Improving the National Response to Catastrophic Disaster: Statement before the Committee on Government Reform, House of Representatives* (September 15, 2005), at www.heritage.org/ Research/HomelandDefense/tst091505a.cfm.

5. Department of Homeland Security, Office of Inspector General, *A Performance Review of FEMA's Disaster Management Activities in Response to Hurricane Katrina* (March 2006), 29, at www.dhs.gov/xoig/assets/mgmtrpts/OIG_06 -32_Mar06.pdf.

6. Senate Committee on Homeland Security and Governmental Affairs, *Hurricane Katrina: A Nation Still Unprepared* (2006), 423, at http://hsgac.senate .gov/_files/Katrina/FullReport.pdf.

7. National Center for Health Statistics, *Health, United States, 2006* (Hyattsville, MD: NCHS, 2006), Table 27, at www.cdc.gov/nchs/data/hus/hus06 .pdf#027.

8. Social Security Online, "Historical Background and Development of Social Security," at www.ssa.gov/history/briefhistory3.html.

9. An excellent history of federal policy in this area is Henry B. Hogue and Keith Bea, *Federal Emergency Management and Homeland Security Organization: Historical Developments and Legislative Options* (Washington, DC: Congressional Research Service, 2006), at www.fas.org/sgp/crs/homesec/RL33369.pdf.

10. Ibid., 6.

11. White House, "President Bush Meets with Gulf Coast Grant Recipients" (March 1, 2007), at www.whitehouse.gov/news/releases/2007/03/20070301-6 .html.

12. Casino Gambling Web, "Beau Rivage Casino Reopening on Katrina Anniversary" (July 28, 2006), at www.casinogamblingweb.com/gambling-news/ casino-gambling/beau_rivage_casino_reopening_on_katrina_anniversary .html.

13. Dauphin Island Real Estate, at http://dauphinislandrealestate.com.

14. Gilbert M. Gaul, "Repeat Claims Strain Federal Flood Insurance," *Washington Post* (October 11, 2005), at www.washingtonpost.com/wp-dyn/content/ article/2005/10/10/AR2005101001465.html.

15. Valerie Bauerlein, "On Topsail Island, Storms Fuel Battle over Right to Build," *Wall Street Journal Online* (December 8, 2005), at www.realestatejournal.com/ buysell/regionalnews/20051208-bauerlein.html?refresh=on.

16. House Committee on Oversight and Government Reform, *More Dollars, Less Sense: Worsening Contracting Trends under the Bush Administration* (June 2007), at http://oversight.house.gov/features/moredollars.

17. Otto Kreisher, "Panel Questions Cost of Contractors in War Zone," *Government Executive* (March 12, 2008), at www.govexec.com/story_page .cfm?filepath=/dailyfed/0308/031208cdpm2.htm.

18. NASA, *Report of Columbia Accident Investigation Board* (2003), at www.nasa.gov/ columbia/home/CAIB_Vol1.html.

19. Government Accountability Office, *Defense Acquisitions: Role of Lead Systems Integrator on Future Combat Systems Program Poses Oversight Challenges*, GAO-07-380 (June 2007), 7, at www.gao.gov/new.items/d07380.pdf.

20. Ibid., "Highlights."

21. P. W. Singer, *Corporate Warriors: The Rise of the Privatized Military Industry* (Ithaca, NY: Cornell University Press, 2003).

22. Lester M. Salamon, "The New Governance and the Tools of Public Action: An Introduction," in *The Tools of Government*, ed. Lester M. Salamon (New York: Oxford University Press, 2002), 2.

23. E. S. Savas, *Privatization and Public-Private Partnerships* (New York: Chatham Publishers, 2000), 3. See also E. S. Savas, *Privatization in the City: Successes, Failures, Lessons* (Washington, DC: CQ Press, 2005).

24. Jody Freeman, "Extending Public Law Norms through Privatization," *Harvard Law Review* 116 (March 2003), 1338.

25. Statement of Stanley J. Czerwinski (Director, Strategic Issues) before the Subcommittee on Oversight, Committee on Ways and Means, House of Representatives: Government Accountability Office, *Nonprofit Sector: Increasing Numbers and Key Role in Delivering Federal Services*, GAO-07-1084T (July 24, 2007), at www.gao.gov/htext/d071084t.html.

26. For an exploration of the role of faith-based organizations, see John J. DiIulio, *Godly Republic: A Centrist Blueprint for America's Faith-Based Future* (Berkeley: University of California Press, 2007).

27. See Czerwinski, *Nonprofit Sector.*

28. See Paul Verkuil, *Outsourcing Sovereignty: Why Privatization of Government Functions Threatens Democracy and What We Can Do about It* (New York: Cambridge University Press, 2007).

29. Office of Management and Budget, memo to the heads of executive departments and establishments on the performance of commercial activities, Circular No. A-76 (Revised) (May 29, 2003), at www.whitehouse.gov/OMB/circulars/a076/a76_rev2003.pdf.

30. David M. Walker, Testimony before the Subcommittee on Readiness, Committee on Armed Services, House of Representatives: Government Accountability Office, *Defense Management: DOD Needs to Reexamine Its Extensive Reliance on Contractors and Continue to Improve Management and Oversight*, GAO-08-572T (March 11, 2008), at www.gao.gov/new.items/d08572t.pdf.

31. Stephen Goldsmith, "What's Left for Government to Do?" *The American* (January/February 2008), at www.american.com/archive/2008/january-february-magazine-contents/what2019s-left-for-government-to-do.

32. Government Accountability Office, *Defense Contracting: Army Case Study Delineates Concerns with Use of Contractors as Contract Specialists*, GAO-08-360 (March 2008), at www.gao.gov/new.items/d08360.pdf.

33. Pew Research Center for the People and the Press, *Trends in Political Values and Core Attitudes: 1987–2007* (Washington, DC: Pew Research Center, 2007), 45, at http://people-press.org/reports/pdf/312.pdf.

34. House Select Bipartisan Committee to Investigate Preparation for and Response to Hurricane Katrina, *Deposition—FEMA Director Michael Brown* (February 11, 2006), at http://katrina.house.gov/brown.depo.doc.

35. Senate Committee on Homeland Security and Governmental Affairs, *Hurricane Katrina*, 136.

36. Kevin Merida and Michael A. Fletcher, "For the Poor, Sudden Celebrity," *Washington Post* (September 22, 2005), at www.washingtonpost.com/wp-dyn/content/article/2005/09/21/AR2005092102396_pf.html.

37. "Great Aviation Quotes," at www.skygod.com/quotes/cliches.html.

38. This notion echoes the plaintive subtitle in the classic, Jeffrey L. Pressman and Aaron Wildavsky, *Implementation: How Great Expectations in Washington Are Dashed in Oakland; Or, Why It's Amazing That Federal Programs Work at All* (Berkeley: University of California Press, 1973).

39. Robert D. Putman, *Bowling Alone: The Collapse and Revival of American Community* (New York: Simon & Schuster, 2000).

40. Theda Skocpol, "Unraveling from Above," *American Prospect* (March–April 1996), 20–25.

41. Hugh T. Miller, *Postmodern Public Policy* (Albany: State University of New York Press, 2002), vii.

42. Jody Freeman, "Extending Public Law Norms through Privatization," *Harvard Law Review* 116 (March 2003), 1285.

43. "Transcript of President Reagan's News Conference," *New York Times* (August 13, 1986).

Chapter 3. Irresponsible Government

1. Spencer Hsu, "Findings on Katrina Trailers Went Undisclosed, Maker Says," *Washington Post* (July 10, 2008), at http://www.washingtonpost.com/wp-dyn/content/article/2008/07/08/AR2008070802315.html.

2. *Prepared Testimony of Lindsay Huckabee, Government Reform and Oversight Committee, U.S. House of Representatives* (July 19, 2007), at http://oversight.house.gov/documents/20070719104250.pdf.

3. House Committee on Oversight and Government Reform, memorandum from the majority staff to members of the committee (July 19, 2007), at http://oversight.house.gov/documents/20070719111406.pdf.

4. House Committee on Oversight and Government Reform, *Committee Probes FEMA's Response to Reports of Toxic Trailers: Chairman Waxman's Opening Statement* (July 19, 2007), at http://oversight.house.gov/story.asp?ID=1419.

5. The findings that follow in the text came from the Department of Homeland Security's own investigators. See *Statement of Richard L. Skinner, Inspector General, U.S. Department of Homeland Security, before the Committee on Homeland*

Security and Governmental Affairs, United States Senate, Hope, Arkansas (April 21, 2006), at www.dhs.gov/xoig/assets/katovrsght/OIGtm_RLS_Katrina_042106 .pdf.

6. Ibid.

7. CNN.com, "FEMA to Move People Out of Trailers with Toxic Threat" (February 14, 2008), at www.cnn.com/2008/HEALTH/conditions/02/14/ fema.trailers.ap/index.html. See CDC's report, "Preliminary Findings on Air Quality in FEMA-supplied Mobile Homes and Trailers" (2008), at www.cdc .gov/Features/FEMAtrailersFindings.

8. "CDC Urges Hurricane Victims Be Moved Out of Trailers with Too Much Formaldehyde," *USA Today* (February 15, 2008), at http://blogs.usatoday.com/ ondeadline/2008/02/cdc-urges-hurri.html.

9. "FEMA's Formaldehyde Foul-up," *New York Times* (February 15, 2008), at www.nytimes.com/2008/02/15/opinion/15fri2.html?_r=1&hp&oref=slogin.

10. Doug Leduc, "FEMA Trailer Sales Worry RV Dealers," *Greater Fort Wayne Business Weekly* (March 23, 2007), at www.kpcnews.com/articles/2007/03/24/ greater_fort_wayne/news/doc4602c4627c73e488227422.txt.

11. See Anna Worden, "Trailer Turnaround," *Philadelphia Inquirer* (January 17, 2008); and Robert Brodsky, "Overcoming Katrina," *Government Executive* (May 15, 2007), at http://govexec.com/features/0507-15/0507-15s4.htm.

12. Government Accountability Office, *Hurricanes Katrina and Rita Disaster Relief: Improper and Potentially Fraudulent Individual Assistance Payments Estimated to Be between $600 Million and $1.4 Billion*, GAO-06-844T (June 14, 2006), esp. p. 7, at www.gao.gov/new.items/d06844t.pdf.

13. *Statement of Richard L. Skinner*, 3.

14. Thomas E. Mann and Norman J. Ornstein, *The Broken Branch: How Congress Is Failing America and How to Get It Back on Track* (New York: Oxford University Press, 2006), 13, 242.

15. Senate Committee on Homeland Security and Governmental Affairs, *Statement of Joseph I. Lieberman, Senate Committee on Governmental Affairs, "The Nomination of the Honorable Tom Ridge to Be Secretary of Homeland Security"* (January 17, 2003), at http://hsgac.senate.gov/public/index.cfm?Fuseaction =Hearings.Testimony&TestimonyID=c117b7a2-a1c2-4883-9d57-f462e6 bea80d&HearingID=7d6dd2fb-6138-4376-bcf7-5570d6fac564.

16. Larry M. Wortzel, *Creating an Intelligent Department of Homeland Security*, Executive Memorandum No. 828 (Washington, DC: Heritage Foundation, 2002), at www.heritage.org/Research/HomelandSecurity/EM828.cfm.

17. National Commission on Terrorist Attacks upon the United States, *The 9/11*

Commission Report (New York: Norton, 2004), 408. Also at www.9-11commis sion.gov/report/911Report.pdf.

18. William Shakespeare, *Julius Caesar*, act 1, scene 2.

19. Author's interview with anonymous public official, November 19, 2007.

20. Joe Lieberman, "Lieberman Supports Creation of National Homeland Security Agency" (September 21, 2001), at http://lieberman.senate.gov/newsroom/ release.cfm?id=208263.

21. Arlen Specter, quoted in Joe Lieberman, "Homeland Security Reorganization Proposed" (May 2, 2002), at http://lieberman.senate.gov/newsroom/release .cfm?id=207958.

22. White House, "President Bush Signs Homeland Security Act" (November 25, 2002), at www.whitehouse.gov/news/releases/2002/11/20021125-6.html.

23. White House, "Press Secretary's Morning Conversation with Reporters" (June 6, 2002), at www.whitehouse.gov/news/releases/2002/06/20020606-1 .html.

24. Michael Scardaville, *The New Congress Must Reform Its Committee Structure to Meet Homeland Security Needs* (Washington, DC: Heritage Foundation, November 12, 2002), at www.heritage.org/Research/HomelandSecurity/ bg1612.cfm#pgfId=1015242.

25. Chris Strohm, "Chertoff Sees Too Many Congressional Hearings, Demands," *Government Executive* (September 5, 2007), at www.govexec.com/story_page .cfm?articleid=37935&dcn=e_gvet.

26. Norman J. Ornstein and Thomas E. Mann, "When Congress Checks Out," *Foreign Affairs* (November/December 2006), at www.foreignaffairs.org/ 20061101faessay85607/norman-j-ornstein-thomas-e-mann/when-congress -checks-out.html?mode=print.

27. John Diamond and Kathy Kiely, "Administration, Agencies Failed to Connect the Dots," *USA Today* (May 17, 2002), at www.usatoday.com/news/washington/ 2002/05/17/failure-usatcov.htm.

28. Keith Bea and Henry Hogue, *FEMA Reorganization Legislation in the 109th Congress*, RL33522 (Washington, DC: Congressional Research Service, 2006).

29. Craig W. Thomas, "Reorganizing Public Organizations: Alternatives, Objectives, and Evidence," *Journal of Public Administration and Theory* 3 (1993), 457–486.

30. Quoted in the editorial "The Next Federal Department," *New York Times* (July 13, 1988).

31. Department of Homeland Security, Office of Inspector General, *A Performance Review of FEMA's Disaster Management Activities in Response to Hurricane Katrina*, OIG-06-32 (March 2006), 109, at www.dhs.gov/xoig/assets/mgmtrpts/OIG_06-32_Mar06.pdf.

32. David R. Mayhew, *Congress: The Electoral Connection*, 2nd ed. (New Haven, CT: Yale University Press, 2004).

33. Theodore J. Lowi, "Toward a Legislature of the First Kind," in *Knowledge, Power, and the Congress*, eds. William H. Robinson and Clay H. Wellborn (Washington, DC: Congressional Quarterly, 1991), 10.

34. "Quotation of the Day," *New York Times* (March 3, 1985).

35. Horst W. J. Rittel, *Dilemmas in a General Theory of Planning* (Berkeley: Institute of Urban and Regional Development, University of California, 1973).

Chapter 4. Routines and Remedies

1. Social Security Administration, "Fact Sheet: Direct Deposit," at www.ssa.gov/pressoffice/direct-deposit-fct.htm.

2. San Diego Environmental Services Department, "Using Technology to Reorganize Trash Collection Routes," at www.icma.org/upload/library/2006-06/%7B99D5BCEB-C900-47C0-8642-822C75BBCF7B%7D.pdf.

3. Martha Derthick, *Agency under Stress: The Social Security Administration in American Government* (Washington, DC: Brookings Institution, 1990), 5.

4. Ibid., 4.

5. Bureau of Justice Statistics, "Felony Sentences in State Courts, 2000," at www.ojp.usdoj.gov/bjs/pub/ascii/fssc00.txt; Bureau of Justice Statistics, "Homicide Trends in the U.S.," at www.ojp.usdoj.gov/bjs/homicide/cleared.htm.

6. Senate Committee on Homeland Security and Governmental Affairs, "Response of the Department of Homeland Security to Hurricane Katrina" (February 15, 2006). There are variants on the name *Keystone Cops*, including *Keystone Kops*. Many scholars insist that the original form was *Keystone Cops*.

7. The quotes and conclusions come from a consultant's report prepared at the request of Governor Ed Rendell following the storm: James Lee Witt Associates, "Independent Report on the Mid-February 2007 Winter Storm Response for the Commonwealth of Pennsylvania" (March 27, 2007), 16, at www.state.pa.us/papower/lib/papower/pa_report_final.pdf.

8. 6ABC.com, "I-78 Expected to Reopen" (February 17, 2007), at http://abclocal.go.com/wpvi/story?section=local&id=5039790.

9. Witt, "Independent Report," 25, 26.

10. Ibid., 4.

11. Ibid., 32.

12. National Academy of Public Administration, *Taking Environmental Protection to the Next Level: An Assessment of the U.S. Environmental Services Delivery System* (Washington, DC: NAPA, 2007), xi, xiii, at www.napawash.org/pc_management_studies/EPA_Summary_Report_5-17-07.pdf.

13. See Laurence E. Lynn Jr., Carolyn J. Heinrich, and Carolyn J. Hill, "Studying Governance and Public Management: Challenges and Prospects," *Journal of Public Administration Research and Theory* 10 (April 2000), 233–261; and Laurence E. Lynn Jr., Carolyn J. Heinrich, and Carolyn J. Hill, *Improving Governance: A New Logic for Empirical Research* (Washington, DC: Georgetown University Press, 2001).

14. See, for example, Brian J. Cook, *Democracy and Administration: Woodrow Wilson's Ideas and the Challenges of Public Management* (Baltimore, MD: Johns Hopkins University, 2007), 125–128. For the administrative-law point of view, see Jody Freeman, "The Private Role in Public Governance," *New York University Law Review*, 75 (June 2000), 543–675.

15. For a thoughtful look at the ideas behind this revolution, see Robert Kanigel, *The One Best Way: Frederick Winslow Taylor and the Enigma of Efficiency* (New York: Viking, 1997).

16. Woodrow Wilson, "The Study of Administration," *Political Science Quarterly* 2 (June 1887), 220.

17. For analysis of the development of these ideas, see Laurence J. O'Toole Jr., "Doctrines and Developments: Separation of Powers, the Politics–Administration Dichotomy, and the Rise of the Administrative State," *Public Administration Review* 47 (1987), 17–25.

18. Frederick C. Mosher, "The Changing Responsibilities and Tactics of the Federal Government," *Public Administration Review* 40 (1980), 541–548; Lester M. Salamon, "Rethinking Public Management: Third-Party Government and the Changing Forms of Government Action," *Public Policy* 29 (1981), 255–275; Donald F. Kettl, *Government by Proxy: (Mis?)Managing Federal Programs* (Washington, DC: Congressional Quarterly Press, 1988); and Paul C. Light, *The True Size of Government* (Washington, DC: Brookings Institution Press, 1999).

19. Ronald A. Heifetz and Marty Linsky, *Leadership on the Line: Staying Alive through the Dangers of Leading* (Boston: Harvard Business School Press, 2002), 14.

20. Marian Burros, "*E. coli* Fears Inspire a Call for Oversight," *New York Times* (December 9, 2006).

21. See World Health Organization, "Update 95—SARS: Chronology of a Serial Killer," at www.who.int/csr/don/2003_07_04/en.

22. Health Canada, *Learning from SARS: Renewal of Public Health in Canada*, Report of the National Advisory Committee on SARS and Public Health (Ottawa: Health Canada, 2003), at www.phac-aspc.gc.ca/publicat/sars-sras/pdf/sars-e.pdf.

23. Ibid., 97, 99.

24. Centers for Disease Control and Prevention, "Basic Information about SARS" (May 3, 2005), at www.cdc.gov/ncidod/sars/factsheet.htm.

25. Mark H. Moore, *Creating Public Value: Strategic Management in Government* (Cambridge, MA: Harvard University Press, 1995).

26. Paul Rioux, "Evacuation Was 'Individual Responsibility,' Blanco Testifies," *Times-Picayune* (New Orleans; August 29, 2007), at www.nola.com/timespic/stories/index.ssf?/base/news-5/1188368563232970.xml&coll=1.

27. Mary Beth Sheridan, "Area Disaster Planning Gets More Muscle," *Washington Post* (September 7, 2007).

28. David Leonhardt, "Technology Eases the Road to Higher Tolls," *New York Times* (July 4, 2007), at www.nytimes.com/2007/07/04/business/04leonhardt.html?_r=1&ref=business&oref=slogin.

Chapter 5. Tectonic Nation

1. "The War against America: An Unfathomable Attack," *New York Times* (September 12, 2001).

2. Indira A. R. Lakshmanan, "Attack on America/Nations Respond," *Boston Globe* (September 12, 2001).

3. In public policy, the best discussion of "punctuated equilibrium" is provided by Frank R. Baumgartner and Bryan D. Jones, *Agendas and Instability in American Politics* (Chicago: University of Chicago Press, 1993). The original concept comes from Stephen Jay Gould's work in paleobiology, especially Niles Eldredge and Stephen Jay Gould, "Punctuated Equilibria: An Alternative to Phyletic Gradualism," in *Models in Paleobiology*, ed. Thomas J. M. Schopf (San Francisco: Freeman, Cooper, 1972), 82–115.

4. The classic statement is Charles E. Lindblom, "The Science of 'Muddling Through,'" *Public Administration Review* 19 (Spring 1959), 79–88.

5. For example, see John Rouse and George E. Berkeley, *The Craft of Public Administration*, 8th ed. (Boston: McGraw-Hill, 2000).

6. James W. Fesler, *Area and Administration* (University: University of Alabama Press, 1949), 152.

7. Paul C. Light, "The Tides of Reinvention," *Government Executive* (January 1997), at www.govexec.com/features/0197s3.htm.

8. David Osborne and Ted Gaebler, *Reinventing Government* (Reading, MA: Addison-Wesley, 1992), 11–12.

9. Fesler, *Area and Administration*, 152.

10. See, for example, Richard Brookhiser, *Alexander Hamilton: American* (New York: Free Press, 1999), ch. 4.

11. Joseph J. Ellis, *Founding Brothers: The Revolutionary Generation* (New York: Alfred A. Knopf, 2001).

12. See Brian J. Cook, *Democracy and Administration: Woodrow Wilson's Ideas and the Challenges of Public Management* (Baltimore, MD: Johns Hopkins University Press, 2007).

13. Theodore J. Lowi, *The End of Liberalism: Ideology, Policy, and the Crisis of Public Authority* (New York: Norton, 1969).

14. Dave Boyer, "Philly International: Vacation Destination," *Philadelphia Inquirer* (August 15, 2007), at www.philly.com/inquirer/opinion/20070815_Philly_International__Vacation_destination.html.

15. Stephen Barr, "Contingency Planning, for Technology and Terrorism," *Washington Post* (August 16, 2007), at www.washingtonpost.com/wp-dyn/content/article/2007/08/15/AR2007081502282.html.

16. US Department of Transportation, *National Strategy to Reduce Congestion on America's Transportation Network* (May 2006), introduction, at www.joc.com/Whitepapers/DOT_Congestion_Plan051606.pdf.

17. *Statement of the Honorable Jeffrey N. Shane, Under Secretary for Policy, U.S. Department of Transportation, before the Subcommittee on Highways and Transit Committee on Transportation and Infrastructure, U.S. House of Representatives* (June 7, 2007), at http://republicans.transportation.house.gov/Media/File/Testimony/Highways/6-7-07-Shane.pdf.

18. See Donald F. Kettl, *Sharing Power: Public Governance and Private Markets* (Washington, DC: Brookings Institution, 1993).

19. Donna Kutt Nahas, "Higher Ground for Freeport's Nautical Mile," *New York Times* (September 27, 1988), at http://query.nytimes.com/gst/fullpage.html?res=9904EED71F30F934A1575AC0A96E958260.

20. James L. Witt, "Forward," *National Mitigation Strategy: Partnerships for Building Safer Communities* (Washington, DC: FEMA Mitigation Directorate, 1995), i, quoted in Multihazard Mitigation Council, *Natural Hazard Mitigation Saves: An Independent Study to Assess the Future Savings from Mitigation Activities*, vol. 2 (Washington, DC: National Academy of Sciences, 2005), 305.

21. Multihazard Mitigation Council, *Natural Hazard Mitigation Saves*, 320.

22. Kit Batten, Jane Bullock, Benjamin Goldstein, George Haddow, Bracken Hendricks, Kari Manlove, and Daniel J. Weiss, *Forecast: Storm Warnings—Preparing for More Severe Hurricanes Due to Global Warming* (Washington, DC: Center for American Progress, 2007), 21.

23. William L. Waugh Jr., *Leveraging Networks to Meet National Goals: FEMA and the Safe Construction Networks* (Washington, DC: PriceWaterhouse-Coopers Endowment for the Business of Government, 2002), 35–36, at www.businessofgovernment.org/pdfs/WaughReport.pdf.

24. Thomas L. Friedman, *The World Is Flat: A Brief History of the Twenty-First Century* (New York: Farrar, Straus and Giroux, 2005).

25. CNN.com, "Pet Owners Join Class-Action Suit over Tainted Food" (March 23, 2007), at www.cnn.com/2007/US/03/22/pet.food.recall/index.html?iref=newssearch.

26. Food and Drug Administration, "FDA Update and Synopsis on the Pet Food Outbreak" (April 5, 2007), at www.fda.gov/oc/opacom/hottopics/petfood_update.html.

27. Association of American Feed Control Officials, "How Pet Food Is Regulated," at www.aafco.org/Portals/0/Public/petfood_regulations.pdf.

28. Joseph Kahn, "China Quick to Execute Drug Official," *New York Times* (July 11, 2007), at www.nytimes.com/2007/07/11/business/worldbusiness/11execute.html?ei=5070&en=216a00380fd639e4&ex=1187841600&pagewanted=all.

29. "Former Head of China's Drug Watchdog Executed," *China View* (July 10, 2007), at http://news.xinhuanet.com/english/2007-07/10/content_6353536.htm.

30. FOXNews.com, "Toxic Recalls Complicate 'Toys for Tots' Drives This Season" (December 18, 2007), at www.foxnews.com/story/0,2933,317351,00.html.

31. Louise Story, "Indictments in Pet Food Poisoning," *New York Times* (February 7, 2008).

32. Dick Durbin, "Durbin Says Pet Food Points to Larger Problem" (April 13, 2007), at http://durbin.senate.gov/record.cfm?id=280932.

33. Government Accountability Office, *High-Risk Series: An Update*, GAO-07-310 (Washington, DC: GAO, 2007), "Highlights," at www.gao.gov/new.items/ d07310.pdf.

34. Walt Bogdanich, "The Drug Scare That Exposed a World of Hurt," *New York Times* (March 30, 2008), www.nytimes.com/2008/03/30/weekinreview/ 30bogdanich.html?_r=1&ref=weekinreview&oref=slogin.

35. For an examination of these issues, see Alyssa Rosenberg, "Features: Stand & Deliver," *Government Executive* (April 1, 2008), at www.govexec.com/features/ 0408-01/0408-01s3.htm.

36. Paul C. Light has charted the periodic nature of government reforms in *The Tides of Reform: Making Government Work, 1945–1995* (New Haven: Yale University Press, 1997).

37. The President's Committee on Administrative Management, *Report of the Committee*, 74th Cong., 2d sess. (Washington, DC: U.S. Government Printing Office, 1937).

38. Commission on Organization of the Executive Branch of the Government [Hoover Commission], Report (New York: McGraw-Hill, 1949). Records of the commission (1947–49) are available at http://www.archives.gov/research/ guide-fed-records/groups/264.html. A second commission followed in 1955.

39. David Halberstam, *The Best and the Brightest* (New York: Random House, 1992, 20th anniversary edition).

40. Bureau of the Budget, Bulletin No. 68–69 (April 12, 1968). The approach originally was developed by Peter F. Drucker in *The Practice of Management* (New York: Harper and Row, 1954).

41. Nixon introduced MBO through two memos from the Office of Management and Budget to federal agencies on April 18 and 19, 1970. For a history, see Chester A. Newland, "Policy/Program Objectives and Federal Management: The Search for Government Effectiveness," *Public Administration Review* (January/February 1976), pp. 20–27.

42. Peter A. Pyrrh introduced the system at Texas Instruments and helped Carter install it in Georgia. See his *Zero-Base Budgeting: A Practical Tool for Evaluating Expenses* (New York: Wiley, 1973).

43. President's Private Sector Survey on Cost Control (Grace Commission), *A Report to the President* (Washington, DC: Government Printing Office, 1984).

44. For an analysis of the impact of the reinventing government movement, see Donald F. Kettl, *Reinventing Government: A Fifth-Year Report Card* (Washington, DC: Brookings Institution, 1998).

45. Statement of Bernice Steinhardt, U.S. Government Accountability Office, *Government Performance: Lessons Learned for the Next Administration on Using Performance Information to Improve Results*, Report GAO-08-1026T (July 24, 2008).

Chapter 6. Rocket Science

1. Lester M. Salamon, ed., *The Tools of Government: A Public Management Handbook for the Era of Third-Party Government* (New York: Oxford University Press, 2002).

2. Tim Read and Nick Tilley, *Not Rocket Science? Problem-Solving and Crime Reduction* (London: Home Office, 2000), 35, at www.homeoffice.gov.uk/rds/prgpdfs/crrs06.pdf.

3. NASA Public Affairs, *The Kennedy Space Center Story* (Kennedy Space Center, FL: NASA, 1991), at www.nasa.gov/centers/kennedy/about/history/story/ch1.html.

4. For a NASA-sponsored history of the Johnson Space Center, see Henry C. Dethloff, *Suddenly Tomorrow Came . . . : A History of the Johnson Space Center* (Washington, DC: NASA, 1993), at www.jsc.nasa.gov/history/suddenly_tomorrow/suddenly.htm.

5. NASA, "The Space Shuttle Launch Team," at http://science.ksc.nasa.gov/shuttle/countdown/launch-team.html.

6. CNN.com, "Coast Guard Admiral to Lead Relief Effort" (September 9, 2005), at www.cnn.com/2005/US/09/09/katrina.impact/index.html.

7. This account comes from the Coast Guard's description of Allen's activities, in "Katrina: The Gulf Response," *Coast Guard* Special Edition 2005, at www.uscg.mil/hq/g-cp/cb/PDFs/Katrina_2005.pdf.

8. A. H. Maslow, "A Theory of Human Motivation," *Psychological Review* 50 (1943), 370–396.

9. For an account of the disaster, see Robert C. North [US Coast Guard], "Assistant Commandant's Perspective," at www.uscg.mil/hq/g-m/insert.pdf; and "The Alaskan Oil Spill: Lessons in Crisis Management," *Management Review* 79, no. 4 (April 1990), 12–21.

10. "Alaskan Oil Spill," 20.

11. Samuel K. Skinner and William K. Reilly, *The Exxon Valdez Oil Spill: A Report to the President (Executive Summary)* (Environmental Protection Agency, National Response Team, May 1989), at www.epa.gov/history/topics/valdez/04.htm.

12. See Matthew Weinstock, "The 2002 Service to America Medals Hero of September 11th Medal Standing Tall," *Government Executive* (December 1, 2002), at www.govexec.com/features/1202/1202samS4.htm; and Service to America Medals, "2002 Homeland Security Medal Recipient," at http://servicetoamericamedals.org/SAM/recipients/profiles/hsm02_concepcion.shtml.

13. James Kitfield. "New Coast Guard Chief Discusses Lessons Learned from Katrina," *Government Executive* (June 2, 2006), at www.govexec.com/dailyfed/0606/060206nj2.htm.

14. For an important analysis of these issues, see Anne M. Khademian, *Working with Culture: How the Job Gets Done in Public Programs* (Washington, DC: CQ Press, 2002).

15. Government Accountability Office, *Coast Guard: Observations on the Preparation, Response, and Recovery Missions Related to Hurricane Katrina*, GAO-06-903 (July 2006), at www.gao.gov/new.items/d06903.pdf.

16. *U.S. Coast Guard: America's Maritime Guardian* (Washington, DC: US Coast Guard, 2002), at www.uscg.mil/top/about/doc/uscg_pub1_complete.pdf.

17. Ibid., 50.

18. GAO, *Coast Guard*, 11.

19. Unless otherwise cited, material on this case comes from the author's interview with LeAnn Jenkins, Executive Director, Federal Executive Board, Oklahoma City, on January 9, 2008; and Oklahoma Department of Civil Emergency Management, *After Action Report, Alfred P. Murrah Federal Building Bombing, 19 April 1995 in Oklahoma City, Oklahoma*, at www.ok.gov/OEM/documents/Bombing%20After%20Action%20Report.pdf.

20. For a searching and gripping analysis, see *Arlington County After-Action Report on the Response to the September 11 Terrorist Attack on the Pentagon*, at www.arlingtonva.us/departments/Fire/edu/about/docs/after_report.pdf.

21. Ibid., 11.

22. For an account of these efforts, see Greg Jaffe, "Midlevel Officers Show Enterprise, Helping Reduce U.S. Violence in Iraq," *Wall Street Journal* (December 29–30, 2007).

23. Captain Patriquin's presentation can be found at http://abcnews.go.com/images/US/how_to_win_in_anbar_v4.pdf.

24. *The Iraq Study Group Report* (2006), at www.usip.org/isg/iraq_study_group_report/report/1206/iraq_study_group_report.pdf.

25. Association of the United States Army, "Remarks as Delivered by Secretary of

Defense Robert M. Gates, Washington, DC, Wednesday, October 10, 2007," *Small Wars Journal* (October 11, 2007), at http://smallwarsjournal.com/ blog/2007/10/secretary-of-defense-robert-m.

26. Jaffe, "Midlevel Officers Show Enterprise."

27. Unless otherwise cited, material on this case comes from the author's interview with Ramsey Green on January 28, 2008.

28. For background, see "Robert T. Stafford Disaster Relief and Emergency Assistance Act (Public Law 93-288) As Amended," on FEMA's Web site, at www .fema.gov/about/stafact.shtm.

29. Sarah Carr, "Schools, FEMA Keeping It Simple," *Times-Picayune* (New Orleans; December 6, 2007), at http://blog.nola.com/times-picayune/2007/12/ schools_fema_keeping_it_simple.html.

Chapter 7. The Political Future

1. Jeffrey L. Pressman and Aaron B. Wildavsky, *Implementation: How Great Expectations in Washington Are Dashed in Oakland; or, Why It's Amazing That Federal Programs Work At All, This Being a Saga of the Economic Development Administration As Told by Two Sympathetic Observers Who Seek to Build Morals on a Foundation of Ruined Hopes* (Berkeley: University of California Press, 1973), esp. ch. 5. Pressman and Wildavsky cite their debt to an earlier work on implementation by Martha Derthick: *New Towns In-Town: Why a Federal Program Failed* (Washington, DC: Urban Institute, 1972), which makes much the same point.

2. Jody Freeman, "Extending Public Law Norms through Privatization," *Harvard Law Review* 116 (March 2003), 1339.

3. Ibid., 1289.

4. Adrienne Héritier and Dirk Lehmkuhl, "The Shadow of Hierarchy and New Modes of Governance," *Journal of Public Policy* 28 (2008), 13.

5. See, for example, Peter Hupe and Michael Hill, "Street-Level Bureaucracy and Public Accountability," *Public Administration* 82 (2007), 279–299.

6. Siobhan Gorman, "CIA Likely Let Contractors Perform Waterboarding," *Wall Street Journal* (February 8, 2008).

7. Paul R. Verkuil, *Outsourcing Sovereignty: Why Privatization of Government Functions Threatens Democracy and What We Can Do about It* (New York: Cambridge University Press, 2007).

8. One of the most thoughtful analyses of these issues is Laurence E. Lynn Jr., *Public Management: Old and New* (New York: Routledge, 2006).

9. Ibid., 180.

10. Jody Freeman, "The Private Role in Public Governance," *New York University Law Review* 75 (June 2000), 672.

11. Ibid., 664.

12. For an analysis of these issues, see Christopher Pollitt, Sandra van Thiel, and Vincent Homburg, eds., *New Public Management in Europe: Adaptation and Alternatives* (New York: Palgrave Macmillan, 2007); and Donald F. Kettl, *The Global Public Management Revolution*, 2nd ed. (Washington, DC: Brookings Institution Press, 2005).

13. For an exploration of these balance-of-power issues, see Thomas E. Mann and Norman J. Ornstein, *The Broken Branch: How Congress Is Failing America and How to Get It Back on Track* (New York: Oxford University Press, 2006).

14. Association of Government Accountants, *Public Attitudes toward Government Accountability and Transparency 2008* (Washington, DC: AGA, 2008), at www .agacgfm.org/harrispoll2008.aspx.

15. Cory Fleming and Bryan Barnhouse, *San Antonio Customer Service/311* (Washington, DC: ICMA, 2006), at http://icma.org/upload/bc/attach/%7B36945528 -1037-4B28-B9FC-3625FB4164C6%7D311%20San%20Antonio%20 Case%20Study.pdf.

16. See https://baltimore.customerservicerequest.org/web_intake_balt/Controller.

17. Robert D. Behn, *What All Mayors Would Like to Know about Baltimore's CitiStat Performance Strategy* (Washington, DC: IBM Center for the Business of Government, 2007), at www.businessofgovernment.org/pdfs/BehnReportCiti .pdf.

18. For an exploration of these issues, see Christopher Hood, Oliver James, B. Guy Peters, and Colin Scott, eds., *Controlling Modern Government: Variety, Commonality, and Change* (Cheltenham, UK: Edward Elgar, 2004).

19. For an exploration of the variety of control mechanisms for government tools, see Lester M. Salamon, ed., *The Tools of Government* (New York: Oxford University Press, 2002); and Freeman, "Private Role in Public Governance," 642.

20. American Health Care Association, "Statement of Bruce Yarwood, President and CEO, American Health Care Association, for the U.S. House Ways & Means Subcommittee, 'Hearing on Trends in Nursing Home Ownership and Quality'" (November 15, 2007), at http://waysandmeans.house.gov/media/ pdf/110/ahca.pdf.

21. John W. Miller, "Private Food Standards Gain Favor," *Wall Street Journal* (March 11, 2008).

22. See Edward P. Weber, *Pluralism by the Rules: Conflict and Cooperation in Environmental Regulation* (Washington, DC: Georgetown University Press, 1998).

23. See the EPA's description of the effort: "Acid Rain Program SO2 Allowances Fact Sheet," at www.epa.gov/airmarkets/trading/factsheet.html. See also Bernd Hansjurgens, *Emissions Trading for Climate Policy: US and European Perspectives* (New York: Cambridge University Press, 2005).

24. Howard Kunreuther, *The Role of Insurance in Managing Extreme Events: Implications for Terrorism Coverage* (Philadelphia: Financial Institutions Center, University of Pennsylvania, 2007), at http://knowledge.wharton.upenn.edu/papers/1146.pdf.

25. See Department of Health & Human Services, "Hospital Compare," at www.hospitalcompare.hhs.gov; and CalHospitalCompare.org, "Rating Hospital Quality in California," at www.calhospitalcompare.org.

26. Author's interview with anonymous OMB official, February 11, 2008.

27. American Consumer Satisfaction Index, "Citizen Satisfaction with Federal Government Lags Private Sector, e-Gov Still a Bright Spot in Federal Services According to ACSI" (Ann Arbor, MI: ACSI, 2007), at www.theacsi.org/images/stories/images/news/1207Gov.pdf.

Appendix. An Action Plan for the Next Government of the United States

1. For an exploration of the process of transforming government agencies, see James E. Kee and Kathryn Newcomer, *Transforming Public and Nonprofit Organizations: Stewardship for Leading Change* (Vienna, VA: Management Concepts, 2008).

2. For an analysis of these systems, see Robert D. Behn, *What All Mayors Would Like to Know About Baltimore's CitiStat Performance Strategy* (Washington, DC: IBM Center for the Business of Government, 2007), at www.businessofgovernment.org/pdfs/BehnReportCiti.pdf.

3. See Governor Martin O'Malley's testimony before the U.S. Senate Subcommittee on Federal Financial Management, Government Information, and International Security, for the Committee on Homeland Security and Governmental Affairs (July 24, 2008), at http://hsgac.senate.gov/public/_files/OMalleyTestimony.pdf.

4. Terry Culler, "Most Federal Workers Need Only Be Competent," *Wall Street Journal* (May 21, 1986).

5. See David B. Walker's testimony before the U.S. Senate Committee on Home-

land Security and Governmental Affairs, *Federal Acquisitions and Contracting: Systemic Challenges Need Attention*, Report GAO-07–1098T (July 17, 2007), 12, at www.gao.gov/new.items/d071098t.pdf.

6. See Donald F. Kettl, *Sharing Power: Public Governance and Private Markets* (Washington, DC: Brookings Institution, 1993).

7. See David R. Mayhew, *Congress: The Electoral Connection*, 2nd ed. (New Haven, CT: Yale University Press, 2004).

8. See testimony of Bernice Steinhardt, U.S. Government Accountability Office, *Government Performance: Lessons Learned for the Next Administration on Using Performance Information to Improve Results*, GAO-08–1026T (July 24, 2008), at www.gao.gov/new.items/d081026t.pdf.

APPENDIX

AN ACTION PLAN FOR THE NEXT GOVERNMENT OF THE UNITED STATES

A merican government is at a turning point. More of the same government is likely to produce more of the same unacceptable results. What we need is a fresh, even revolutionary approach to governance. What should be the action plan for this approach—to the next government of the United States?

As this book has shown, we have been here before: critical points in American history at which old ideas have run out of gas and where new reforms have been needed to replace them. Reform 5.0, which dominated American government since the beginning of the Reagan administration, is no longer up to the big challenges we face, as both the Mildred and Katrina cases have shown. American government needs the next generation of reform—a fresh, even revolutionary, Reform 6.0 strategy. In previous tectonic shifts, the reform path was clearer. There were big ideas—ideological, pragmatic, and theoretical—to guide reformers. With the natural end of Reform 5.0, however, the problems are big, but there is no map for the next stage. Without a new Reform 6.0 strategy, American government is doomed to be mired in more disappointing Katrina-style results. It's time now to develop the plan for Reform 6.0, the *next* government of the United States.

The action plan must begin by charting what reformers should *not* do. As Katrina showed, the biggest risks come from charging blindly down the wrong road. Indeed, the initial step in Reform 6.0 is a Hippocratic Oath for governance: first, do no harm. The second step is avoiding the temptation to promise sweeping symbolic changes that, at best, produce only a quick flash and no lasting results—and, at worst, create mischief that will only make the problems worse. For example, reformers regularly pledge to eliminate the unholy trinity of waste, fraud, and abuse. There surely is waste, fraud, and abuse in public programs, and government needs to relentlessly root it out. But that can't be the plan for Reform 6.0, because it wouldn't get at the core problems. It is tempting to promise cuts in earmarks and narrow spending programs without a broad public purpose, but that won't produce substantial budget savings or attack the underlying governance problems. It is tempting to juggle organization charts, but as this book shows, the core issues aren't fundamentally structural. More transparency will help, but opening the window wider won't help if what is inside doesn't work any better. Moreover, Reform 6.0 shouldn't toss away the best efforts of Reforms 4.0 and 5.0, especially the Clinton and Bush tactics of bringing improved citizen service to a leaner government. The government needs to push public officials to define goals and improve outcomes, so more of this approach would move us in the right direction.

But none of these tactics can be the core of Reform 6.0. Some of them might help, but none of them will solve the core problems. If we use old reforms to attack new problems, we will surely fall short.

What *should* Reform 6.0 look like? As I concluded in Chapters 6 and 7, America needs *rocket science leaders* to take the nation to the next level. It needs a *government of transformation and collaboration* to grow these rocket science leaders and to ensure they have what they need to work effectively.[1] Much—perhaps most—of government is not a vending machine into which citizens insert taxpayers and government officials dispense goods and services. It is increasingly a system in which government officials must leverage the activities of partners, some governmental and many not, toward public purposes. Many local government social workers do not do social work; instead, they manage contractors who do much of the work with the young and elderly who receive public help. Most state transportation department officials do not build roads but work with federal and local partners to design transportation systems, and work with private contractors who do most of the actual construction. Most federal EPA workers do not themselves clean the environment but, rather, work through state officials who administer many of the environmental regulations and through contractors who clean up toxic waste sites.

Government needs to redefine its role. Government, and only government, can leverage complex partnerships to achieve public goals. It needs *transformation* to create and lead these partnerships and to ensure the public interest is paramount. And government needs *collaboration* to build the networks that can get the job done.

To produce this Reform 6.0, government must focus squarely on results. We need to provide citizens with effective, efficient, and responsive programs, in the manner that this book's rocket scientists do. Accountability built on last-generation procedures would serve twenty-first-century government as well as a Model T would serve interstate highway travelers. At best, the trip would be slow, bumpy, and unpleasant. At worst, we might not get where we're going. We need Reform 6.0, built on five balanced elements.

Focus on results. Citizens care little about government's organizational building blocks. They don't really care about the Federal Aviation Administration or the Food and Drug Administration per se. They want to be able to get on a plane and arrive safely at their destination. They want to shop for food and eat it safely. Producing results that matter to people, and that do not focus narrowly on managing government agencies, must lie at the core of Reform 6.0. This, in fact, is the central lesson of Katrina. FEMA's efforts failed because the agency's leaders tried to solve big problems by managing them within the agency's borders, instead of FEMA working to bring together the capacity, based in many agencies, needed to help the storm's victims.

Moreover, the fundamental realities of the Mildred paradox— that government funds many services without itself providing them—and of the Mildred corollary—that many services depend on complex networks in which no one is in charge—means that trying to solve problems simply by managing agencies is a fool's errand. Successful government increasingly depends on building and managing networks, and successful networks emerge only when their members share a common vision of the results they are trying to produce. *We need to put the pursuit of outcomes at the center of the government's work.* That means agency managers must see their job as getting the job done—of looking past the boundaries of their agencies to accomplish the broad mission, rather than simply managing the more narrow activities within their agency's walls.

This step will be critical throughout government, for as we have seen in this book, no single agency can control any program or fully shape any outcome that matters. Federal transportation officials do not just distribute grants and administer regulations. They seek a transportation system that moves people and goods smoothly and that minimizes congestion and hassle. Federal labor officials do not just run job training programs, but try to use the federal government's leverage to promote job growth and safe workplaces. No agency can successfully do what must be done if it tries to do it alone. Focusing narrowly on an individual agency's processes only blinds it to the broader results that matter most and cripples its ability to build the partnerships it needs.

2. *Develop place-based performance measures.* State and local governments, especially in Baltimore and New York, have demonstrated that real-time, place-based, performance-driven systems can help them drive public programs to effective results.[2] As Maryland Governor Martin O'Malley, who created Baltimore's CitStat process as the city's mayor, explained, there are four key steps: "timely, accurate information, shared by all; rapid deployment of resources, so that we can respond in real time; effective tactics and strategies; and relentless follow-up and assessment."[3] This approach has led to the creation of new systems for tracking problems (such as the occurrence of crimes or the accumulation of storm-sewage problems), identifying the location by neighborhood, and developing cross-agency, neighborhood-based responses. The strategy transformed Baltimore's service systems. If the recurring problem of Reform 5.0 is the inability of agencies to leverage results for actions that lie outside their boundaries, the great promise of Reform 6.0 is to use place-based and citizen-based service systems to build the coordination mechanisms we need. This local government approach has spilled over to the state level, including Maryland. At the federal level, the EPA has begun charting quarterly performance measures on maps that show the progress being made toward a cleaner environment.

Focusing on results that matter to citizens, and then integrating the functional components of government's activities so that they work effectively for people where they live and work, are the core elements of Reform 6.0 practice. The next-generation performance measures need to build on the Clinton and Bush efforts by creating better data on outcomes—the results produced—instead of just activities—the things that agencies do. They also need to bring national policies to sharp reality in communities by linking agencies that share a contribution to solving a particular problem, and by bringing together the data that bear on each community. *We need to focus on outcomes to drive collaboration across functional boundaries if we are to produce the results citizens expect.* Local governments could overlay the locations of their schools and the placement of their recreation and nutrition centers to improve the coordination of services for children. State governments could link the location of Medicaid recipients with the location of senior centers and transportation programs to help seniors. The federal government could even further strengthen its mapping of public health problems, including disease outbreaks, with the programs designed to counter them. We need to manage our problems through functionally organized agencies. We need to solve our problems in the communities where people live. Reform 6.0 must provide a powerful mechanism for linking functions with places and people.

Create rocket science leaders. The lessons of government's rocket scientists—the leaders who have found ways to make transformation and collaboration work—is that they *are* leaders. They have discovered how to bring together the resources they have available to them to solve the problems people care about. The good news is that the government has produced so many rocket science leaders. The bad news is that, except for a handful of agencies such as the Coast Guard, the process for producing these leaders has been haphazard. To make government work, we have had to rely too much on the leaders' own drive to solve the problems we all face. We have not worked hard enough to develop a system to produce a steady stream of such leaders. Thus, when big crises arise and when big challenges face government administrators, we have had to rely too much on the luck of having the right person at the right place at the right time. That's too risky a strategy for twenty-first-century government, where wicked problems quickly punish governments that do not rise quickly enough to the challenges they face.

The more complex government's policy strategies become, both technically and organizationally, the more government needs skilled rocket science leaders. However, the government over the last generation has systematically underinvested in its people. Government workers have often been seen as impediments to efficiency, as dead weights that clog government's operations, or often simply as assets that do not matter. The nadir came during the Reagan administration, when Terry Culler, who once headed the federal government's efforts to improve workforce effectiveness, wrote a 1986 *Wall Street Journal* op-ed that argued "most federal workers need only be competent." Better, he argued, to put society's smartest workers in the private sector, where they create more value.[4] In fact, as we slide deeper into the Mildred paradox and its corollary, government needs a large and steady supply of smart leaders. Government's results are only as good as the government officials who build the bridges among the complex components of public programs—and the private sector can only be successful when these bridges work.

The Office of Personnel Management has historically been charged with developing the federal government's managers, but it increasingly has fallen short in this mission. The powerful lesson of successful private sector companies is that they look on their people as their most important asset. The government must do the same, with an aggressive program to hire and develop skilled managers. *We need to devise a government-wide strategy of developing rocket science leaders, because only skilled leaders can drive the next generation of government.* In homeland security, we need skilled leaders who can reach across government's many organizational boundaries and complex cultures to weave a more seamless system for preventing and responding to problems. In agriculture and environmental protection, we need officials who can link the processes of saving trees with the need to produce sustainable forest products. In human services, we need officials who know how to build a safety net whose web is tight enough to keep society's needy from falling through. We need rocket scientists throughout government—and a strategy to produce a strong and steady supply of them.

Sort out the who-does-what. The deep patterns identified in this book—the growing privatization of government and the publicization of the private sector—are irreversible. Some reformers are looking for a solution that will draw clear boundaries, once and for all, but that is a fool's errand. The boundaries between the sectors have become blurred, and interdependence between the two is here to stay. However, government's reliance on the private sector, not only for administrative support but also for fundamental policy decisions, threatens both the effective administration and democratic control of government action.

We've simply pushed government's dependence on the private sector too far. We have defense contractors who not only build weapons systems but design them and oversee other contractors. We have had crises in space because NASA struggled to evaluate the advice it was getting from its contractors. We have local social workers who are trained to help society's needy but who spend most of their time managing contracts with nonprofit organizations who do most of the work: they are not doing what they were trained to do, they weren't trained for the jobs they're doing, and the very people for whom the programs were created often suffer in the process. As then-head of the U.S. Government Accountability Office, David B. Walker argued in 2007, "there is a need to focus greater attention on what type of functions and activities should be contracted out and which ones should not."[5] The fundamental problem is not the ideological debate between conservatives and liberals, which characterized the Reagan-era debates over Reform 5.0. Rather, the issue is the Reform 6.0 question of how government can best accomplish the people's work, who ought to do it, and how the people can hold government accountable for getting that work done.

To govern well, government needs to be a smart buyer: to make the fundamental decisions about what goods and services to buy and how well they are working.[6] As Reform 5.0 advanced, government's capacity to act as a smart buyer diminished. In many areas, anything that could be contracted out *was* contracted out. This not only blurred the lines of public and private roles but made it vastly more difficult to ensure that taxpayer-funded programs served the public purpose. We do not need to pretend we can (or should) put the privatization genie back into its bottle. Indeed, tight partnerships among government, the private sector, and non-profit organizations are irreversible and useful, for they provide government valuable flexibility and expertise. But *we do need to enhance government's capacity to oversee the complex interdependence that has emerged.*

This does not mean we need to grow government, because a very small number of government workers can leverage a vast network of public and private partners. But if government does not enhance its own capacity—to do the things that only government can do and that government must do in a democratic society—the quality of public services and the accountability of public programs will inevitably diminish. We will have more waste, fraud, and abuse because of contractors who steer public money to their narrow interest. From defense policy to environmental protection and from home-land security to drug safety, we will have private partners who work to the narrow letter of the law but miss making the connections among programs that are needed to make these programs work. We will inevitably find ourselves mired in more crises like 2007's mortgage meltdown, in which the tunnel-vision decisions of private rating agencies and mortgage lenders crippled the economy and pulled the government into a multibillion dollar bailout.

Drive commitment to results from the very top. On each of these steps, government needs a commitment from the very top. We need top-level officials focused on producing results that matter to citizens. They do not need to do it themselves, but they need to make sure it gets done. In particular, the president needs a performance czar, a White House official whose sole job is to focus the efforts of the executive branch on producing results. The president also needs someone who, in a crisis, can bring to the table the management instincts required to solve problems. There is little political payoff for government doing hard things well, but there is a large, growing, and inescapable political cost for doing important things badly. Indeed, this proved to be the central political problem for the George W. Bush administration. Despite the roller coaster of the administration's problems with the war in Iraq—and the big changes in public opinion polls that resulted—the point at which the president's negative ratings exceeded his positive ones and remained there was in the month after Katrina struck, when the public concluded the administration had bungled the response to the storm.

The history of presidential "czars" is a checkered one, but *we need—and the president needs—a point person whose sole job is to make the pursuit of outcomes the federal government's top priority.* A senior member of the president's staff, present in the West Wing for important meetings on big issues, could bring a who-does-what-and-how perspective to the important decisions. The president is a political leader but also the nation's chief executive officer, and the president needs a management consultant at hand to ensure that the law is in fact faithfully executed. Such a management czar would have saved the Bush administration tremendous heartache in the days after Katrina.

On Capitol Hill, Congress must grapple with the powerful instincts for fragmentation of policy making among the scores of congressional committees and subcommittees and for selective intervention in areas of credit-claiming, casework, and micro-management.[7] Congress has at its disposal a powerful tool, the Government Performance and Results Act of 1993, which requires agencies to identify the outcomes they are seeking to achieve and to measure their success in doing so. Federal agencies are already producing GPRA reports, although there is little evidence that they take them very seriously.[8] But Congress can change that. In their oversight hearings, congressional committees ought on every occasion to call on agency managers to summarize the outcomes they are seeking to achieve and to inform members of Congress of their success in achieving them. Budget hearings ought to begin with a careful look at the objectives of federal programs, agencies' success in achieving outcomes, and what plans they have for improving their success in the future. *We need to make these simple questions—what government agencies are trying to do and how well they are doing it—the core of every congressional hearing.*

Too often, Congress reinforces the executive branch's instinct toward tunnel vision by holding hearings focused on hyper-narrow (and often headline-grabbing) issues. It isn't reasonable to try to change the laws of politics. But it is essential that when the Secretary of Labor appears before a committee, members of Congress ask about the department's broader mission and its success in achieving it: jobs created, workers trained, workplaces made safe. The head of the FDA needs to answer on a regular basis for the overall health of the American public and for the safety of the drugs citizens take. Such a dialogue doesn't need to be lengthy, but it needs to remind everyone—the members of Congress asking the questions and the members of the executive branch answering them—about the broader goals they all seek.

These five elements in Reform 6.0 focus mainly on the federal government. However, state and local governments can—indeed, must—take the same steps. The nation's government system has become so interdependent that government does not work well unless all parts of government work. This, in fact, is the lesson of Katrina. Reform 6.0 requires a seamless focus on effective governance.

This strategy requires elected officials to step away, even if only periodically and momentarily, from the short-term political behavior that focuses administrators on narrow areas in which they can deflect scrutiny and control results. That kind of defensive administration, however, ducks the big problems—and often makes them worse. Solving the problems of the twenty-first century requires government administrators to take risks on the job, in an environment that often provides few rewards for good results and strong penalties for public failure. The rise of government's rocket scientists—of skilled leaders who have discovered smart transformation and collaboration strategies that get results—is proof that taking risks to make government work better can in fact produce better government. It is also proof that government can build a culture in which the quest for high performance produces its own rewards.

We know what the government needs to work better. And we know how to take the steps we need. An increasingly complex world and increasingly wary citizens will surely punish a government that fails to rise to the challenges of the twenty-first century with a governance system that works: one that mobilizes government in the public interest and ensures collaboration to achieve results that matter for people. This is the core of Reform 6.0, and it must drive the next government of the United States.

If we fail to rise to the challenges of Reform 6.0, we'll end up with a government that works poorly, proves unacceptably expensive, and is unresponsive and unaccountable. And for the first time in American history, we will have failed to rise to the challenge of our founders: adapting America's robust democratic system to the tectonic shifts we have regularly faced and conquered. Should we fail, it is no exaggeration to conclude that American democracy and the nation's place in the world will be at risk. And—this is not too big an exaggeration—the future of American democracy will be at risk. We know how to do this. We will be punished if we fail.